'The welfare state has been an essential part of our national story for the past two hundred years. Its history is excellently recounted in this comprehensive, scholarly survey ... It is a thoroughly worthwhile work' Kenneth O. Morgan, *Literary Review*

'A myth-busting history ... *Bread for All* is written for the intrigued layman rather than the academic specialist, and it is all the better for that ... a readable book with an important point to make' Philip Collins, *The Times*

'It tells the story of the development of the Welfare State with clarity, intelligence and rigorous scholarship ... makes a powerful argument' Tristram Hunt, *The Times Literary Supplement*

'Chris Renwick's fresh and inspiring study shows the long-term history of the British welfare state and its liberal underpinnings. He reminds us all of its remarkable significance as a means of making a good society' Mike Savage, author of *Social Class in the 21st Century*

'In lively and incisive fashion Chris Renwick tells the story of the remarkable men and women whose ideas and decisions led, by accident as much as by design, to the creation of a distinctively British welfare state' Paul Addison, author of *The Road to 1945*

'An excellent book ... With a combination of scholarship and panache, he traces the origins of sustained thinking about the state's role in the alleviation of poverty' John Bew, *New Statesman*

'Formidably learned ... the kind of book that gives academic history a good name ... *Bread for All* ends with the Attlee government's implementation of William Beveridge's blueprint for a postwar welfare state. In Renwick's account, this is best seen as the final act in a long drama, rather than a revolutionary moment ... the product of endless compromises with private and local interests, built on the legacy of the past and designed to improve capitalism rather than to replace it' Dominic Sar~ "

'Makes a gripping human sto   e policy achievement of any Stuart Maconie, *Ne*

D1354044

'A brilliant book, full of little revelations – my personal favourite is that Britain's leading eugenicist also invented the dog whistle. *Bread for All* anchors the creation of the welfare state deep within 19th-century science ... It is written with real agility in an accessible style, and is bound to figure in "books of the year" lists – it will in mine'
Jon Cruddas, *Prospect*

'I greatly enjoyed Chris Renwick's colourful and clever *Bread for All*'
BBC History Magazine Books of the Year

ABOUT THE AUTHOR

Chris Renwick is Senior Lecturer in Modern History at the University of York, where he has taught since 2010. His main area of expertise is the relationship between biology, social science and politics, especially how the interaction of the three has shaped the way we think about, study, and govern society since the early nineteenth century.

CHRIS RENWICK

Bread for All
The Origins of the Welfare State

PENGUIN BOOKS

PENGUIN BOOKS

UK | USA | Canada | Ireland | Australia
India | New Zealand | South Africa

Penguin Books is part of the Penguin Random House group of companies
whose addresses can be found at global.penguinrandomhouse.com.

Penguin
Random House
UK

First published by Allen Lane 2017
Published in Penguin Books 2018
001

Set in 9.35/12.4 pt Sabon LT Std
Typeset by Jouve (UK), Milton Keynes
Printed and bound in Great Britain by Clays Ltd, Elcograf S.p.A.

A CIP catalogue record for this book is available from the British Library

ISBN: 978-0-141-98035-5

www.greenpenguin.co.uk

For Ivy

Contents

Introduction: A Very British Revolution   1

1   Atmospheric Impurity   11
2   Below the Poverty Line   35
3   Reinventing Liberalism   58
4   The Health of the Nation   82
5   The Well-being of the Whole   104
6   The Greatest Argument for
    Socialism Ever Produced   126
7   The Man You Can Trust   148
8   Will the Machine Work?   170
9   In the Long Run We're All Dead   192
10   Half-way to Moscow   214
11   Constructive Progress   237

Conclusion: This New Entity Composed
    of Old Elements   259

Essay on Sources   269
Acknowledgements   293
Index   295

Introduction

'A Very British Revolution'

On the afternoon of Tuesday, 16 February 1943, William Beveridge – a slightly built 64-year-old economist with a distinctive head of white hair parted on the left – was sat in the gallery at Westminster listening to MPs, who were meeting in the House of Lords after Luftwaffe bombs had destroyed the Commons' chamber nearly two years earlier. Back in the summer of 1941, Beveridge had made a nuisance of himself, criticizing the government when it had been struggling to make a breakthrough in the war with Germany, calling on it to let him play a bigger role in helping turn things round. Tired of his demands, the coalition government, led by Conservative Prime Minister Winston Churchill, had looked for ways to keep him out of sight and mind. A time-consuming and deeply involved investigation into Britain's complex state-run insurance schemes, which covered almost 15 million people against short periods of unemployment and enabled nearly 5 million more to see a doctor when they were ill, seemed as good an answer as any. Now MPs had convened at Parliament to discuss the results – a 299-page report called *Social Insurance and Allied Services*. While Beveridge had been compiling his report, things had changed. Lieutenant-General Montgomery had secured a major victory at El Alamein in Egypt in November 1942 and the war seemed to have turned in the Allies' favour. But the government still wanted Beveridge to go away, along with his report.

In the report, Beveridge had outlined an ambitious and expensive system of social security, wrapped in a 'comprehensive policy of social progress', and told the public it was nothing less than they deserved for their wartime sacrifices. Judging by the half a million copies of the report that had been sold by the time of the parliamentary debate, the public agreed.

At around three o'clock, a few hours into the debate, Beveridge left Parliament and headed two miles north, past St James's Park and through Soho, on his way to Manson House in Marylebone, where he was due to deliver a lecture entitled 'Eugenic Aspects of Children's Allowances'. Later in the twentieth century, any hint of an association with ideas of eugenics would be enough to terminate a political career. In the mid-1970s, the Conservative reformer Keith Joseph, one of Margaret Thatcher's mentors, ran for the leadership of the Party: when he gave a speech warning that Britain would degenerate if something was not done about teenage mothers and other groups he suggested were a threat to British 'stock', his campaign promptly collapsed. In 1943, however, attitudes to eugenics were quite different. Beveridge, a man with deeply progressive ideas about society, was himself a fellow of the Eugenics Society and would join its consultative council after the war. But he also thought the idea of a welfare state that he had outlined in his report had eugenic implications – albeit ones quite different from those that later concerned Joseph – and believed they needed to be taken seriously by both government and society.

Beveridge was far from alone in having some kind of connection to either the Eugenics Society or the broad range of conversations on which it impinged. In the first half of the twentieth century, British people were fascinated by questions about fertility and what these questions meant for the country's future. While the public digested scientific research that warned, plausibly (though with important caveats), that Britain's population could dwindle to as few as 5 million within a century, social researchers inquired into people's lives to find out why they seemed to want fewer children than their parents and grandparents. Mass-Observation, created in 1937 by the journalist Charles Madge and Tom Harrisson, an anthropologist, with help from the filmmaker Humphrey Jennings, aimed to access what Madge called the 'collective unconscious' by documenting the kinds of ordinary voices that went unheard in most newspapers and magazines. Initially based in London and Bolton, Mass-Observation had upwards of a hundred active volunteers around the country who responded to surveys and kept diaries about life around them, which the organization then used as the basis for reports and books. By the early 1940s, attitudes to parenthood and families was a topic that had piqued Mass-Observation's interest. They interviewed more than a thousand men and women in London and Gloucester, Britain's metropole and a town thought typical of life beyond it, analysed hundreds of letters sent to family planning clinics and radio shows, and carried out observational studies of ordinary households, all in an effort to understand why British people, particularly middle-class people, were having smaller families than they had in the past. According to Mass-Observation's report, *Britain and Her Birthrate* (1945), the situation was indicative of a deep and decades-old malaise that had been brought into focus by the war. People lacked

> faith in the future. Not a belief that things are going to be tough, and
> it will take a long time to get right . . . But a belief that nobody's going
> to *try* and put things right and improve them, that the nation is going
> to muddle on through the chaoses [*sic*] of another 1919–39 to another
> world war in 1965.

These concerns seemed to prove Beveridge right. People were likely to muddle through whatever happened, but when it came to big decisions, like whether or not to have a child, their behaviour was guided, often unconsciously, by whether they thought there was a light at the end of the tunnel. The plan Beveridge had presented to the government in late 1942, more than two months before Parliament was finally allowed to debate it, was ambitious. He promised it would end poverty in Britain and allow people to live with dignity, thanks to a system that would take care of them 'from the cradle to the grave' – as others, including Churchill, put it – and all for a simple, flat-rate weekly payment from everyone who had a job. There were all kinds of questions about his proposals. Would there be enough jobs for everyone so they could pay the taxes that were required to make the scheme work? Would the benefits Beveridge's system offered make some people lazy and complacent? Would there be families who expected everyone else to pick up the tab for the cost of raising their children (as the more reactionary members of the Eugenics Society argued)? But, as hundreds of thousands of copies of *Social Insurance and Allied Services* flew off His Majesty's Stationery Office's printing presses, to be seen later in the hands of people in libraries and cafés, and on trains and buses, there was a sense that Beveridge had gone a long way to showing politicians what the country wanted.

Yet for all the interest in his report, not to mention the government's displeasure at being forced to discuss such a significant programme of reconstruction and reform when there was still a war to win, the vast majority of what Beveridge had presented his readers with was far from new. A technocrat who excelled when it came to detail and pragmatism, he had looked at a century's worth of ideas developed by myriad politicians, social scientists, social reformers, campaigners and businessmen from across the political spectrum. Indeed, he had drawn extensively on the principles underpinning the existing social insurance legislation passed by both Conservative and Liberal governments during the previous four decades. Beveridge thought implementing his proposals would mean immediate and significant improvements in people's lives. He also described them, however, as the capstone of a 'British revolution': a process that had evolved over the previous 150 years, whose strands he was helping to tie up.

Few of the MPs who debated Beveridge's report in 1943 wanted to argue with his headline-grabbing promise to end poverty, which had captured the imaginations of those who had joined the armed forces and kept the country going through aerial bombing, evacuation and shortages of everything from food to clothes to fuel. Many of them were uneasy, however, with the breadth and depth of his vision, which implied even greater change. Beveridge had told people that it was time to slay 'five giants': want, disease, ignorance, squalor and idleness. He argued that, to achieve this, Britain needed to do much more than make incremental improvements to its existing system of benefits and contributions, as the government had imagined Beveridge would suggest when it sent him away in June 1941. He told Parliament and the public that tinkering would achieve little on its own. The country had to commit to the creation of new and costly institutions, including a National Health Service, not to mention markedly different economic policies to the ones that had been commonplace before the war. Beveridge had described what he thought the British people not only wanted but truly deserved: a society where there were cash benefits for anyone who required them, but in which few people actually needed to ask for them in the first place. All that was required was the political will to make it happen.

When it comes to the history of the British welfare state, there are good and obvious reasons for starting in early 1943, with William Beveridge. *Social Insurance and Allied Services*, usually known simply as the Beveridge Report, made him synonymous with the welfare state in popular and political culture and a central figure in the story of the general election of 1945, when the British people said thank you but goodbye to Winston Churchill and voted Clement Attlee's Labour Party into power by a landslide. Thanks to this handover, there is a tendency in popular culture to see the welfare state as Labour's achievement – a socialist triumph, built out of the wreckage of the Second World War. Labour were certainly key actors in that moment, creating something the Tories were unlikely to have assembled in precisely the same way or using exactly the same parts had they been in government. But institutions as huge as the welfare state are seldom constructed in one moment or by one person. Indeed, while Beveridge had made his name in politics more than forty years earlier when Churchill, then a member of a Liberal government, had invited him to help establish state-backed unemployment insurance for specific groups of workers, he was not a socialist either. Although he refused to declare his political allegiance for most of his career, Beveridge was a Liberal MP by the closing stages of the war, albeit one who lost his seat in the electorate's unforgiving judgement of July 1945.

The story of the British welfare state's origins is clearly longer and more complicated than a focus on the 1940s and the Second World War allows us to see. Charting that history and, in the process, pulling apart the strands that Beveridge helped weave together are this book's central aims. Doing so will see us encounter some of the most eminent names in modern British political history, from Tories like Neville Chamberlain, to Liberals including David Lloyd George, and socialists such as Sidney and Beatrice Webb, members of the Fabian Society who helped found the modern Labour Party. It also features social scientists and investigators, from nineteenth-century theorists such as Jeremy Bentham, the founder of utilitarianism, and John Stuart Mill, his most distinguished intellectual successor, through to their twentieth-century heirs, such as Seebohm Rowntree, the York-based confectionary manufacturer and social surveyor who made famous the idea of a 'poverty cycle', and John Maynard Keynes, the Cambridge don and public intellectual who pioneered the then-new field of macroeconomics during the 1920s and 1930s. It will also involve politicians, commentators and campaigners with eyes on an assortment of different problems, from public health to women's rights to child poverty, not to mention the different and constantly evolving structures of government, from high political debate in the Houses of Parliament to the frequently more mundane but no less important world of local government.

This book has its centre of gravity in the ideas about the welfare of the British public and the thinkers, politicians, campaigners and social investigators who produced, argued about and legislated for them during the century and a half leading up to 1945. As we will see, these ideas were constantly in motion; products of particular times and places, they inspired people to act in different ways and some-times changed significantly once they were put into practice. Popular movements – the kind of agitation from below that some commenta-tors believe is central to social and political change – of course played their part, not least by giving the individuals and groups I discuss leverage to put their ideas into action at key junctures. But the intel-lectual framing and content of ideas about the welfare of the British people often came from people with power – elites, as they are often called – whether they be in political parties, universities, business or any of the other institutions that shape society. Sometimes these reformers met with resistance, at other times they found the wider political and intellectual climate more accommodating. At each stage, however, far-reaching ideas about concepts such as human nature were embedded into both political discourse and the seemingly un-remarkable administrative structures encountered in everyday life.

As we will see, the welfare state was an intergenerational project, built by a variety of different and sometimes conflicting individuals and groups, not all of whom fit neatly within the 'progressive' or 'radical' tradition or who understood themselves to be contributing to a process that would end up where it did after the Second World War. These people lived in different eras, were located on different parts of the political spectrum, had different aims and interests, and played different roles, from formulating the questions – and, indeed, causing the problems – that others would grapple with to providing the ideas and tools that would be used to answer them. The welfare state that emerged from that process – which spanned the Victorians' efforts to align society and their new notions of progress, the early twentieth-century struggle to adjust old political ideas to new economic realities, and post-war reconstruction – was not simply a moral enterprise intended to protect the weakest members of society or reward people who had given up so much in not one but two world wars. The welfare state was certainly those things, but it was also a project that integrated different aspects of social, political and economic life with the aim of making Britain fit for the challenges of the modern world. Sentiment played its part, but so did hard-headed thinking about things like economic productivity. As Beveridge put it shortly after *Social Insurance and Allied Services* was published, there should be 'bread for all . . . before cake for anybody'.

In the decades that followed its foundation, the welfare state's modernizing credentials were often obscured as politicians and commentators focused their criticisms and complaints, as their predecessors had done, on quite narrow aspects of its overall job. Unemployment benefits have been a favourite target, with critics, including Keith Joseph, claiming they have a negative impact on economic growth and moral character. As we will see, though, the welfare state – understood as not simply cash benefits but, as Beveridge and his contemporaries saw it, a general approach to shaping people's social environment – was intended to be a tool for social and economic progress. Rather than a rejection of capitalism and industrialization, the welfare state was meant to make those things work better. During the nineteenth century, Britain had gone as far as any country when it came to unleashing the forces of economic liberalism. In the process, however, people had come to realize that markets would not always right themselves or produce the kinds of social outcomes they thought desirable. Problems such as long-term unemployment and chronic ill health often looked like matters for individuals, but, as observers across the political spectrum conceded, they were capable of combining in ways that threatened the stability of the system as a whole, as anyone who had lived through the Great Depression of the 1930s could testify.

Underpinning all these developments was a relatively simple idea: that society could be shaped and controlled according to the will of those in charge. By the mid-twentieth century, politicians, bureaucrats and intellectuals believed Britain could run an economy in such a way that the number of people who were unemployed at any given point would be below a specific proportion of the available workforce. They thought they could keep overall welfare expenditure down, and economic productivity up, by spending money on things such as health services, including public health infrastructure, and schools. The results of this way of thinking were often stark: a free prescription that cured a condition someone had been suffering from for years; an end to parents deliberating over which of their children would get to see a doctor; a house with bedrooms for everyone and an indoor toilet; a pension on retirement. But there were rules, regulations and institutions too. These made the aims of welfare politics clear, though sometimes through the formal language of administrators, and made entitlements and practical achievements secure. Despite their seemingly mundane nature, however, those rules and regulations were also a significant statement on the kind of society people wanted to live in – most notably on the matter of who was included and who was excluded from the benefits and services on offer. In these respects, it is important to remember that the British welfare state was founded not as a system of handouts, as critics often claim, but as a partnership between the state, individuals and private business, each contributing to a project from which they all derived benefits. None of this was inevitable and, as experiences in other countries make clear, it could have been organized very differently. Indeed, the seeds of alternative ways of calibrating the relationship between people, the state and capitalism, such as the idea of a 'property-owning democracy', were sown in the midst of these developments.

One of the most important arguments I make in what follows is that, while the British welfare state has roots in different political camps, it owes most to liberalism. This debt is easily obscured by a temptation to equate liberalism with the Liberal Party, which went into near terminal decline after the 1920s, and the fact that a Labour government presided over the construction of institutions like the National Health Service after 1945. Political philosophies are not static entities, though; they change over time, are frequently renewed, and sometimes find new leases of life in different settings. Nineteenth-century liberalism played a central role in both causing and defining problems that have loomed large in debates about welfare and social policy over the past two hundred years. Conversely, however, liberal thinkers' efforts to reform their ideas in response to their obvious failings were crucial in the development of welfare provision during the early twentieth century. This was true not only legislatively but also intellectually, with thinkers such as John Maynard Keynes, a Liberal Party supporter, working out ways to reconcile new economic realities with old ideals. In so doing, solutions such as Keynes's may very well have been one of the major factors in the Liberal Party's decline as an electoral force, primarily by creating the levers that other parties could pull to achieve ends that satisfied not only the Liberals' traditional supporters but their own too. Liberalism was woven into the welfare state's identity, something that is essential to understand if we are to appreciate what its founders hoped it would achieve.

I

Atmospheric Impurity

If you could not support yourself or your family in nineteenth-century England there was a system to help. It was called the Poor Law and it had been in place since 1601. By the beginning of the twentieth century, however, these three-centuries-old arrangements were falling apart. Despite constant battles to keep costs down, the Poor Law was increasingly expensive and, as many commentators were prepared to admit, doing a less-than-perfect job of serving the people who needed it and those who paid for it. As a mark of how seriously it was taking these concerns, the government appointed a Royal Commission, made up of experts and politicians, whom it asked to diagnose the causes of the Poor Law's widely perceived problems and suggest ways to fix them. Yet in 1909, after four years of work, the eighteen-member commission was so deeply divided over the purpose and remit of the Poor Law its members refused to sign up to the same set of recommendations. According to the four commissioners who eventually signed what became known as the 'minority report', the problem with the Poor Law was clear. 'The mere keeping of people from starving' might have been a suitable aim in earlier times, when the political classes used the Poor Law as one means of 'averting social revolution'. But everyone had the right to expect much more by the early twentieth century. 'The very conception of relieving destitution starts the whole service on a demoralising tack,' they argued.

For the authors of the minority report, this 'demoralising tack' had been fixed back in the 1830s, a little more than three-quarters of a century earlier, when the government had last asked a Royal Commission to consider whether the Poor Law was fit for purpose. Strict new rules to decide who qualified for help had been imposed on local Poor Law administrators by MPs, who insisted that the dark, dank and unforgiving conditions of the workhouse should be what people thought about when deciding whether or not they really needed the government's help. Before too long, though, the authorities started to wonder if they had got things horribly wrong. The new Poor Law was supposed to be a deterrent, driving away all but the most obvious cases of need, and to cut costs through rational new approaches to administration. Yet the 1834 reforms had not delivered everything that their champions had promised. Abstract rules and principles devised in Westminster had proven problematic. Officials, who had been used to a significant degree of autonomy when it came to deciding how much help to offer their communities, had struggled with the distance between what they saw day to day and the world the new Poor Law described. Before too long, however, even those who had helped write that description realized they needed to help fill in the gaps.

THE 43RD OF ELIZABETH

David Ricardo (1772–1823) came from one of the thousands of Jewish families that had fled Portugal during the seventeenth century at the height of the Inquisition. His father, Abraham, had made a fortune in stockbroking, which would become the family trade, first in Amsterdam and then London, where there was a large immigrant Jewish community. Abraham and David did not always see eye-to-eye when it came to matters of faith or parental authority, however. The final straw for Abraham came when the 21-year-old David married the daughter of a local Quaker surgeon. Abraham banished his son from the family firm, wrote him out of his will and refused to talk to him until after David's mother had died. Yet David Ricardo was stronger and more determined than his small stature and high-pitched voice suggested to many people encountering him for the first time. He threw himself into work on the London Stock Exchange and, before long, had amassed a fortune of his own. He owned a house at one of the capital's most fashionable and expensive addresses, on Grosvenor Square in Mayfair, and a country residence – a nine-bedroom Gloucestershire manor house complete with library, billiard room and extensive grounds (which would later be bought by the royal family).

Ricardo believed there was much more to life than money, though. He thought deeply about the world around him, and imagined how his own journey to riches might be the foundation for a better society. He wrote a number of essays and pamphlets on economics that caught the attention of influential political thinkers and commentators. Then, in the mid-1810s, he started work on *Principles of Political Economy and Taxation* (1817), in which he set out to explain what he believed were the laws governing the economy and the production of wealth. When they read it, many of his contemporaries and successors reckoned the book was so good it made him second only to Adam Smith – the recently deceased Scottish author of *The Wealth of Nations* (1776) who was revered as the Enlightenment's greatest political economist – when it came to understanding the relationship between individual freedom, economic activity and prosperity. Some commentators had their doubts about the unusually precise way Ricardo presented his ideas, which could be so abstract they seemed to bear little relation to the messy reality of the economy most people experienced. But Ricardo was adamant these criticisms missed the point: he was a political reformer who was explaining not only how the economy worked but also how its laws could be the basis for a better society.

Ricardo's mission had strong connections with the Whig faction in British politics. Like 'Tory', the name of their aristocratic opponents in Parliament, 'Whig' was originally a term of abuse – one that referred to the Presbyterians who fought the royalists in Scotland and believed James II, a Catholic, should have been excluded from the line of succession in 1685. Whereas the Tories believed in the importance of the royal prerogative over parliamentary opinion, the indissoluble link between the Church of England and the state, and the centrality of tradition in political and social life, Whigs believed the best form of government involved power being evenly distributed between monarchy, aristocracy and popular representation, which would ensure no single group dominated any other or threatened key rights like private property. Whigs looked for inspiration to events such as the 'Glorious Revolution' of 1688, when Parliament had deposed James II and invited the Dutch Protestants William and Mary to take his place, and to the philosopher John Locke, whose patron, the Earl of Shaftesbury, was one of the Whig movement's founding figures. As he explained in *Two Treatises of Government*, published the year after the Glorious Revolution in 1689, Locke believed governments have a contract with the people they rule. In contrast to Tories, who thought monarchs derived their authority from God, Locke argued that people had certain inalienable rights and that governments were legitimate insofar as they carried out a clearly defined set of duties, including maintaining public order. Rulers who failed to fulfil these duties had broken their contract, meaning people had the right to replace them with someone or something else. With this check in place, Whigs argued, British history had been a story of gradual but inevitable progress.

By the early nineteenth century, however, this moderate reformism had been joined by divergent strands known as 'radicalism', which had roots in the European Enlightenment. The political programmes and ideologies that emerged from this milieu were frequently based on controversial philosophical foundations. Whereas constitutional Whiggism was focused on inalienable rights endowed by God, radicals engaged with systems of thought such as materialism, in which everything was underpinned by physical principles and properties. The best known of the radical late Enlightenment programmes was utilitarianism, which was founded by the English philosopher and social reformer Jeremy Bentham (1748–1832), whose wealthy London attorney father had hot-housed his son's educational experience, forcing him to learn Latin when he was just three years old, and got him to the University of Oxford before his thirteenth birthday. Driven on by a belief that social conventions, political rules and public institutions could be shorn of ideas that were relics of eras less advanced than his own, Bentham's hugely influential, though often frustrated, career was based on a deceptively simple idea: that 'nature has placed mankind under the governance of two sovereign masters, *pain* and *pleasure*'. If one accepted this as true, he argued, then it was easy to evaluate the right course of action, because it was that which followed from what he called the 'principle of utility': the proposition that things be judged in terms of their tendency 'to augment or diminish the happiness of the party whose interest is in question', as he put it in *An Introduction to the Principles of Morals and Legislation* (1789). The right thing to do was always that which increased happiness.

The political economy that emerged during the later stages of the Enlightenment, which Adam Smith believed was a central component of a project he called the 'science of the legislator', found a natural home among these radical thinkers. Individuals should be encouraged to pursue self-interest, they argued, because their endeavours would produce not only greater national wealth within a stable social order, but also rational and mature individuals who were less dependent on the paternalistic aristocracy. Ricardo, whom Bentham allegedly called his 'spiritual grandson', was prominent among these thinkers. A close friend of Bentham's most famous disciple, the Scottish political philosopher and historian James Mill (1773–1836), who had argued in *An Essay on Government* (1820) that government should exist only to secure the happiness of the governed, Ricardo applied his economic reasoning to a host of political questions. One issue Ricardo considered to be among the most important was the laws and customs that dictated when the poor were entitled to help from public authorities, which he believed were so misguided they should ultimately be abolished.

The specific object of Ricardo's criticism was known as the '43rd of Elizabeth' because it had been passed by Parliament in 1601, the forty-third year of Elizabeth I's reign. At the time, the law was unique in early modern Europe. Relief of the poor had once been a matter of charity only but, after experimenting with different arrangements throughout the late Middle Ages, the governing classes had accepted the need for legislation setting out rules and responsibilities. The result was a government-mandated system that gave individuals in England the right to relief in the case of distress. Local parishes, each typically home to around six hundred people, were in charge of this system, which was administered by an unpaid overseer who was appointed by magistrates and answerable to a vestry of local people who funded the system by paying poor rates – a progressive local tax levied in proportion to the value of their households and property. Parliament was prepared to legislate to create uniformity in certain matters, as it did in the 1662 Settlement Act, which clarified that individuals were entitled to poor relief in parishes where they had a connection via birth, marriage, apprenticeship or inheritance. For the most part, however, parishes decided for themselves how to run and pay for things, and varied their rules and practices in response to economic, social and demographic circumstances, such as war, inflation and disease.

Poor rates were meant to help three groups of people. One was the 'impotent' poor who were unable to support themselves through no fault of their own, usually because they were sick or old. Then there were the able-bodied poor, such as children, who could not work for legitimate reasons. Finally, there were the able-bodied but 'idle' poor, who were judged to be simply unwilling to work. Each of these groups were understood to have different needs. While the idle were seen as requiring punishment of some kind, children were often given the opportunity to learn a trade. The old and sick, on the other hand, were offered places in poorhouses and almshouses – institutions that took care of their basic needs. Anyone who was able to work was expected to offer something in exchange for relief, though. They frequently entered a 'house of correction', where they would be told to perform tasks such as picking apart old rope, beating hemp and breaking stones, because it was believed to be important to 'set the poor to work'.

While rates were set by overseers, relief was given both 'indoors' and 'outdoors'. Indoor relief was typically for those who were unable to support themselves at all. Outdoor relief, on the other hand, was distributed in the form of cash allowances, goods and services, and was usually for people who worked but still could not meet their basic living costs, usually because they had dependants. The most famous and often notorious form of outdoor relief was the 'Speenhamland system', named after a meeting at the Pelican Inn in Speenhamland, Berkshire, where it was devised in 1795. With steep rises in the price of grain putting extreme pressure on family budgets and the number of people asking for help spiralling, local magistrates decided to pay labourers an allowance, pegged to the cost of bread, so they could feed their families. Over time, however, 'Speenhamland' became shorthand for a wide range of approaches to outdoor poor relief, including rates exemptions and allowances for children, which were increasingly popular in parishes across the country during the early 1800s.

Political economists had a number of problems with this system. While Smith believed the laws of settlement restricted the free movement of workers, Ricardo thought poor relief, and outdoor relief in particular, was an unearned payment – money handed over for nothing – that interfered with market mechanisms, stopping it, for example, from setting wages at their correct level. But the most famous criticism came from Ricardo's great rival, Thomas Malthus (1766–1834). The son of a rich literary radical who once entertained the Enlightenment philosopher Jean-Jacques Rousseau at the family home, Malthus had been educated at Cambridge and overcome the challenges of a cleft palate to become a well-regarded curate in Surrey and the country's first professor of political economy, at the East India Company College in Hertfordshire, where prospective employees of the company that held the monopoly over trade with the Indian subcontinent and China were educated. Unlike his father, however, Malthus was not an optimist; he thought society was constrained by potentially devastating natural laws and tendencies.

Malthus explained his ideas about these topics in the wildly popular (and equally controversial) *An Essay on the Principle of Population*, which was initially published anonymously in 1798 and ran through six editions until 1826. According to Malthus, human populations increase at a geometric rate, doubling every twenty-five years or so, but their means of subsistence increase at a much slower, arithmetic rate. The only thing stopping complete disaster was what he called 'checks', which slowed down the rate at which populations grew. Some of these were natural, like disease and famine; others were what he called 'artificial', such as sexual abstinence. Malthus thought the Poor Law was a problem because it interfered with these checks. With the availability of poor relief, he argued, people could have as many children as they wanted, regardless of the economic consequences, because they knew somebody else would always pick up the bill. The periodic result was the opposite of what well-meaning poor law officers intended: hunger and misery, as too many people fought over a dwindling pool of resources. This vision was deeply gloomy but, when even Adam Smith estimated that eighteen out of every twenty babies born to poor parents failed to survive to adulthood, it made intuitive sense to many people.

Although Ricardo and Malthus disagreed about much, they agreed that the Poor Law had a profound and demoralizing impact on individuals, by reducing the value of independence and making charity the norm. Yet even they were forced to recognize a number of its more pragmatic benefits. For one thing, the Poor Law helped ward off rebellion and revolt among the poor by ensuring that the kinds of famines and shortages that happened in other countries throughout the seventeenth and eighteenth centuries were not common features of life in England. Less obviously, however, the Poor Law helped create one of Europe's most mobile workforces. The young were freed from some of the responsibility for elderly relatives, who faced destitution if they could not share living costs with or get help from family, which their counterparts on the Continent were burdened with. Moreover, by giving all ratepayers a voice through local vestries, the law ensured a reasonable level of flexibility and accountability within communities. In theory, at least, dominant local individuals could not dodge their financial liabilities or exert disproportionate influence over Poor Law administration.

By the 1830s, though, Poor Law critics seemed to be growing in number and influence and it looked possible that serious reform might happen. One reason was costs. Expenditure on poor relief in England in 1776 was around £1.5 million; in 1803, the total had risen to over £4.2 million; by 1820 it was approximately £7 million. Although these increases had good explanations, from population growth to price rises caused by the Napoleonic Wars, and were small compared to a massive national debt that had stood at £834 million when France was finally defeated in 1815, the idea of profligate administrators and queues of feckless poor seemed to resonate in a way they had not done before. The reason was a shift in the balance of power between Whigs and Tories in Parliament.

ELEVATING THE GREAT MASS OF SOCIETY

The Tories had dominated British politics during the late eighteenth and early nineteenth centuries, with an unbroken series of governments under the likes of Pitt the Younger from the early 1780s through to the 1820s. As Whigs liked to complain, this situation was made possible by a system that favoured the Tories. The electorate was tiny – about 500,000 men in Britain and Ireland were, for a variety of reasons (mainly because they owned property), entitled to cast votes in public ballots. Furthermore, the geographical distribution of parliamentary seats did not reflect the economic and social changes that were well under way by the 1810s. While places such as Leeds and Manchester did not have representatives at all, the infamous 'rotten boroughs', where there were just a handful of voters, continued to return members to Westminster. Seats in such places were often held by families and were known to change hands for cash. Even Ricardo, looking for a way to influence government, bought the seat of Portarlington in Ireland, where there were roughly twelve electors, in 1818 as part of a £25,000 loan he made to its owner.

Whig hopes that this situation might change were raised several notches in 1830, when the then Tory Prime Minister, the Duke of Wellington, whose administration was increasingly unpopular thanks to its tax and foreign policies, lost a parliamentary vote after refusing to let Parliament scrutinize its civil list, as governments were entitled to. A new Whig administration, the first for almost forty years, took over and then won a convincing victory under Earl Grey at the ballot box a year later. The new government had a number of pressing issues to tackle. Rebellions such as the Swing Riots, when agricultural workers in the south started smashing machines that were putting them out of work in the summer of 1830, had broken out, raising concerns about the stability of the social order. But the Whigs wanted to pursue a broader programme of reforms too. The most obvious emblem of that ambition was the Great Reform Act of 1832, which abolished the rotten boroughs and enfranchised men who owned or were the sole occupants of property worth £10 or more, almost doubling the size of the electorate. No less important, however, was the agreement known as the Lichfield House Compact after the building where the Whigs met with radicals and the Irish Repeal Party, led by Daniel O'Connell, to discuss it in 1835. The compact established a basis for working together in Parliament and keeping the Tories out of power. By most measures, the agreement worked: the Tories, split during the 1840s over economic policy, managed to form just one majority government and a number of short-lived minority governments in the next thirty years.

The Whig ascendency provided the grounds for the appointment of a Royal Commission on the Poor Law in 1832. Although it was nine members strong, the commission was dominated by two men. One was Nassau Senior (1790–1864), an Eton-educated grandson of a merchant trader who had practised law in London following his graduation from Oxford, but who returned to Oxford in 1825 as a professor of political economy after taking a deep interest in the economic causes of poverty. The other was Edwin Chadwick (1800–1890), a fellow lawyer who also saw a strong connection between scientific study and social problems. The author of a number of provocative pieces on the reform of public institutions, he had been drawn into London's network of philosophers and social reformers, through which he came to live for a year with Jeremy Bentham in his Westminster home in 1831, when he served as the utilitarian philosopher's assistant. Bentham was a controversial public figure – an honorary citizen of the revolutionary French republic – but his published writings were just the tip of the iceberg. He wrote piles of manuscripts on subjects ranging from the legalization of homosexuality to the application of the principle of utility to the Poor Law, which never saw the light of day during his own lifetime but to which Chadwick was privy.

While Senior was known for his unconventional opinions on issues like Church of England finance, he was also a popular figure on the capital's intellectual and social scene. Chadwick, on the other hand, possessed an uncompromising manner and gave short shrift to people who disagreed with him, making him something of an acquired taste. Senior saw value in Chadwick's determination and focus, though, and was instrumental in having him promoted from assistant to full commissioner during the early stages of their work. Together, they dominated the writing of the Royal Commission's final report, which was published in 1834 and drew on evidence about Poor Law administration and practices supplied by parishes across the country. The report's central message was that the country was burdened with a confusing, inconsistent and unfair patchwork of services. Local overseers were well meaning, the report argued, but they were too ready to be generous to people who said they needed help, often because they had deep connections within the local community. As a result, many of the lowest class of labourers found that poor relief paid better than the work they could find and decided to take the easy option of living among the highest class of paupers. Indeed, Senior and Chadwick believed it was their 'painful duty' to pass on the news that throughout the country money was being used for 'purposes opposed to the letter, and still more to the spirit of [the Poor Law], and destructive to the morals of the most numerous class, and to the welfare of all'.

Senior and Chadwick's arguments depended on a number of sleights of hand. Although their report acknowledged that the Poor Law dealt with all kinds of cases, including the sick, the aged and children, they had concentrated almost entirely on labourers, particularly agricultural labourers in the south of England, who formed many of their examples and case studies. In fact, Senior and Chadwick's main concern was outdoor relief, which they argued was the main cause of most of the problems the commission had uncovered. 'In all extensive communities,' they wrote, 'circumstances will occur in which an individual, by the failure of his means of subsistence, will be exposed to the danger of perishing' and there was a moral and social obligation to help. 'But in no part of Europe except England,' they went on, 'has it been thought fit that the provision, whether compulsory or voluntary, should be applied to more than the relief of *indigence*.' Somehow, and at some point in the past, they argued, the Poor Law had got the country into the ill-advised business of relieving poverty – that is, aiding people who either worked or could work.

Of course, Senior and Chadwick did not believe all was lost. They thought it was quite possible to administer a decent, fair and economical system – one that 'elevates the condition of the great mass of society' – and the final third of their report outlined what it might look like. They identified three central principles. The first and most important was that there should always be an incentive for people to choose work over relief. This would be achieved if what people could expect from poor relief was worse than what they could secure by working; or, in the words of Senior and Chadwick's report, if the system aimed to make sure that those in receipt of relief 'shall not be made really or apparently so eligible as the situation of the independent labourer of the lowest class'. The second principle was that poor relief should only be dispensed indoors at workhouses. These institutions would enable administrators to keep the impotent poor, children, able-bodied females and able-bodied men apart, preferably in separate buildings. For this reason, the third principle was of significant centralized control. Local decision-making created chaos at the national level, Senior and Chadwick argued, so there needed to be a central board, empowered to enforce uniform regulations across the country. Parishes would have to band together to form new Poor Law Unions, which would be responsible for enforcing the rules this central board devised.

Senior and Chadwick believed this system would involve spreading the approach that had already been introduced in a number of places, and scaling it up into a coherent, streamlined and evidence-based programme. They argued that the resulting system would be simpler and drive down costs. But they also wanted to convince their readers that it would have a whole host of other social, economic and moral benefits. Those able-bodied labourers who had experienced something like it had seen their industry 'restored and improved', their 'frugal habits . . . created or strengthened', their likelihood of entering into an unwise marriage reduced, and their chances of obtaining better paid employment increased. In 'every instance', Senior and Chadwick suggested, these labourers' 'discontent has been abated, and their moral and social condition in every way improved'.

A SOUNDER OR MORE HEALTHFUL STATE?

Senior and Chadwick's proposals, packaged as the Poor Law Amendment Act of 1834, were presented to Parliament strategically. The Act was an effort to establish a single, uniform system across the country. But the bid to constrain decision-making within local communities was framed as both proven good practice and a return to the true spirit of the 43rd of Elizabeth, with several ideas, including the principle of 'setting the poor to work', being well known to MPs and the public. The Poor Law Amendment Act committed the government not only to discharging its basic and long-standing responsibilities to the poor, but to modernization, with the means of helping the poor presented as the foundation of social, economic and moral progress. This approach appealed to both the landed classes, who saw the chance to reduce their poor rate liabilities, and Whig reformers, who thought they needed to adapt the country's political institutions to new economic and social realities. The big question was whether the theoretical structure would deliver in practice.

Initially, and according to some longer-term measures, the new Poor Law seemed to follow a course its designers had predicted. The total amount of money being spent on able-bodied paupers was less during the middle third of the nineteenth century than it had been during the three decades before. Indeed, according to official figures, the percentage of the population receiving poor relief declined by around a quarter, to 4.6 per cent by the 1870s, as spending per head went down too. Yet these figures told only part, and often not the most important part, of the story. The economy had been experiencing an upturn when Senior and Chadwick wrote the Royal Commission report, making it easy to implement their system first in the south. As the roll-out reached the north of England, home to the nation's most industrially developed areas, a few years later, when the economic picture was not so positive, the limitations of their reforms became apparent.

There were numerous problems when it came to administering the new system. One of the most important was that the commission's report had focused almost entirely on a specific case: able-bodied agricultural labourers, particularly those in the south of England. While agricultural labourers were often tied to year-round contracts, mill and factory workers, who were mostly found in or near rapidly growing urban areas in the north, were less secure in their employment. Peaks and troughs in the business cycle could mean significant and unpredictable fluctuations in the amount of work available throughout the year, and even prolonged periods of unemployment. People who needed poor relief in those circumstances were often unhappy with a system that was rooted in the idea that there should almost always be sufficient paid work available. Yorkshire and Lancashire, where the country's mills and factories were concentrated, were particularly dissatisfied with the reforms. While rate strikes were common, army detachments were deployed in Bradford in 1837 to control large crowds, often hundreds strong, bent on disrupting the administration of the new rules. Concerned by the potential for serious social unrest, officials in other towns, including Huddersfield, Bolton and Oldham, often refused to do things such as implement the workhouse test, at least in its strictest form.

Creating a single, uniform system of poor relief across the whole country at the pace reformers wanted to implement change turned out to be much harder than they had imagined. In addition to resistance from those who expected to be able to access poor relief, there were problems with establishing the administrative structures the Royal Commission had recommended. There were meant to be new Poor Law Unions, which merged different parishes that had run the old system on their own. This meant arguments over boundaries and authorities, with officers who took great pride in their positions in their local communities unhappy about having to give them up. Indeed, contrary to expectations, and despite the reformers' centralizing tendencies, the new Poor Law Commission, and its successor in 1847, the Poor Law Board, actually lacked a number of what seemed like crucial powers, such as being able to compel Unions to build huge new segregated workhouses.

The consequence was that many of the practices that had so riled Senior and Chadwick actually carried on. Outdoor relief, including for people who were working but unable to make ends meet, which the Royal Commission report had called the 'master evil' of the old system, continued on a massive scale. According to the Local Government Board, almost 148,000 able-bodied paupers, and more than 880,000 paupers of all classes, including children, were still receiving relief outdoors in 1871, more than thirty years after it was supposed to have been abolished. Successive governments had tried to deal with these difficulties with new legislation, including the Outdoor Relief Prohibitory Order in 1844. Yet the proposal to ban the practice completely had to face up to hard realities. In Bradford, for example, the workhouse had a capacity of around 260 people. At one point in 1848, however, the city had more than 13,000 claims for relief.

The Royal Commission had argued that these people should be helped in specially constructed workhouses that were so bleak they would hold demand down through deterrence. Some Unions were able to build these ominous-looking and claustrophobic institutions. Poorly lit and heated, new reformed workhouses had a main entrance to a reception where claimants would be evaluated before being handed an uncomfortable and badly fitting uniform. From there, families would be broken up and sent to different wings with their own dormitories, exercise yards and work spaces, where people would be given jobs to do in exchange for their bed and board. Barely adequate meals were prepared in the workhouse kitchen but mass food poisoning was common, especially in the summer months thanks to the absence of refrigeration. All of this was overseen by a master (former soldiers were a popular choice) who liberally dispensed beatings or spells in solitary confinement to those accused of misdemeanours.

With the best will in the world, though, nowhere had the money to build facilities of this kind for the number of people asking for help in places in like Bradford. Especially in the north, the trend was to convert old workhouse facilities in ways that either upped capacity or allowed limited amounts of segregation, often by converting attics and basements. Though often filled with damp, these adapted workhouses displeased reformers, who objected to their high-ceilinged halls as too welcoming and to their practice of keeping families together. What worried them more, however, was Unions tackling high demand by continuing with outdoor relief. Unable to stop this practice, the government fell back on the long-standing tradition of requiring a labour test before Unions could dispense such relief.

Although the Poor Law reformers had seen these difficulties as having interrelated administrative and moral solutions, it was clear the economy could throw up problems that were not susceptible to that approach. Britain had emerged from the downturn that greeted the roll-out of the new Poor Law during the late 1830s, and had gone further down the path recommend by the likes of Adam Smith and David Ricardo in 1846 when it abolished the Corn Laws, removing the tariffs on imported grain and helping to make food, especially bread, cheaper at the expense of landowners' profits. But importing more grain only highlighted that the country had a growing economy that was part of widening and deepening international networks that were not limited to agriculture and finance. It was easier than ever to source goods and trade with people in different countries. Economic and political events in those places now took on a new significance.

Nowhere was this driven home to people more than during the Lancashire cotton famine of the early 1860s. With Manchester, 'Cottonopolis', at its heart, Lancashire was dominated by the textiles industry, with some 2,500 factories importing cotton from around the world and spinning it into fabric that was sold throughout the UK and abroad. Aside from employing more than 400,000 men, women and children in these factories, the textile industry indirectly supported hundreds of thousands of others, from workers in Liverpool's ports, where cotton came into the country and was then exported in finished goods, to the City of London, where money was invested in America's cotton businesses, to families and the owners of businesses where workers spent their wages. According to *The Economist*, during the 1860s almost a quarter of the country's 20 million people made a living that was connected to cotton in one way or another. It was therefore a catastrophic moment when, during the American Civil War of 1861–5, the Unionist North blockaded the Confederate South, one of the world's biggest cotton-growing areas, cutting off the supply to the outside world. Prices spiralled as reserve stocks of cotton were run down. Hundreds of thousands of people in Lancashire were thrown out of work as mills closed their doors.

The Poor Law Unions in the north-west of England were completely overwhelmed by this economic disaster. Soup kitchens started to open as local administrators, church groups, trade associations and other voluntary groups did what they could to plug the gap between the meagre help available through the under-strain Poor Law and the huge demand for relief. For some commentators, the American North was to blame. But Lancashire was home to a huge number of religious dissenters and political radicals who supported the North's anti-slavery stance, as they had done the Whigs' move to abolish slavery in the British Empire in 1833. Emboldened by a message of gratitude from Abraham Lincoln, workers and employers attended public meetings to show they were willing to suffer for the cause, as the government watched and waited for what it thought was a likely victory by the North. As Lancashire's mills and factories closed, funds were set up to collect donations to help those who had been thrown out of work. When such charity started to run down, however, the Poor Law had to pick up the slack. Although disorder was relatively uncommon, riots in Stalybridge, where officials' homes, businesses and property were attacked, forced a rethink on whether the workhouse was an appropriate response to people whose predicaments were so clearly out of their hands. The Public Works (Manufacturing Districts) Act was passed in 1864 and allowed local authorities to borrow money to pay for improvements in their communities. These projects, like paving streets and building parks, created much-needed jobs.

Yet what was also clear by the 1860s was that economic events were far from the only major pressure on the Poor Law. Less than 15 per cent of poor relief claimants in Bradford in 1848 were able-bodied labourers, meaning most were prepared to knock at the workhouse door for reasons other than the ones the Poor Law reformers had imagined. With sick wards and infirmaries attached to workhouses, illness and disease turned out to be one of the most important factors. In theory, access to the Poor Law medical service involved the same principle of less eligibility that governed relief more generally, with help supposedly kept to a level below that which the lowest paid labourer would be able to purchase outside the workhouse. This principle was believed to be particularly important in the case of health, because hospital care outside the workhouse was divided into two separate sets of institutions with predictably different levels of resourcing: one for those who were wealthy enough to pay; and a voluntary service, reliant on charitable donations and funds from 'sick clubs' into which working-class people paid as a protection when they needed care, for those who were not. In practice, however, the idea that Poor Law officers should decide who was entitled to healthcare had not always followed during the middle decades of the nineteenth century.

The fact that Poor Law Unions were bigger, and therefore had more money, than the old parish units helped when it came to dealing with sickness. Some Unions put money into things like dispensaries – institutions where local doctors who treated the poor banded together to achieve economies of scale – with the aim of keeping people away from the workhouse. Others invested in facilities attached to their workhouses. These infirmaries could be small, providing care for just a handful of people, though they could also be quite large, with separate wards for men and women. But, thanks to the principle of less eligibility and huge demand, they were often bleak and depressing places. It was not uncommon for three people to be expected to share a bed; wards were staffed by female occupants of the workhouse, rather than trained nurses, and basic resources were often scarce. In 1860s Paddington, for example, the workhouse infirmary had one towel for every thirty-one people. Yet under pressure from public health campaigners, including Florence Nightingale, this situation started to improve. Poor Law officials were put in charge of the smallpox vaccination programme, which was made compulsory by the government in 1853. Then, from the late 1860s onwards, hospitals were slowly separated from workhouses as Poor Law Unions were instructed to centralize their medical services in order to redistribute funds between districts with different levels of needs. The result was something like an extremely limited national hospital service: more than three-quarters of the country's hospital beds were attached to workhouses.

INEFFICIENCY AND DISEASE

Edwin Chadwick would have seemed to be one of the least likely sources of insight when it came to the problems of the new Poor Law. But professional disappointment had forced him to reflect on his creation. Chadwick had been passed over for a post on the permanent Poor Law Commission, primarily because the government did not think he was of a suitable social standing to win over the kinds of people whose co-operation was necessary to make the system work. Instead, he was forced to accept a consolation prize, the post of secretary to the commission, from which vantage point he had to observe others taking charge of a machine he had helped design. Yet this new role turned out to be an important turning point in his career, and in the history of public health more generally. Although he was excluded from policy decisions, Chadwick's responsibility for gathering and passing on information about the Poor Law to the commissioners meant he got to know much more about the day-to-day workings of the reformed system than he otherwise might have done. Almost immediately he noticed the pressures that bad health had on poor relief – something he had overlooked during the early 1830s.

Chadwick, of course, was far from the only person to observe that, in early nineteenth-century Britain, illness and disease had consequences for more than the individuals directly affected. Industrialization had brought significant population growth and caused people to move to areas where trading and manufacturing were creating new jobs. Cities such as Leeds, Manchester and Liverpool more than doubled in size in the first three decades of the nineteenth century, as people looking for work crammed into new housing that was thrown up quickly to accommodate them. These dwellings seldom, if ever, had adequate provision for sanitation. Waste and dirt were prevalent, with soil heaps and cesspools common sights. Communal water supplies were often contaminated; there were frequent outbreaks of cholera that affected people of all social and economic ranks, but especially the working classes who shared the worst conditions and facilities.

The exact cause of cholera was widely contested. The era's most popular theory was that illness spread through contact with 'miasmas': cloud-like entities emanating from rotting matter. But the accumulation of more and better information during the middle decades of the nineteenth century enabled statisticians and medical professionals to investigate those causes in new ways. Spikes in death rates and the geographical clustering of cases highlighted not only the important differences between rural and urban areas, but also that illness was linked to environment. Some local authorities, like the Poor Law Guardians in the East End of London, decided to start removing hazardous waste, from faeces to rotting corpses, in their districts in the hope they could stop outbreaks of disease before they started. Yet these initiatives were the subject of fierce criticism. Why, some people argued, should ratepayers' money be used to clear up the mess that other people were leaving behind?

The Poor Law Commissioners, urged on by the Whig Home Secretary, Lord John Russell, asked Neil Arnott and James Phillips Kay, two London-based doctors, to investigate these issues. Their report, which appeared in 1838 in the far from inspiring form of a supplement to an appendix on unnecessary expenditure in the Poor Law Commissioners' annual report, concluded that it was certainly illegal to use the poor rate funds to pay for programmes like waste removal. Nevertheless, they also pointed out that there was a strong body of evidence to support the claim that such practices helped reduce the spread of disease. There needed to be some hard thinking that weighed a political principle against pragmatic action.

Chadwick was fascinated by these developments. Feeling marginalized in a system he thought he had earned the right to run, he wanted a project he could call his own: now, he believed, the quest to improve working-class living conditions might be it. Drawing on his considerable contacts book, Chadwick managed to convince Parliament to commission him to investigate, and in 1839 he put himself at the head of a network through which Assistant Poor Law Commissioners, clerks of the Boards of Guardians and medical officers funnelled information. The outcome – *Report on the Sanitary Condition of the Labouring Population of Great Britain* (1842) – was a mammoth, 450-page document, filled with detailed charts and tables, that was testament to the three years of work that went into it.

Chadwick's report made one of the most important and compelling cases for state intervention ever written. Yet it was also a dry account that was never likely to light the coals of revolution. Leaning heavily on the miasmatic concept of disease (which would be disproved by the French chemist Louis Pasteur, among others, less than forty years later), Chadwick expressed his conclusions about the link between disease and environment in the staid language of a serious public official. Disease was caused 'by atmospheric impurities produced by decomposing animal and vegetable substances, by damp and filth, and close and overcrowded dwellings' that were common in the poorest parts of modern cities. Disease was 'always found in connexion with [those] physical circumstances', he explained; moreover, it almost always went away when 'those circumstances are removed by drainage, proper cleansing, better ventilation, and other means of diminishing atmospheric impurity'.

Chadwick's proposals for tackling these problems – which were essentially right, albeit for the wrong reasons – were ambitious and expensive. He wanted improved sanitation through a massive public works programme that would involve building a new system of clean water supply to and waste removal from houses in cities. The cesspools, soil heaps and decomposing waste and matter that were common sights in poor districts would become a thing of the past as enclosed pipes carried waste away from homes and into a new system of sewers, where it would be disposed of appropriately. Ever the technocrat, Chadwick insisted there had to be new rules, regulations and public officials, including salaried medical officers, to stop bad practices and to enforce behaviours that would cut the chances of illness and disease spreading in the ways they had done in the past.

To the casual observer, Chadwick looked as if he had made a dramatic U-turn on the position he had taken ten years earlier. Now, he seemed to be asking the government to spend a huge sum of money fixing a problem that less sympathetic commentators thought people living in slums could and should tackle themselves. Chadwick's transformation, though, was skin-deep. His proposed solutions to public health problems were products of the same heavy emphasis on scientific evidence, administrative efficiency, technical expertise and economic measures. He wrote at length in his sanitary report about the importance of protecting 'the labouring classes and . . . the ratepayers against inefficiency and waste' by ensuring 'all new local public works are devised and conducted by responsible officers qualified by the possession of the science and skill of civil engineers'. He also suggested that the new enclosed pipes could go all the way out to the countryside, where treated waste could be turned into manure for farming. In other words, the problems could be fixed by people like himself and in a way that had direct economic applications.

The overall design of the new sanitary system also looked a lot like the reformed Poor Law. Chadwick was adamant that public health problems could not be solved if local authorities were left to their own devices. There needed to be 'uniformity in legislation and in the executive machinery, and of doing the same things in the same way'. There had to be one approach, 'calling the same officers, proceedings, and things by the same names', if disease and illness were to be tackled effectively. Like the Royal Commission on the Poor Law's report, Chadwick's sanitary report insisted that good administration did not just solve problems; it also built good character. Bad environments caused disease, which in turn caused poverty – but, Chadwick stated, they also produced 'an adult population short-lived, improvident, reckless, and intemperate, and with habitual avidity for sensual gratifications'. Overcrowded and dirty living conditions were 'destructive to the morality as well as the health of large classes of both sexes'. Better and more rational rules and regulations would not only bring down costs; they would help produce better citizens.

Chadwick believed his case was so persuasive and his solutions so well thought out that legislation would follow quickly. There were, however, big and obvious obstacles in the way. Who was going to pay for the infrastructure he had described? If the proposal was for money to come from taxation, was it right that the middle classes, whose homes had adequate waste disposal that they had paid for themselves, should be asked to put their hands in their pockets again? Even with seemingly overwhelming evidence linking dirty environments and disease, could the state compel people to fund any of the solutions Chadwick suggested? Progress was much slower than he had envisaged. Further investigations were undertaken and reports written. Some of the largest cities, including Leeds and Manchester, were given more powers to deal with the problems they faced, while local authorities were made responsible for dealing with waste thought to cause the worst epidemics, including cholera. But it took another six years to establish the General Board of Health, the single national health authority Chadwick had recommended and of which he was appointed the commissioner.

Chadwick's excitement at having the opportunity to turn his administrative dreams into reality – denied him after the Royal Commission on the Poor Law – was short-lived. His strong tendency towards an authoritarian form of technocracy made him nigh-on impossible to negotiate with, suggesting MPs had been wise to overlook him a little over a decade earlier. Increasingly frustrated by his inability to push through his plans, Chadwick struggled on until 1854, when, on the brink of collapse, he decided to retire. From his home in Richmond, Surrey, he spent the next thirty-six years writing unsolicited letters to public officials pointing out what he believed were flaws in their work, and repeatedly failing to secure a seat in Parliament.

Nevertheless, Chadwick's mission was not lost with him. His successor, John Simon, was a fully trained medical professional who worked as a surgeon at both St Thomas' and the new King's College Hospital in London. Like Chadwick, he believed in the power of scientific evidence and poured public money into medical research, including studies of typhoid and smallpox. This turned out to be an important characteristic when ideas about the causes of disease were moving away from the miasmatic theories that Chadwick had believed in and towards something that would later be called the 'germ theory of disease', as people such as John Snow, a London-based doctor who traced an outbreak of cholera in 1854 near his Soho home to a single water pump on what is now Broadwick Street, threw doubt on the existence of disease-spreading clouds. But, well read in literature and philosophy and a friend of the art critic John Ruskin, Simon was also a skilled diplomat who knew how to get people to work for him. He committed years to the painstaking process of holding coalitions of interested parties together, sometimes making breakthroughs – as he did when local authorities were empowered to tackle industrial pollution as well as street waste – but at other times with less success, as was the case with the 1866 Sanitary Act, a well-intentioned but vague effort to establish binding public health responsibilities for local authorities that left enough room for those who wanted to escape them to do so. Yet his patience and perseverance were rewarded during the final decades of the century with legislation like the Public Health Act of 1875, which made it compulsory for every district to have a medical officer of health.

An important feature of these developments was a step back from the strong centralizing tendencies that had motivated Chadwick during the early 1830s. Westminster may have been the source of legislation and, in some cases, money, but local government was expected to shoulder a huge amount of responsibility when it came to delivering things like public health programmes, not to mention the cost-cutting and efficiency aspects of other initiatives. By the end of the nineteenth century this kind of approach had animated a whole new attitude to local government and organization in places that had seen the worst effects of industrialization. Birmingham, under its Liberal mayor Joseph Chamberlain in the 1870s, had started to pioneer what became known as 'municipal socialism', whereby utilities such as gas and water were brought under community ownership and control, often through compulsory purchase, and slums were demolished. The intention was not to make a financial profit but to deliver services that were recognized to have wider, and often cost-saving, benefits to local people who might otherwise not be able to afford or receive them. Only local authorities could do this, politicians and administrators like Chamberlain argued, because they had the connections with and knowledge of the areas that were meant to be improved.

The intention of scaling back expenditure on poverty had produced consequences that few of its architects, including Chadwick, would have predicted forty years earlier. Although it was a long way from being a general principle of government, the idea of spending money in one area in order to save much more in another had been established. Furthermore, having been shunned by reformers during the 1830s, the idea that the solutions to large and seemingly national problems should involve input from local government and other actors had been renewed. But what was also quite clear was that reform had thrown up many more questions than answers. Poverty, in particular, seemed to be a consequence of more than just poor decisions or bad character and, as a result, a much more difficult concept to understand than many confident but cavalier observers had suggested during the early nineteenth century. While Chadwick had thrown light on the role played by illness and disease, others started to wonder if other factors beyond individuals' control played a role too. The process of finding out would help set the cause of social reform in new directions.

2

Below the Poverty Line

Although Edwin Chadwick had boasted that the Poor Law Amendment Act of 1834 was 'the first great piece of legislation based upon scientific or economical principles', the Royal Commission on the Poor Law's report had conceded they did not know the answers to a number of important questions. In particular, and somewhat remarkably given the changes the report wrought, the Royal Commission admitted they had difficulty specifying what 'less eligibility' – the principle that relief inside the workhouse should always fall short of what the lowest-paid job could pay for outside – actually was. When it came to the lives of independent labourers, about whom Chadwick and his colleague Nassau Senior were so willing to moralize, the Royal Commission's report had actually conceded that 'little is really known . . . by those who award or distribute relief'.

This omission mattered, because 'less eligibility' had to be put into practice. Across the country, administrators were obliged to create conditions that deterred people from seeking help. All too frequently the result was horrifying, with reports of people being forced to live in degrading and – to modern eyes – barely believable conditions. There was a public outcry in 1845 when newspapers, including *The Times*, told their readers about the workhouse in Andover, a town in Hampshire, where men were so hungry they had been driven to gnawing putrid gristle and marrow from the animal bones they had been told to crush to make fertilizer in exchange for a pitiful level of relief. Less eligibility might have had an intuitive theoretical attractiveness, but many observers, not to mention people reading about events far away, were deeply troubled when such cruel scenes were the consequence. Nevertheless, they were a logical end-point of the new approach to poor relief and, it seemed, what reformers wanted.

By the early twentieth century, however, the terms of the argument had changed. In the intervening time, social investigators had immersed themselves in overcrowded and filthy slums and discovered a web of forces that seemed to stop even the most determined people from breaking free of the grinding poverty that surrounded them. A complex, dynamic and new understanding of society had emerged, one in which people's lives and fates were seen to be connected in ways they had never been understood to be before. Thrift, hard work and individual character – the qualities that earlier Poor Law reformers had believed were both the only path out of poverty and the foundations of national prosperity – seemed to be only a part, and often not the most important part, of the explanation of why someone might not be able to make ends meet. But while most observers, including Chadwick, had accepted that events such as illness and disease helped explain why some people fell on hard times, others wondered if poverty was a problem that was embedded into the very structure of modern life. The question, then, was what a Poor Law fit for such conditions looked like. The answers contained not only the kinds of moral judgements about poverty that had been features of the discussion since the 1830s, but a whole host of ideas about its possible eradication that had previously been considered untenable.

ECONOMIC GROWTH AND ITS DISCONTENTS

When MPs and political economists thought about the relationship between state and society around the time the Poor Law had first been established at the start of the seventeenth century, they were often concerned with stability. By the end of the century, however, merchants and financiers had become increasingly vocal in arguing that governments should encourage trade with and investments in the rest of the world. They believed Britain should be producing and selling more and better goods than anywhere else. As commercial activity increased, the Enlightenment's political economists (and the philosophers who followed in their footsteps) linked economic growth with access to expanding markets. Thinkers such as Adam

Smith explained that mills, factories and firms could succeed in those markets through innovations like the division of labour. In his most famous and celebrated example, Smith demonstrated that ten workers in a pin factory, each of whom could produce no more than twenty pins a day on their own, could make more than 48,000 a day if they were part of a mechanized production line that divided the task into eighteen different jobs. This, Smith argued, was progress of the highest order, which was helping Britain to lead the world in industrial and economic terms.

The Great Exhibition of 1851 has often been seen as a symbolic moment in this story. With Queen Victoria's husband, Prince Albert, enlisted as a patron and organizer, foreign manufacturers and designers were invited to send examples of their wares for display alongside Britain's best work in the spectacular Crystal Palace, which was made of 300,000 sheets of glass and covered almost 70,000 square metres of land. More than 6 million visits were made by people who poured into London on trains and arrived at Hyde Park by omnibus and carriage so they could wonder at 100,000 objects, from printing presses to tapestries to folding pianos, spread over two floors. The French, Germans and Americans all sent highly advanced and sophisticated displays, but many far-from-unbiased observers thought Britain's own presentations triumphed – if only because they took over half the available floor space.

Political economists were keen to take credit for these developments, claiming that economic growth and its spoils had followed directly from their ideas about free trade, to which the Whig-dominated governments of the middle third of the nineteenth century were sympathetic. Their favourite example of their influence was the Tory Prime Minister Robert Peel's decision in 1846 to repeal the Corn Laws: taxes on imports of grain. Many Whigs and radicals had considered these taxes as symptoms of the structural bias towards the Tories in British politics. Landowners wanted to keep food prices high to protect their profits, the Whigs argued, and they were able to do so because a small electorate and unrepresentative distribution of seats across the country, and especially the 'rotten' boroughs, meant the Tories, the landowners' political representatives, controlled Parliament. As David Ricardo put it in an argument that would be an important influence on Karl Marx, the landowning class were in conflict with other classes because they did well out of situations that were bad news for everyone else. Indeed, the corn tariffs had a number of direct impacts on the public purse, including the Poor Law, because high food prices were one of the common reasons people sought relief.

Peel's decision to back repeal of the Corn Laws, taken during the second year of the disastrous and epoch-making famine in Ireland, was momentous: it split the Tory party and, in the process, made free trade the new centre ground in British politics. For the Whigs and radicals who had long argued for such reforms, the repeal was a triumph. It was no surprise, political economists argued, that after this stranglehold had been broken Britain entered a twenty-year period of economic growth subsequently dubbed the 'Great Victorian Boom'. For the third quarter of the nineteenth century, Britain had what was by some measures the most productive economy in the world, with the highest GDP per head and a share of the global trade in manufactured goods that was measured at more than 35 per cent in the early 1880s.

Nevertheless, not everyone thought this was a story of unquestionable progress. Economic growth involved travelling on a winding and sometimes bumpy road on which some people were often left behind. Real wages did not rise continuously or steadily and there were periodic slumps, such as the Lancashire cotton famine during the 1860s, and different rates of development in different parts of the economy. Moreover, as the economy moved from the world of what historians call 'gentlemanly capitalism', dominated by land and financial services, to industrial capitalism with its smoking chimneys, iron, coal and steel, during the first half of the nineteenth century, people worried about the impact all these changes were having on the workers who toiled away at the bottom of society and lived in the kinds of conditions that shocked Edwin Chadwick during the early 1840s.

Among those raising concerns were capitalists, industrialists and mill owners. One of the earliest and most famous was Robert Owen (1771–1858). An energetic character who had lost his religious faith, Owen made his money from developing new cotton-spinning machinery before moving into mill management in the 1790s. At the turn of the century, however, he made what looked like an unusual decision:

he bought shares in a recently founded Scottish mill town called New Lanark. He had done so with the intention of showing he could run it as a profit-making venture that also improved, rather than degraded, his workers' physical and spiritual conditions. Owen encountered scepticism, but he was successful enough to persuade a group of investors, including the utilitarian Jeremy Bentham, to provide him with capital for a wholesale buyout of New Lanark in 1813. This enabled Owen to turn the town into a fully-fledged experiment in philanthropic management and socialist living – one based on the idea that meaningful participation in economic and social life would be achieved through self-organization. His theory was that people's enthusiasm for their work, and their behaviour outside it, would improve if they were treated better and encouraged to live in what he thought was a more rewarding way. He reduced working hours to eight per day, introduced communal cooking, and put a sixth of workers' wage packets into a fund that was used for sick pay and pensions. Owen even tried to export his model to the USA, buying New Harmony in Indiana in 1825.

Tory MPs also worried about the effects of industrialization, particularly its potential for wearing down traditional social ties and moral values. As members of the party of social order, hierarchy and paternalism, many Tories reacted with horror to a world of mills and factories where men, women and children toiled for long hours, sometimes seven days a week, among noisy and dangerous machinery for bosses who seldom showed Owen's broader concerns for their welfare. What kind of a country would Britain be in fifty years' time if children, often younger than ten, were forced into work, leaving little time for things like religious instruction at a crucial point in their moral development? Lord Shaftesbury, an evangelical aristocrat who pressed for strict Sunday religious observance and spoke out about the treatment of workers in Britain's new factories, played a leading role in campaigns to improve working conditions, especially for children, during the middle decades of the nineteenth century. Criticized by factory owners and economic liberals as restraints on trade, legislation, including the Factory Acts of the 1830s and 1840s, cut the working week to five and half days and sixty hours in total, which helped create the modern concept of Sunday as a day of rest.

Workers themselves also found ways to resist the worst aspects of capitalism and industrialization. The Combination Laws of 1799 and 1800 had banned people from forming work-related organizations with political aims because there were fears Britain might go down the same revolutionary path as France. When those laws were repealed in 1824 workers were permitted to set up trade-based bodies, the forerunners of today's trade unions, which offered limited forms of collective protection. By the 1850s, the co-operative movement had also laid down roots in the north of England, with the Rochdale Society of Equitable Pioneers, founded in 1844, often cited as the first successful enterprise of its kind. Co-operatives provided goods and services via their shops but, thanks to their collective purchasing power and supply chains that included their own factories, they insulated their members from price swings and profiteering. These organizations became important sources of pride and identity, often integrated with existing community infrastructure like churches.

People wanted to know more about the new economy and society that was emerging through these processes. Karl Marx's patron and collaborator, Friedrich Engels, whose family owned a successful textiles business, had come to England from Prussia in 1842 to work in their Manchester mill. Already a political radical, Engels had taken to systematically observing and recording his thoughts on his surroundings so that he could report them to the wider world. The resulting work, *The Condition of the Working Class in England* (1845), first published in German, argued that, far from spreading wealth as the classical political economists had promised it would, capitalism and industrialization functioned in a way that was bad for the working classes, making them poor, demoralized and, as Edwin Chadwick had been finding out, ill. Other famous works included Charles Dickens's novels *Oliver Twist*, *Hard Times* and *Great Expectations*, first published as serials from the late 1830s through to the early 1860s and which captured the attention of an even wider middle-class audience, who read about death, disease and poverty forcing children into lives of crime, people ground down by a society that treated them as little more than numbers, and how their own wealth was ultimately built on these people's suffering.

Often-shocked readers of those works wanted to know what they could or should do in response. While writers and campaigners like Marx and Engels thought the answer was a new political programme, such as communism, organizations like the Manchester Statistical Society and its counterpart in London, which would be granted a royal charter in 1887, offered a different kind of hope. Statisticians and social investigators studied official statistics, like census returns and Poor Law records, in the belief that doing so would uncover laws behind seemingly random but common events: births, deaths, marriages and sickness. The most popular of the bodies frequented by these researchers, including Chadwick and the liberal philosopher and political economist John Stuart Mill, during the late nineteenth century was the National Association for the Promotion of Social Science. More widely known as the Social Science Association, it met annually from 1857 to 1886, during which time it hosted more than 3,000 presentations on legal reform, penal policy, public health and 'social economy'. Particularly popular with lawyers, doctors and educators – those whom the Tory periodical the *Spectator* called 'volunteer legislators of Great Britain' – the Social Science Association was built on the idea there were scientific answers to all manner of political questions. Although few of the laws they assumed would be discovered were forthcoming, the continuing flow of information about society and the economy kept their hopes alive.

The issue that connected almost everything these thinkers and organizations discussed was the continued existence of poverty. Not only did poverty seem puzzling when so many people could be heard lauding the extent of progress in Britain at this time, it also continued to be mysterious. Engels, Dickens and others pulled the curtain back on a world that shocked the middle and upper classes because few of them experienced or understood it. But by the 1880s, books such as Andrew Mearns's *Bitter Cry of Outcast London* and George Sims's *How the Poor Live*, both published in 1883, had taken the argument one step further for the middle-class reading public. Impressionistically, at least, it seemed that the poor were a much bigger group than the one that showed up in Poor Law statistics. Unfamiliar parts of British cities seemed to house significant numbers of people who went about their business on the margins of society, away from prying eyes. What were these people's lives like? How many of them were there? Did they live that way out of choice? How did they survive if they were not taking money from Poor Law officers? In short, what did these people's lives tell everyone about what being poor actually meant in nineteenth-century Britain?

LIFE AND LABOUR ON THE STREETS OF LONDON AND YORK

One of the most significant investigations into these questions was conducted by Charles Booth (1840–1916), a wealthy Liverpudlian who had made a fortune from his family's shipping firm and who had married into political aristocracy: his wife, Mary Catherine Macaulay, was the niece of Thomas Babington Macaulay, the eminent Whig MP and author of *A History of England*. Not only had Booth not been to university, where increasing numbers of privileged young men were being introduced to the 'social question', he also lost touch with his family's Nonconformist faith, a faith that was a common spur to becoming involved with poverty relief and charity. Booth, though, had moved to London at a critical moment, in 1871 just as the 'Great Victorian Boom' was giving way to a prolonged period of economic depression. By the 1880s the situation had become much worse and, for many commentators, a matter of great concern. A particularly severe winter in 1886 had stretched people's limited resources, and a host of sometimes violent trade disputes about pay and conditions, including one particularly fractious strike on the docks in the East End of London, had occurred. In February 1886, a demonstration following a rally in Trafalgar Square, where 20,000 unemployed workers had gathered to call for a programme of public works to alleviate their suffering, had turned into a riot. Trouble flared as the demonstrators spilled into the West End, where shop windows were smashed and the well-to-do were robbed.

After fifteen years tending to his transatlantic business interests and mixing with the capital's intellectual and social elites to which his wife had introduced him, Booth approached the subject in 1886 with the utmost seriousness and a determination to transform the debate about poverty with hard facts. Tapping into the capital's network of social reformers through organizations like the Royal Statistical Society and the Charity Organisation Society, he assembled a team of research assistants whom he sent out onto the streets of London with instructions to come back with information about the everyday lives of the people they saw. The project was a magnet for social investigators and activists trying to make their mark on politics and social policy. Booth's recruits included Beatrice Potter (1858–1943), who later married Sidney Webb and, via her leading role in the Fabian Society, would help found the London School of Economics and the Labour Party, and Octavia Hill (1838–1912), whose philanthropic work was an influential model for social housing projects.

Beginning in the east London slums of Tower Hamlets, Booth's assistants – around eight full-time workers who were aided by countless other contributors – tried to find out what went on behind closed doors in London's poor neighbourhoods. Reprising an undercover role she had performed three years earlier when, as part of another investigation into working-class life, she visited Lancashire disguised as the daughter of a Welsh farmer, Beatrice Potter found a job making trousers in a tailor's on Mile End Road, where she anonymously observed what life was like for people working in one of the capital's most notorious sweated trades. Other assistants were asked to dig into the details of life in poor homes. Yet with the communities they encountered proving understandably suspicious of their intentions, Booth's assistants were forced to be as inventive as Potter had been. The most fruitful way in was interviewing school board visitors. Following the Liberal MP William Forster's Elementary Education Act of 1870, which had established the principle of basic schooling for all children from the ages of five to thirteen, the 1880 Elementary Education Act had made attendance compulsory, though not free, until the age of ten, with fines issued both to families that did not comply and to employers who took on children under thirteen who could not produce a certificate proving they had not been absent. School board visitors had the power to enter homes to enforce those rules, which gave them first-hand knowledge of some of the people in which Booth was interested. There were obvious flaws with this method, including the fact that school board visitors only gave researchers access to information about households with children aged twelve years and under. Nevertheless, Booth and his researchers amassed an unparalleled body of information, which was published in seventeen volumes from 1889 through to 1903 called *The Life and Labour of the People in London*.

Booth divided the capital's population into eight different groups based on measurements such as household income, which gave the impression of scientific objectivity. However, these categories often involved value-laden judgements about the lives his subjects led. In 'Class A', Booth grouped people that he described as vicious borderline savages and criminals; 'Class B', meanwhile, categorized casual labourers who had fallen from higher classes thanks to what he believed were character failings of some kind and who lived in a state of perpetual want. 'Class D', on the other hand, were what Booth considered decent people – factory labourers, porters and so on – who worked hard to make ends meet, while 'Class H' were the respectable and wealthy upper-middle classes. In addition to the hundreds of pages of tables, charts and detailed analyses, Booth and his assistants produced a series of colour-coded maps that showed, street by street, where those people could be found, creating a visually powerful topography of London.

Booth's main finding, and the one that gained the most attention, was that 30 per cent of the capital's population, including wage earners, lived in poverty. This figure was even higher than the 25 per cent Henry Hyndman of the Social Democratic Federation had suggested to a widely disbelieving public, including Booth himself, in 1885. Booth had come to this conclusion by defining poverty by looking at whether people were in regular employment, how they spent their leisure time, and whether their income was enough to buy the items he thought were necessary for a modest life – a calculation that involved some of the many judgements he dispensed throughout the inquiry. For many people, Booth's 30 per cent figure was mind-boggling. It challenged their deepest assumptions about the relationship between poverty and wealth and their sense of who was benefitting from Britain's industrial power. To be sure, Booth attributed poverty to a range of different factors, including economic downturns, low wages and a weakness for drink, meaning there was plenty of scope in his conclusions for blaming the poor for the situation in which they found themselves. When a third of the population were judged to be living in poverty, however, moralizing could only go so far.

One person who became caught up in this debate was Seebohm Rowntree (1871–1954), a member of a Quaker family of confectionery manufacturers based in York. Under the leadership of Seebohm's father, Joseph, who had joined the company in the early 1860s, Rowntree's had developed into a business motivated by the idea that profit and conscience went together. This conviction manifested itself in a number of ways. Trade was conducted to what Joseph Rowntree considered the highest ethical standards, and the company developed a paternalistic relationship with its employees. Joseph tried to know each of his employees by name and introduced a variety of welfare schemes, beginning with an eight-hour working day in 1896 and gradually increasing in scale and ambition. This paternalism peaked during the first decade of the twentieth century, with the construction of an entirely new town, New Earswick, near the company's main factory on the city's outskirts.

Many of these projects were funded by a business that boomed after Fruit Pastilles went on the market in 1881. But success also meant a significant expansion, from 200 workers during the early 1880s to almost 4,000 twenty years later. Joseph Rowntree found it impossible to keep up certain practices, such as remembering his employees' names, in these circumstances. The question that interested the Rowntrees was how to continue with their social ideals in a company that was operating on such a massive scale. Seebohm, who joined the firm in 1889 and later become its first director of labour, was central to developing their answer.

Although Seebohm continued to promote the family's Quaker faith – refusing, for instance, to let his workers take a day off to attend York races, where they were likely to drink and gamble – he also blazed a modernizing trail, pioneering the use of industrial psychology and scientific management in the company's factory and offices. Booth's research caught his attention because, if also true of York, its estimates of the level of poverty suggested that he and his family might not know their employees quite as well as they thought they did. Rowntree decided to carry out his own survey in 1897. But, rather than rely on hearsay and third-party testimony, as Booth had been forced to in many situations, he wanted to be comprehensive. Rowntree resolved to make actual visits to working-class homes and interview the people who lived in them. Armed with a list of pre-set questions, he and his assistants visited 11,560 families, totalling 46,754 individuals. 'Among the other questions upon which I desired to obtain information were the following,' Rowntree wrote:

> What was the true measure of the poverty in the city, both in extent and depth? How much of it was due to insufficiency of income and how much to improvidence? How many families were sunk in a poverty so acute that its members suffered from a chronic insufficiency of food and clothing?

As they travelled through York, Rowntree and his team built a detailed picture of life in a city which had retained much of its Roman and medieval architecture but had seen slums grow around it. Although they were more successful than Booth's researchers when it came to gaining access to working-class homes, they also encountered some of the same problems. Some people were simply unwilling to divulge the information Rowntree was interested in. Others, no doubt wary of what might happen if someone in authority, or even their wife, found out how much they earned, were happy to lie in order to get rid of the inquisitive strangers at their doorstep. Rowntree and his investigators were forced to cross-reference their interviewees' answers with information from other sources, including employers, who helped Rowntree figure out how much around 60 per cent of York's workers were paid. Rowntree even produced his own colour-coded map. His, however, was of the location of every public house and off-licence in York – a decision that revealed much about his Quaker preoccupations.

The result of these efforts was *Poverty: A Study of Town Life*, which was published in 1901. Rowntree's main conclusion was clear and simple: Booth's 30 per cent claim was not an anomaly. York, a representative and average-sized provincial city, had a similar level of poverty as London, which made it highly likely other cities did too. Yet by delving deeper into the concept and definition of poverty,

Rowntree went beyond Booth's work in a number of ways that would be crucial for subsequent debates about the subject.

The first was the 'poverty line' – an idea that had been around for some time but which Rowntree defined in a new and rigorous way. Drawing on information such as the latest medical estimates of the minimum number of calories an adult should be consuming on a daily basis, Rowntree calculated the income that was required to purchase the basic amenities of life, which he declared the poverty threshold. The second was Rowntree's distinction between 'primary' poverty – that caused by income insufficient to keep people above the poverty line – and 'secondary' poverty, caused by excessive or frivolous expenditure. Like the decision to map York's public houses, this distinction owed much to Rowntree's beliefs about what constituted the 'right' kind of lifestyle. Just as Booth had done in London, Rowntree passed judgement on what counted as essential and non-essential expenditure.

Rowntree's third – and most important – contribution, the poverty cycle, was his attempt to map those concepts on to the lives people actually lived. Rather than there being a single homogeneous group that could be labelled 'the poor', Rowntree observed that large numbers of people seemed to spend their lives trapped in an unrelenting battle against forces that pulled them below the poverty line and then pushed them back above it. 'The life of a labourer is marked by five alternating periods of want and comparative plenty,' Rowntree explained. The first was early childhood, when 'unless his father is a skilled worker, he will probably be in poverty.' This would last until they or one of their siblings got a job, giving them their own money and freeing up some of their parents' income. The second came after a brief period when people earned their own wage, had no dependants or responsibilities, but could continue living with their parents. This, Rowntree wrote, was a man's 'chance to save money. If he has saved enough to pay for furnishing a cottage, this period of comparative prosperity may continue after marriage until he has two or three children, when poverty will again overtake him.' Ten years or more of struggle would follow, until their own children had started to earn money, freeing them from a number of financial responsibilities. 'While the children are earning, and before they leave the home to marry, the man enjoys another period of prosperity.' Yet, Rowntree reflected, gloomily, he was likely to 'sink back again into poverty when his children have married and left him, and he himself is too old to work, for his income has never permitted his saving enough for him and his wife to live upon for more than a very short time'.

Poverty, then, was a periodic but inevitable experience for many wage earners – a fact that went a long way to explaining a whole range of things, including why poor relief was constantly in demand, regardless of the wider economic context, why the principle of less eligibility was seldom enforced as strictly as it was supposed to be, and why few Poor Law Unions had got anywhere close to creating the institutions, such as separate workhouses for different classes of claimant, that the reformers of the 1830s had demanded. Rowntree's work showed that when public officials acquiesced to demands for help or to make relief more generous, they did so less out of misplaced sympathy, as the Royal Commission of the 1830s suggested, and more because they knew they confronted needs that were a basic feature of life in modern industrial capitalism. It was clear to most observers that something needed to be done, both for the people Rowntree described and for the integrity of the system itself. Quite what that something was, however, was deeply contested.

'SOMETHING IN OUR SOCIAL ORGANIZATION IS SERIOUSLY WRONG'

The Royal Commission on the Poor Laws and Relief of Distress was appointed in 1905. It was one of the Conservative Arthur Balfour's last acts as Prime Minister. Nicknamed 'Hotel Cecil' in tribute to the number of Cabinet members who belonged to the aristocratic Cecil family, including Balfour himself, the Conservative–Liberal Unionist administration, a coalition that had been in power for most of the previous twenty years, was ravaged by splits that suggested profound changes might be about to take place in British politics. The most serious of its disagreements was over free trade, which had been the economic policy consensus for fifty years. 'Tariff reformers', as free trade's opponents were known, argued that taxes on imports could boost the British economy by protecting businesses and industries that were under threat from abroad. Yet some, like the former mayor of Birmingham, Joseph Chamberlain, who saw tariff reform as a modernizing project rather than a return to the days of the Corn Laws, were beginning to make arguments that challenged the claim that free trade and its principles were best not only for the economy but social welfare too. What if the proceeds from import tariffs could be used to pay for things that free trade did not provide, like pensions for the elderly, Chamberlain argued.

On the face of it, the new Royal Commission looked like it had the potential to make changes to the Poor Law every bit as dramatic as the ones Nassau Senior and Edwin Chadwick had instigated more than seventy years earlier. The commission's eighteen members all had knowledge and experience of either administering a system that most commentators agreed was in need of reform, or of life around its edges. At sixty-seven years old, Octavia Hill was a veteran of London's voluntary assistance and charity scene. She had worked on Booth's survey and was renowned for her pioneering small social-housing projects, which offered people high-quality homes in return for strict tenancy conditions. Thomas Hancock Nunn was a founding resident of Toynbee Hall, a university settlement in east London that offered aspiring social researchers and politicians, including a young William Beveridge, the chance to live among the poor so they could see first hand the problems they wanted to solve. Charles S. Loch was the honorary secretary of the Charity Organisation Society, which had been founded in 1869 with the aim of co-ordinating these varied organizations and turning them into a professional operation guided by a single philosophy. Although many of these thinkers shared a belief in self-reliance and hard work as the routes out of poverty, they had contrasting and sometimes surprising ideas about not only the Poor Law but also the proper relationship between individuals and the state. Hill, for example, did not support the growing calls for women's suffrage, arguing that women's roles were limited to the domestic sphere, or old-age pensions, which she thought were examples of the state overreaching itself.

Two women with very different perspectives on the Poor Law (and poverty more generally) dominated the Royal Commission, though.

One was Booth's former research assistant Beatrice Potter, now Beatrice Webb. She had been born in 1858 into the wealthy and well-connected Potter family, and her home was frequented by the leading social reformers and thinkers of the day, such as the Derby-born philosopher Herbert Spencer, coiner of the phrase 'survival of the fittest'. The independent-minded Beatrice had spent her teenage years searching for a sense of purpose in a world where many of the bourgeois intellectuals she encountered were disillusioned with the cultural and spiritual ideas that dominated Victorian society. Like them, she struggled with her Christian faith and looked for alternative ways of understanding and experiencing the world. She immersed herself in politics and the debates about social reform, which took her to the Charity Organisation Society and Booth's survey of London. In the process, she embraced socialism, and in 1892 she married Sidney Webb, a steady rationalist who was every bit Beatrice's intellectual equal but from a humbler, lower-middle-class background. Given the frankness with which she expressed her feelings towards his 'tiny tadpole body, unhealthy skin, cockney pronunciation, [and] poverty', some people wondered exactly what it was that attracted Beatrice to Sidney. But theirs was a meeting of minds; a joint commitment to socialism was the basis of a marriage that lasted until her death in 1943.

Beatrice first encountered Sidney in 1889 through an essay he contributed to a book published by the Fabian Society, a socialist organization named after the Roman general Fabius Maximus 'Cunctator', whose military strategy of gradual, almost attritional, warfare was their inspiration. Beatrice and Sidney were dominant members of the Fabian Society from the moment they joined in 1891. They shaped its distinctive version of socialism, which ignored revolutionary politics and was sceptical about the working classes' potential to effect social change: for the Fabians, socialism would instead be realized through experts and bureaucrats. Using Beatrice's contacts and those of fellow Fabians, including the writers George Bernard Shaw and H. G. Wells, the Webbs' strategy was to embed the organization in the era's networks of political and intellectual power. They wanted to capture the attention of important individuals in literary and scientific circles, put down roots in government and the civil service, and, in the process, exert an influence that far outweighed their numbers.

They even founded a university, the London School of Economics and Political Science, in 1895, to promote research and teaching they thought would be a catalyst for the kind of social changes they wanted to see.

Webb's major rival on the Royal Commission, Helen Bosanquet (1860–1926), had quite different ideas. A home-educated Mancunian, Bosanquet had a reserved manner that barely hinted at her profound intellect. One of the first women to be awarded first-class honours in the Cambridge moral tripos, the name given to the university's tripartite structure of examinations, she had become interested in political economy and was convinced that Adam Smith, David Ricardo and their followers were broadly right about the economy, government and everyday life. Like Webb, she took an interest in the Charity Organisation Society, through which she met her husband, the philosopher Bernard Bosanquet. In contrast to her Fabian rival, however, Helen Bosanquet was deeply suspicious of the state's capacity to do good and threw herself into the society's mission to co-ordinate and improve voluntary efforts to tackle poverty, becoming its district secretary for Shoreditch. As Bosanquet explained in her widely read books, including *Rich and Poor* (1896) and *The Strength of the People* (1902), every major city and town had its own provident or relief society, whose members would collect donations and dispense essential items like food and clothing, not to mention charities dedicated to particular causes, and religious organizations such as the Salvation Army. She believed these organizations were well-meaning and had a great deal of untapped potential, but needed more professional attitudes if they were going to make a more significant impact on poverty by turning the recipients of aid into thrifty, self-reliant and, above all, deeply moral individuals.

Helen Bosanquet and the Charity Organisation Society saw the Poor Law as a major obstacle to these goals. They believed that local community organizations were the best vehicles for social change because they understood the people and places around them better than anyone in Whitehall ever could. Bosanquet took issue in public with anyone she thought was encouraging the idea that poverty and economic hardship should be understood as anything other than moral issues. The task was quite simple, she argued: building better character among the people so that when they found themselves in difficult circumstances they were capable of pulling themselves out of them. She even clashed with Seebohm Rowntree after the publication of *Poverty: A Study of Town Life* for suggesting otherwise, and openly questioned his findings about primary poverty, arguing that such hardship was nowhere near as common as he had claimed.

The Royal Commission's wide-ranging and complex investigations did much to hide these differences for a while. There were relatively few occasions when all eighteen members would gather together. Instead, there were a number of different committees, including 'statistical' and 'documents' groups, which commissioners could attend as and when they wished. They pored over written reports from Poor Law officials, central government departments, trade unions, large employers, economists and social researchers. They also visited Poor Law Unions around the country and went abroad to look at the way poor relief was handled in other places, including Belgium, Switzerland and Germany. When commissioners did meet they did so in venues across Westminster, including the palatial surroundings of the Foreign Office opposite 10 Downing Street, which many people considered superior to the Prime Minister's residence. The hub of this activity was a series of meetings that took up 159 days from January 1906 to April 1908, when hundreds of witnesses, including medical officers, administrators, charity workers and social investigators (including Rowntree and Beveridge), sat at a table with the commissioners to be cross-examined on their written evidence. The sheer weight of the material they considered was demonstrated by the thirty-five volumes of minutes, reports and assorted indexes and appendices that eventually appeared under the Royal Commission's name.

While Bosanquet proceeded quietly and slowly through her questions, standing up for the charities and voluntary groups who worked tirelessly and with limited resources, Webb saw a golden opportunity to put the Fabian programme at the heart of an official investigation. Even mild compromise was off the table as Webb tried to make the case for dispensing with the old system entirely and envisaging something new. While Webb was successful in drawing attention to the gulf that separated Bosanquet's commitment to individuals and voluntarism from her own Chadwickean faith in technocracy and bureaucratic solutions, many of her fellow commissioners were put off by her adversarial style. The result was deep division over not only the recommendations they should make but the very nature of the problem they were discussing.

'THE MERE SIGNING OF CHEQUES?'

The Royal Commission on the Poor Laws and Relief of Distress's 1,200-page densely packed report was eventually published in 1909. Unlike the earlier Royal Commission, however, there was no unity of judgement or persuasive clarity in their vision for the future. The final document that emerged from His Majesty's Stationery Office was in fact two reports: a 700-page one signed off by fourteen of the eighteen commissioners, and a further 500 dissenting pages produced at the insistence of the other four, led by Webb.

The majority report, signed by Loch, Hill and Bosanquet, argued that the Poor Law, as currently constituted, was a significant problem. There was certainly good news about the progress that had been made over the previous century: ratepayers, for instance, could take comfort in the fact that they were contributing less per head – approximately 8s 3d, down from 8s 10d – than they had been when the Poor Law was reformed in 1834. That, however, was about as far as it went. Any apparent savings were a product of population growth, which meant there were more people paying rates. The amount being spent on poor relief to each needy individual had actually doubled during the previous forty years. On any given day, 900,000 people – a number roughly equal to the population of Liverpool, the largest provincial city in England – were seeking relief, with around 1.7 million different individuals asking for help across the year. When the state's increased responsibilities in areas such as public health and education were factored in, it was clear governments were spending money hand over fist. The lesson, the report argued, was clear:

> the expenditure incurred and the results attained by it prove that something in our social organization is seriously wrong, and that whatever may be the evils, they are not of such a nature as to be improved or removed by the mere signing of cheques or the outpouring of public funds.

If money was not the answer, what was? The majority report argued that their predecessors in 1834 had been right. Poverty would only be solved if individuals had sufficient motivation to help themselves; the state should keep its distance, lest that motivation be eroded. The problem was that Poor Law Unions had never properly implemented the programme set out almost three-quarters of a century earlier. Now, the Royal Commission majority wanted the government to impose order on this situation – and to do so without expanding its day-to-day liabilities or inviting significant extra expenditure. There should be a spirit of collaboration between public and private bodies, they argued, with a clear agreement not to tread on each other's toes. The government, for example, should drop any plans it might have to enter the field of social insurance: schemes that offered people things like pensions and unemployment benefits in exchange for regular financial contributions. Trade unions and friendly societies already provided their members with services of this kind and were much better positioned to do it well. Not only did they understand the needs of their members but their schemes were voluntary, meaning individuals had to take the initiative when it came to joining. What good would come from the state stepping in?

The main reforming task for the majority of the commissioners was figuring out how to relate those voluntary organizations and schemes to the poor relief jobs the state would have to do. The administrative system they proposed was one they believed would promote self-reliant and industrious behaviour in the population. Each district should be served by four 'separate but cooperating' bodies. Two would be 'representative of self-help and voluntary effort, and will be worked through voluntary organizations', with one providing unemployment insurance and the other voluntary aid. The other two bodies would be down to the state to organize: a labour exchange managed by the Board of Trade, which would provide the unemployed with information about where to find work, and a 'Public Assistance Committee', replacing Poor Law Boards, which would pass legitimate applicants for relief on to relevant bodies, whether that was the kind of strictly segregated, state-run workhouse reformers had described in 1834 or a charity that could help someone with a specific problem, like alcoholism.

This system would depend on officials trained to high but specific professional standards, which would be endorsed, of course, by the Charity Organisation Society. The state's role would be as regulator: checking that the same rules, standards and procedures were being enforced everywhere. As they explained in their conclusions, this all had a clear purpose. 'The causes of distress are not only economic and industrial,' the majority argued; 'in their origin and character they are largely moral.' For this reason, 'government by itself cannot correct or remove such influences. Something more is required.' It was certainly the case that there were problems with the way poor relief, and poverty more generally, were approached, they explained. But 'the weak part of our system is not want of public spirit or benevolence, or lack of funds or of social workers, or of the material out of which these can be made. Its weakness is lack of organisation, of method, and of confidence in those who administer the system.'

Beatrice Webb could not have disagreed more. At her side stood the Rev. Prebendary H. Russell Wakefield, a Church of England minister who headed up the committee that co-ordinated unemployment relief in London; Francis Chandler, the General Secretary of the Amalgamated Society of Carpenters and Joiners, who had been added to the commission after complaints that trade unions were under-represented; and George Lansbury, an Independent Labour Party representative who would become leader of the Labour Party in the 1930s. To be sure, they agreed with some of the recommendations the majority had made. But they had a commitment to administrative reconstruction that looked more like the conversion Edwin Chadwick had undergone after 1834 than the return to first principles the majority of the commissioners wanted to see.

The word 'poor' encapsulated everything Webb's group thought was wrong with the Poor Law. The existing Poor Law, they reasoned, was not about poverty in the sense that it should be understood in light of the work by Booth, Rowntree and others. Rather, it was about destitution – because that was the condition people had to be in if they wanted help, and in which they had to remain as long as they received it. While there were all kinds of voluntary organizations that struggled to help people trapped in the poverty cycle, it was unconscionable for the state to continue to ignore both the huge numbers of people affected by poverty and the sheer range of factors that played their part in causing it. The kinds of good will and intentions that filled the majority report were admirable, they concluded, but useless when it came to fighting back against the powerful forces that had been unleashed by the industrial and economic development of the previous 150 years.

Webb and her allies had a radical modernizing vision for change. They wanted to abolish the Poor Law and replace it with something completely new. They argued that the powers invested in the Poor Law Guardians should be transferred to local government, which should be charged with running a completely integrated system of relief that covered education, health and employment. Demoralizing mixed workhouses should be shut down and replaced by specialist institutions and services, such as asylums and schools, that were appropriate to the problems being tackled. In fact, efforts should be made in as many cases as possible to enable those deserving of relief to remain in either their homes or the community, thereby bringing to an end the embarrassing sight of the elderly trudging through the workhouse doors because they had no other choice. Local governments should also develop and maintain sophisticated bureaucratic systems, run by expert administrators, capable of maintaining an overview of people's lives and delivering joined-up aid; seeing, for example, whether members of the same family were receiving help from different departments and investigating whether their problems were connected. There should also be a health service in which 'neither the promptitude nor the efficiency of the medical treatment [was] in any way limited by considerations of whether the patient can or should repay its cost'.

These institutions and policies were going to be expensive but, the minority report argued, only in the short term. Tackling the root causes of things like disease and poverty, rather than treating the symptoms on an ad hoc basis, was a much more productive and humane long-term policy. Conditions such as unemployment were not opportunities to reset people's moral compasses, as Bosanquet and her fellow travellers seemed to imagine them to be; they were profoundly debilitating experiences that scarred people for life. Britain should not be a country where the avoidable suffering of 30 per cent of its population was considered an acceptable price to pay for other people's comforts. The time had come, asserted Webb and her colleagues, for a coherent policy that shaped the social and economic environment.

Thanks to such significant divergences of opinion, the 1909 Royal Commission became an emblem of all the things that people considered wrong – but many politicians have often rather liked – about the format. Their report contained not only extensive and often exhaustive analysis, it featured innovative ideas and policy prescriptions. But there was no agreement, as one might expect from eighteen individuals with expertise in different aspects of the problem. Furthermore, the report had taken four years to produce – twice as long as Senior, Chadwick and their colleagues had spent on their investigation during the early 1830s. Aside from the fact that a split verdict meant it was easy for politicians to bury the report, the wider context had changed significantly. Appointed by a Conservative-led administration, the Royal Commission reported under a new Liberal government that had pressed ahead with its own plans for what looked like a revolution in social policy and taxation. Given that the Liberal Party traced its history back to the Whigs, who had been the most enthusiastic supporters of Poor Law reform during the 1830s, one might have expected them to side with the majority report's recommendations. The Liberal government, however, had embraced a vision of social policy – one that included free school meals and old-age pensions – that looked much more like the one the minority faction had urged the state to embrace. How had a transformation of this kind come to pass?

3

Reinventing Liberalism

Unlike the Royal Commission on the Poor Law on which Edwin Chadwick had served during the early 1830s, the Royal Commission on the Poor Laws and Relief of Distress that reported in 1909 made little immediate impact on government or public institutions. But the split verdict of 1909 that resulted in two reports – one that kept faith with ideas about self-help and individual endeavour, and one that argued the time was right for more extensive government intervention in social life – was a barometer of the changing attitudes to poverty at the beginning of the twentieth century. This point was made particularly clear by the Liberal government, the first for more than a decade, elected in a historic landslide in 1906. Rather than wait for the Royal Commission to report, it had pressed on with a number of ground-breaking schemes, including pensions for the old and social insurance for the unemployed and sick, and had devised new taxes on the rich to pay for them. Indeed, it had even threatened to go to war with the House of Lords, one of the country's unreformed institutions that ensured politics was still biased towards the Tories, to get the measures through Parliament. The Liberals' plans were a long way from what Beatrice Webb and her allies had demanded in their minority report. Yet they were a major departure from the ideas Liberals – and their Whig and radical predecessors – had endorsed for most of the previous hundred years.

The Liberals' new social programme owed much to the transformation of British liberalism over the course of the nineteenth century. By the 1880s, a new generation of thinkers had concluded that the long-standing reforming goal of a society made up of independent and resourceful individuals was going to require significant input from the state. The tradition of political thought known as liberalism went from being the maker of the new Poor Law, which emphasized the importance of providing the destitute with the bare minimum they needed to survive, to the force behind significant forms of government intervention that would have been completely unacceptable to earlier eras. Pragmatism played its part. Politicians such as David Lloyd George, who emerged as the dominant Liberal Party politician of the early twentieth century, realized, much as Chadwick had done before them, that doing something about some problems might be better – and, in some cases, cost less money – than doing nothing. But new ideas were involved too. Britain had been changed dramatically by capitalism and industrialization. With socialists and the emerging Labour Party claiming to have answers to the problems that had accompanied those developments, liberals were forced to reconsider what ideas like freedom, independence and responsibility meant in practice.

FREEDOM, PROGRESS AND GOVERNMENT

The Lichfield House Compact of 1835, when Whigs, radicals and the Irish Repeal Party agreed to co-operate in Parliament against the Tories, did not create an organization we would now recognize as a political party. There was no headquarters, logo or campaigning literature. Forty years later, however, the Liberal Party was firmly established as the Tories' main opposition. The exact date when the Liberal Party appeared is disputed. Many historians suggest 1859, when Viscount Palmerston met MPs at a London social club and persuaded them to unite under his leadership, and this date is as convenient as any other. Whigs and radicals, whose relationship had defined reforming politics during the early nineteenth century, were joined by Tory supporters of the former Prime Minister Sir Robert Peel, who supported free trade over the landed interest. A two-party political system was inaugurated, with the Liberal William Gladstone, one of the former Peelite Tories, and the Tory Benjamin Disraeli sparring across the House of Commons' floor through one of the most famous and celebrated periods in Victorian high politics.

The Liberal Party was committed to continuing the programme of constitutional and social reform that had emerged during the first half of the nineteenth century. While free trade, including the abolition of duties they believed were hindrances to business, was their agreed position on economic matters, the party legislated for greater freedoms for religious non-conformists, including the right to attend the universities of Oxford and Cambridge (which had previously been restricted to those who belonged to the Church of England), and reforms to the judiciary, the army and the civil service. Meanwhile, the inheritors of the radical tradition continued to push for more dramatic change, such as land reform – breaking up the elite's stranglehold on land ownership.

Debates about these issues raged in the pages of periodicals such as the *Edinburgh Review* and the *Westminster Review*, and were discussed in the private members' clubs and philosophical and literary societies that sprang up in the towns and cities that had grown prosperous through free trade and the industrial revolution. A whole way of thinking, often called 'classical' liberalism, which was rooted in the ideals of free speech, limited government interference in matters of individual conscience (particularly religion) and free trade developed out of this milieu. For the likes of Herbert Spencer (1820–1903), who had started his career as a sub-editor at *The Economist* (which was founded in 1843 as part of the campaign for free trade), mid-nineteenth-century Britain had reached an unprecedented moment of political, economic and social development. As he explained in books like *The Man versus the State* (1884), Spencer believed that destroying entrenched privileges, especially those of the aristocracy, and scaling back government would free individuals to realize their inner potential, making Britain more wealthy in the process. In popular culture, the likes of Samuel Smiles, author of *Self-Help* (1859) and *Character* (1871), extolled the virtues of thrift and hard work that were seen as necessary products of this emerging settlement.

The major political issue of the mid-nineteenth century, however, was electoral reform. Following the Great Reform Act of 1832, which had doubled the size of the electorate by lowering the property qualification threshold, and abolished the rotten boroughs, the Chartist movement had called for universal male suffrage and election by secret ballots. Although the Chartists ran out of steam during the

1840s, failing to achieve their major goals when the revolutions that swept major European cities in 1848 seemed to offer a warning of where political instability might lead, they were successful in keeping the franchise on the agenda. At the heart of the discussion was the question of what it meant to participate in the political process: was it a right that everyone should have, or something that should only be granted on certain conditions?

These questions mattered because they cut to the heart of many liberals' assumptions about the relationship between political, social and economic development. Despite the move towards free trade as the official economic policy of the British state, there was little evidence that what we would now call democracy followed. Most obviously, few people, even among radicals and reformers, entertained the idea that women should be able to vote, meaning half the population was excluded from the political process. Even among men, though, political participation was modest. For all the Tories' worries about the implications of expanding the electorate for the stability of the state and their economic interests, six out of every seven men were still unable to vote by the midway point of the nineteenth century. Indeed, despite the Second Reform Act of 1867, which extended the franchise further, it was not until the mid-1880s that more than half of the adult male population had the right to vote. The property qualification remained in place until the early twentieth century – a barrier to mass participation but, for its supporters, an indication that voters had not only a stake in society but also the kind of character that strongly suggested they were capable of acquiring and then holding on to that stake.

Tories, however, were not the Liberals' only opponents. Co-operative and trade organizations, which had grown in working-class communities as responses to the challenges they faced in a capitalist and industrial society, provided fertile ground for a whole host of political ideas that would come to be called 'socialism'. Like reformism, socialism had many different strands. Some thinkers, inspired by radical indigenous traditions dating back to the Levellers and the Diggers during the English Civil War of the mid-seventeenth century, not to mention continental thinkers like Karl Marx and the French politician Pierre-Joseph Proudhon, believed property was theft and that revolutionary activity was necessary to force social change. Much more popular, however, was the side of the socialist movement that kept faith with Parliament and democracy as the means of achieving a fairer deal for everyone, particularly those towards the bottom of society. They believed that the fact there could be shortages of essential items and periods of mass unemployment in an economy that was apparently capable of generating so much wealth was a sign something was wrong. They thought social, not just individual, needs should be factored into political and economic decision-making. Objecting to anything that looked like an impediment to free trade, many liberals found it easy to reject such calls, especially because the socialists lacked representation in Parliament during the middle decades of the nineteenth century.

Not every liberal was deaf to such criticisms, or thought liberalism could safely ignore them. John Stuart Mill (1806–73), the son of the Scottish political philosopher James Mill – the most famous disciple of Jeremy Bentham – was one. James had decided to turn his son's early life into a utilitarian experiment and took charge of his education himself. John started learning Greek at the age of four, Latin at eight, was well versed in the classics, philosophy and logic by twelve, and then started to study political economy, in particular the works of his father's close friend, David Ricardo. Mill was a child prodigy, but his astonishing breadth of knowledge came at a huge price. He struggled to be at all times the rational, calculating, utilitarian machine his education was meant to create, but found no help in anything his father had permitted him to read and suffered an emotional breakdown at the age of twenty.

Mill had a prolific and long career after his year-long recovery, when he embarked on a quest to broaden his intellectual horizons. As he explained in *Utilitarianism* (1863), he had not concluded that his father's philosophy should be abandoned, just that it required important modifications. Benthamism tended to flatten the world when it came to happiness, attributing the same numerical value to everything. This approach was incredibly democratic, Mill argued, but it did not reflect the reality of human experience, in which some things, like art and literature, simply made a greater and longer-lasting contribution to human happiness than other, more trivial pursuits.

Indeed, as he explained in *On Liberty* (1859), his most famous work, he believed that individual freedom could justifiably be constrained if it caused harm to others.

Mill's political economy also followed this reforming path, as shown by his widely read *Principles of Political Economy* (1848), which ran through eight editions and increasingly exhibited the influence of Harriet Taylor, the proto-feminist and socialist sympathizer with whom Mill conducted an allegedly adulterous twenty-year relationship. He departed from the Ricardian economics he had learned by dividing production and distribution into two different books, making a distinction between what would later come to be known as 'positive' and 'normative' economics, or economic laws and the art of economic governance. As Mill explained to his readers, he believed that, 'unlike the laws of Production, those of distribution are partly of human institution: since the manner in which wealth is distributed in any given society, depends on the statutes or usages therein obtaining.' For this reason, although he did not think governments could 'arbitrarily determine how those institutions shall work', he was convinced there was a great deal of choice when it came to questions about who was rich and who was poor, or how big the gap between the two groups was. Indeed, it was quite possible, he argued, to be a good Ricardian about free markets and international trade and support specific socialist ideas, such as more bargaining power for trade unions and the imposition of inheritance tax, which most liberals opposed.

Mill declared himself to be a supporter of 'advanced Liberalism' – a state in which governments were permitted to interfere with markets and provide services in the name of securing liberal freedoms for people who would stand no chance of obtaining them otherwise. His challenge was to persuade critics that it could deliver the kind of society liberals had set their sights on. Like Adam Smith before him, he believed education was an obvious example of the kind of thing governments should be interested in providing their citizens with. In part, Mill thought so for utilitarian reasons: the bill the state would foot for an ignorant population was much larger than the upfront cost of educating it. Yet he also thought the state should be providing education because it was an important means of producing the kinds of self-reliant individuals on which liberal society was dependent. The problem for many liberals, of course, was that education looked like the thin end of the wedge. If education could be justified, and others were embracing the idea that the state should be heavily involved in areas like public health, what else might governments start to think were their responsibility? A new generation of liberals had answers to these questions and they looked very different to the ones their predecessors had given less than a century earlier.

NEW LIBERALISM

The liberals who came of age in the 1880s entered a completely different world to the one inhabited by the Whigs who had inaugurated the era of reform half a century earlier. A Third Reform Act had been passed by William Gladstone's second administration, giving most adult men the vote. Industrialization had generated huge amounts of wealth and transformed the landscape and working lives of ordinary people. In the realms of science and ideas, Charles Darwin's *On the Origin of Species*, published in the same year as *On Liberty*, had revolutionized people's understanding of themselves and the natural kingdom. But any optimism about further reform had to be tempered by new realities. While the mid-century Whig ascendency had given way to a frequent exchange of the keys to 10 Downing Street between Liberal and Tory Prime Ministers, the economy had entered a difficult period. The 'Great Victorian Boom' had come to an end in the early 1870s as international competitors such as Germany and the USA had caught up with Britain, eating into its share of world trade. Following in Mill's footsteps, a new generation of liberals set about reshaping and recasting their predecessors' ideas so they were fit for that new and often uncertain world.

Perhaps the strongest indicator of the differences between new and classical liberalism were the philosophies they were associated with. By the late nineteenth century, calculating the greatest happiness for the greatest number, even in Mill's revised methods, did not hold the appeal it once had. Indeed, for Leonard Hobhouse (1864–1929), who had studied and then taught philosophy at the University of Oxford during the late 1880s, utilitarianism was embarrassingly out of date. A tall, shaggy-looking man affectionately known among friends for his occasional forgetful clumsiness, Hobhouse bought into the vision of liberalism as a modernizing project. He believed the future of liberal modernization, however, was Idealism – a school of thought usually associated with continental, particularly German, philosophers such as Immanuel Kant and G. W. F. Hegel. Idealism was far removed from the kind of hard-headed empiricism British thinkers were believed to value. But it transformed the way people like Hobhouse thought about the world around them and, in the process, left an indelible mark on politics.

The leading British Idealist was the Yorkshireman Thomas Hill Green (1836–82). Born into a church family – his father was the rector of Birkin – Green was quiet, uncomfortable with public speaking, frequently dressed in black and grey clothes, teetotal, and almost always wore a weary look. He was not at first sight an obviously inspirational figure. Yet in the years after his untimely death from septicaemia at the age of forty-five, he was revered as one of the most important and influential thinkers of his generation, thanks in large part to the stream of former students who made their mark on public life, including the Liberal Prime Minister Herbert Asquith and the social reformer and political economist Arnold Toynbee. These graduates spoke fondly of Green as a person and credited him with lighting fires within them that stayed lit for the rest of their lives.

Green wrote about and taught conventional philosophical topics, most notably ethics and metaphysics, but in a way quite different to his contemporaries who continued the tradition of empiricism dating back to John Locke in the seventeenth century. Humans are born as blank slates, empiricists argued, and we learn about the world as we experience it. Although that process was problematic – the senses, for example, could be deceived quite easily – empiricists believed these problems could be overcome if the right methods of observation were used. For Green, however, these beliefs were all wrong. He was convinced it was impossible to separate out what we think we know from the minds that think they know it. There was no clear distinction between the human mind and the external world. Instead, there was something more like a continuum. The human mind, Green told his readers and students, is an active and constituent agent in creating the world that we experience.

Following this line of logic, Idealists argued that society is an organism composed of highly specialized pieces, which created a living entity that, like humans themselves, was somehow more than the sum of its parts. People are connected to each other in this organism, Idealists explained, and therefore part of something much bigger than themselves. The implication was that everyone contributed to the health of the organism. If people acted selfishly or with little regard for anyone else they would head in different directions, gradually stretching the tissues that held them together. In this vision, the common good and the ability of individuals to lead meaningful and fulfilling lives were interdependent. People were not just individuals, they were citizens too.

As he explained in his influential lectures and essays, including the posthumously published *Principles of Political Obligation* (1885), Green believed governments, both national and local, could help prevent individuals pulling away from the social body. A committed Liberal Party supporter, he believed in the ideal of self-reliant and rational individuals. But he also thought that the common good required the state to take on positive responsibilities that went far beyond maintaining social order or removing barriers to trade. An assistant commissioner on Lord Taunton's Schools Inquiry Commission during the mid-1860s, Green was passionate about the case for the state becoming more involved in the provision of education, both as a means of helping individuals realize their potential and insuring society against the problems that might arise when the electoral franchise was extended. Governments had a moral duty to help create a society where everybody had the chance to experience the liberal conception of freedom, Green argued, while also contributing to the common good.

Green's ideas were illustrations of important shifts in middle-class attitudes towards the poor in late nineteenth-century Britain. Thanks to the economic downturn, the mid- and late 1880s had been tough for the working classes. Some commentators thought a new Chartism was on the horizon, this time driven by socialists, particularly the Social Democratic Federation, which had organized the rally in

Trafalgar Square that had so worryingly descended into violence in 1886 and who included among their number Eleanor Marx, Karl's youngest daughter, William Morris of the Arts and Crafts Movement, and Keir Hardie, who would later become the Independent Labour Party's first MP. With sections of the working class once again pushing for greater political representation, middle- and upper-class concerns about social breakdown spoke volumes for their ignorance of the lives of people less fortunate than themselves.

New liberals were among the journalists, writers and social investigators who, like Charles Booth, wanted to know more and who were convinced they could help. Some were inspired by Green, who encouraged his students to think about the world outside their college walls. Hobhouse, for example, was inspired to engage with local politics in Oxford and became deeply interested in trade unionism. He also spent time at Toynbee Hall, the university settlement in London's East End (named after Green's former pupil), where he struck up friendships with the likes of Sidney and Beatrice Webb. Such was the impact of those experiences that Hobhouse decided to quit his life as an Oxford don in 1897 and head to the North West, where he became a journalist for the *Manchester Guardian*. This had been the leading radical newspaper of the early nineteenth century, which now C. P. Scott, its new editor, was in the process of dragging away from its traditional strict adherence to laissez-faire liberalism.

In addition to exploring the places politicians and social reformers claimed to be talking about, new liberals also immersed themselves in the ferment of progressive politics, where lines between positions such as 'liberal' and 'socialist' were nowhere near as stark as they had once seemed. The Rainbow Circle was a London-based discussion group, named after the public house on Fleet Street where it first met in 1894, and a favourite intellectual haunt of new liberals, including J. A. Hobson, Fabian socialists such as the journalist William Clarke and the diplomat William Pember Reeves, Liberal MPs like Herbert Samuel and Noel Buxton, and Ramsay MacDonald, then a struggling writer but thirty years later the first Labour Prime Minister. One of their main points of common interest was the question of whether liberals and socialists could be reconciled in the way Whigs and radicals had been half a century earlier. Since the moment the

Third Reform Act had been passed in 1884, many commentators had considered it inevitable that a new workers' party would be created and would dominate Parliament. Yet progress had been slow. Skilled workers associated with the growing trade union movement, which expanded from 500,000 members in 1880 to 2 million twenty years later, certainly wanted their interests to be represented. But, thanks to their long-standing attachments to the values of self-organization and self-reliance – products of a world where the state refused to provide the help workers thought they needed – trade union members (and the skilled working class more generally) were not convinced that meant socialism. Liberal intellectuals pondered whether this conclusion applied to them too.

While these issues were being thrashed out during the late nineteenth century a co-operative set of arrangements, known as the 'Lib-Lab' system, emerged. Liberal associations in areas where industry was concentrated and trade union representation most dense preserved their status as the political party for working men by putting forward candidates whom unions also endorsed. These deals neutralized the threat of a second candidate splitting the reform vote, allowed the Liberal Party to hold on to seats it might otherwise have lost, and enabled trade unions to put issues that concerned them on the parliamentary agenda when the Liberals returned to power, albeit briefly, under Gladstone for a final time, during the early 1890s. Several pieces of trade union-promoted legislation, including a forty-eight-hour limit to the working week in War Office factories, made it onto the statute books. Nevertheless, the Liberals' wealthy supporters were more than willing to block proposals that posed more significant threats to their economic interests, including the Employers' Liability Bill, which would have made them responsible for compensating employees injured at work.

In this context, the major question for people who considered themselves to be on the progressive side of politics was simple: was the Liberal Party the future? For the likes of Beatrice and Sidney Webb, the Liberals were well-meaning but incapable of embracing the kind of far-reaching change that the British economy and society required. New liberals remained convinced, however, that the Liberal Party was the only organization capable of delivering political change in the tradition begun by the Whigs and radicals. As Hobhouse had explained in his first political book, *The Labour Movement* (1893), there were plenty of reasons to consider social ownership of specific services and industries, not to mention co-operative organizations, as rational responses to the demands of modern capitalism, rather than a rejection of it. Yet what Hobhouse and his allies envisaged was not socialism but a radical form of Mill's 'advanced' liberalism. State interference would be permitted anywhere that individuals were unable to exercise the kind of freedom that liberals wanted them to have.

New liberals, including the MPs R. B. Haldane and J. M. Robertson, stood firm with older liberals on all manner of issues. They fought a fierce battle in Parliament and the press against Liberal Unionists, who had broken away from the Liberal Party when Gladstone made Home Rule for Ireland the new frontier for constitutional reform and had responded to the country's changing economic fortunes by suggesting it was time to bring free trade to an end. Furthermore, and building on the idea that free trade was a means of not only creating prosperity but also spreading liberal values, new liberals became prominent opponents of empire and the jingoism that was becoming increasingly popular through new newspapers like the *Daily Mail* and the *Daily Express*. Most notably, they became passionate critics of the Tory government during the Second Boer War. This saw the British army deployed against settlers of Dutch descent in two provinces of what is now South Africa for what seemed like an embarrassingly long period, from 1899 to 1902. The government and its allies accused their critics of supporting the enemy, with Hobhouse and his sister Emily, a member of the South African Conciliation Committee and founder of the South African Women and Children Distress Fund, targets for the 'pro-Boer' accusations that were thrown around.

The way new liberals saw the connections between these different issues was illustrated most clearly by the self-proclaimed 'economic heretic' John Atkinson Hobson (1858–1940). Although he was Oxford educated, Hobson had been more interested in athletics than Idealism as a student, and failed to excel academically. He looked set for a career as a provincial school teacher until the late 1880s, when he suddenly decided to head for London, where he lectured for

Oxford's university extension scheme, which made academic ideas available to wider audiences. The reason for his move was his wife, Florence Edgar, an American poet and women's rights campaigner. Hobson had always been interested in the 'social question' but, thanks to Florence, who ran a soup kitchen in London in 1888, he pursued it with more vigour than ever before. He integrated himself into the capital's network of social reformers, including the Fabians and their radical associates, and discovered a passion for the kind of political economy that engaged with, rather than explained away, the problems with and injustices of free markets.

Widely credited with coining the term 'unemployment' in the 1890s, Hobson is most famous for his theory of 'underconsumption', which is often cited as one of the roots of Keynesian economics. According to Hobson, a wide variety of late nineteenth-century economic and social phenomena, including unemployment and trade depressions, were symptoms of a much deeper problem. The wealthy simply had more money than they knew what to do with, meaning they saved and invested rather than spent, causing blockages and gluts. Indeed, Hobson believed underconsumption was behind European nations' foreign policy. Financiers and merchants looked overseas for new markets to flood with their excess capital, encouraging the creation of empires. In this respect, Hobson argued, questions usually discussed in isolation were actually closely related. Many of the problems of modern industrial society, not to mention in international relations, could be fixed, he suggested, if the wealthy simply spent more at home, or the state did it after taxing them.

These kinds of prescriptions were given ballast by shifts in the international economy during the late nineteenth century, when some commentators feared Britain was in a throes of a national decline thanks to competition from Germany and the USA. What made the country's shrinking share of world trade difficult to handle for some observers was the fact that not all of its competitors had adopted the economic and social template Britain had claimed was essential for its success earlier in the century. Germany, unified by Otto von Bismarck, the 'Iron Chancellor', in the 1870s, had developed a very different approach to economic issues, and in particular the difficulties confronting German workers. Less wedded to free trade than Westminster, the German state worked with large indus-trial organizations and employers to provide workers with insurance against unemployment due to ill health and disability. The motiv-ation for doing so was to grow the economy by providing the country's most mobile workers with a reason to stay put when they could find higher wages elsewhere. At the same time, providing protection against tough times was part of Bismarck's strategy of immunizing the working classes against the lure of revolutionary socialism.

In Britain, new liberals carried the spirit of these German ideas forward when they argued that government should be much more involved in what Mill had described as economic distribution. The state had, of course, dipped its toes into interventionist waters throughout the nineteenth century, but new liberals regarded meas-ures like the Factory Acts to be matters of regulation in production. They wanted to see new policies, not a continuation of the same old administrative themes; above all, they wanted much more purposeful and creative state action. As L. T. Hobhouse put it in his renowned exposition of his political tradition, *Liberalism* (1911), 'it was the leading "principle of 1834" that the lot of the pauper should be made "less eligible" than that of the independent labourer'. For him and his new liberal colleagues, however, 'the duty of society is rather to ensure that the lot of the independent labourer be more eligible than that of the pauper'.

Although these ideas were scandalous for liberals committed to the classical formulation of the creed, they were a largely academic con-sideration during the final decade of the nineteenth century. Gladstone, Prime Minister on four separate occasions between 1868 and 1894, was the towering Liberal of the period. Yet he also did significant damage to his party's electoral fortunes when he pressed for Home Rule for Ireland – a legacy of Daniel O'Connell's Irish Repeal Party's involvement in the Lichfield House Compact of 1835. Despite his undeniable commitment to the cause, Gladstone also thought that making Ireland the next big constitutional reform project was a use-ful way of avoiding calls for more radical economic interventionism. When his efforts to force the Government of Ireland Bill through the Commons were defeated in 1886, however, the Liberal Party split in two. The biggest group stayed loyal to Gladstone and the Irish cause.

A smaller faction, who called themselves Liberal Unionists and were led by Joseph Chamberlain, the pioneer of 'municipal socialism', chose instead to prop up Lord Salisbury's Tories. With the exception of a short minority government during the 1890s, the Liberal Party would be out of power for the rest of the century as some of its wealthiest supporters deserted it. At the turn of the twentieth century, though, its fortunes seemed to take a turn for the better.

1906 AND ALL THAT

The Conservative MP Arthur Balfour had been a ruthless Chief Secretary for Ireland during the late 1880s. But as the author of several largely forgettable works of philosophy he also had a popular image as a cosmopolitan man and thinker, whom many of his colleagues thought had the intellect to steer the Tories through choppy early twentieth-century waters. He became Prime Minister in 1902 when Lord Salisbury, his uncle, resigned in poor health, shortly after the Boer War had been won. Balfour's Conservative–Unionist government, which had a majority of more than one hundred in the Commons, quickly ran into trouble, though. Religious dissenters, the Jewish community and Liberal Unionists themselves were three of the groups alienated or antagonized by Balfour's administration. Yet the loudest rumblings were coming from the trade unions. The Taff Vale Railway Company had sued striking workers for damages in 1901 and won, making unions legally responsible for employers' losses during trade disputes. Worried about such consequences of their exclusion from Westminster, more than a hundred unions affiliated with the Labour Representation Committee (formed in London in 1901) within two years, swelling the committee's political fund which paid for approved candidates to stand at elections. Ramsay MacDonald, the secretary of the Labour Representation Committee, knew it was a long way from being able to win enough seats to become the main opposition in Parliament, but in 1903 he renewed the agreement with the Liberals not to split the anti-Tory vote in key constituencies, creating what was called the Progressive Alliance.

The Conservative–Unionist government's major problem, however, was a much older one. With the USA and Germany leading the nations eating into Britain's previously dominant share of world trade, and surpassing it in new growth areas such as chemical engineering and the electrical industry, 'tariff reform' had made it onto the political agenda. Other countries protected their domestic industries by taxing imports, so Britain should do the same; at the very least, tariff reformers argued, the country could restrict free trade to its empire. Balfour tried to be pragmatic but his life was made more difficult by Joseph Chamberlain's decision to throw his weight behind the tariff reform cause, arguing that its proceeds could be used to pay for things the country would not otherwise be able to afford. While deep-seated working-class fears about rising food prices and declining living standards came to the surface, principled free-traders like the young Conservative MP Winston Churchill crossed the floor to the Liberals at the sign of the change of direction from the government.

Increasingly unpopular, Balfour decided to resign in early December 1905, leaving the Liberals to form a government. He thought that this move would cause the Liberals problems, but they quickly called a general election and rallied around slogans like 'Big Loaf, Little Loaf' – the consequences, as they saw it, of free trade and tariff reform respectively. The result was a landslide victory for 69-year-old Henry Campbell-Bannerman's Liberal Party and an absolute horror show for the Conservatives. The Liberals increased their 184 seats to 400, which were bolstered by the Labour Representation Committee's 30 MPs, who quickly decided to call themselves simply the 'Labour Party'. The Unionist parties were reduced from 402 seats to just 157, with just 3 members of the previous Cabinet holding on to their seats. Not even Balfour made it back to Westminster.

The Liberals had run on a manifesto that, in its general outlines, would have been familiar to observers of campaigns during the previous forty years. They stood as defenders of working-class living standards and the free trade settlement that they believed underpinned it. Yet there were signs of change. In his 1907 budget the Chancellor of the Exchequer, Herbert Asquith (1852–1928), introduced differentiated income tax – different rates for incomes that were earned, such as wages, and unearned, such as that from property. This innovation was an important revenue-raising mechanism for an increasingly cash-strapped state. In addition to the burden of debts incurred during the Boer War, the government was tied into the expensive 'two power standard' by the Naval Defence Act of 1889, which committed Britain to maintaining a navy that was at least the equal of the two next-most powerful navies in the world combined. But differentiated income tax also had an intellectual attraction, thanks to the long tradition of radical thinkers dating back to David Ricardo, who believed landlords' and rentiers' interests were at odds with everyone else's, and that they should pay their fair share. Indeed, it was an idea that appealed in particular to the significant number of radical social reformers associated with new liberalism who were among the party's new ranks of MPs, including forty journalists, five from the *Daily News*, the radical liberal newspaper whose first editor had been Charles Dickens.

A move towards a position closer to these new liberals became apparent eighteen months into the government's term, when recession hit and the administration's popularity nosedived. After a series of five by-election defeats, Campbell-Bannerman, seriously ill after a series of heart attacks and still mourning his recently deceased wife, resigned in April 1908, to be replaced as leader by Asquith. The new Cabinet contained its fair share of constitutional liberal reformers, but the real beneficiaries were on the radical progressive side of the party. Into the government came the likes of Charles 'Charlie' Masterman (1873–1927), a former president of the Cambridge Union whose experience living in a south-east London tenement block had moved him to write a number of impassioned books, including *From the Abyss* (1902), in which he tried to educate the wider public about the daily struggles and constant depressing grind of urban poverty.

The first evidence of the new government's break with the past was the Old Age Pensions Act of 1908. Pensions had made it onto the agenda by the turn of the century because politicians had realized that old age, a product of economic growth and improvements in public health, was an issue the country was going to have to tackle sooner rather than later. The number of people living past sixty-five in Britain had doubled, to almost 1.5 million, during the second half of the nineteenth century. Some of these people were able to work well into old age. Others, however, had spent their lives working in physically demanding industrial jobs. There were businesses where there was a tradition of moving older workers into simpler and less demanding, albeit poorly paid, roles, from backroom work to sweeping the floors. But with increasing workplace automation, there were fewer of those jobs around. While families could sometimes help relatives who were no longer able to work, there was an increasing number of people who were economically inactive but unable to retire.

A variety of pension schemes had appeared during the nineteenth century in response to these new circumstances. The Northcote–Trevelyan Report of 1854 had argued that giving civil servants a pension was an important part of modernizing the civil service because older and less efficient workers could be replaced. A number of groups of government employees, including policemen – who became entitled to one after twenty-five years' service in 1890 – and elementary school teachers – awarded one from the age of sixty after 1892 – gained from these trends. However, manual workers rarely, if ever, acquired the same benefits in the private sphere, where only white-collar workers at a tiny number of firms, such as railway companies, were offered a pension. Trade unions, co-operative societies and voluntary organizations offered welcome but often meagre schemes to their working-class members. But, as was the case with health and unemployment insurance, availability was dependent on factors such as the size of a person's local trade union. Huge numbers of people simply did not have sufficient money to retire, and many did not even try to save for a pension, because they did not expect to live long enough to benefit. This meant that they worked until they dropped or, if they had no help from family, went cap in hand to the Poor Law authorities after they had sold all their worldly belongings, with some married couples suffering the indignity of being split up when workhouse segregation rules were applied strictly. According to Charles Booth, around 45 per cent of working-class people aged over sixty-five became paupers at some point every year.

Pensions seemed like the only way to keep the old away from the Poor Law, and the provision would allow more generosity towards them. But who would pay for them? The left's preference was for pensions to be funded by general taxation as a matter of social justice – an idea that actually appealed to many businesses that hated the dilemma of what to do about long-standing employees whose age made them less valuable workers. But this proposal raised the spectre of a new and economically inactive category of people – the retired – drawing money from the state for an indefinite period of time. Joseph Chamberlain thought tariff reform might be the answer to these difficulties. Why not use the money raised from taxes on imports, he argued, to pay for worn-out workers to retire with dignity? Yet for some people, such as Helen Bosanquet and other members of the Charity Organisation Society, state-funded pensions of any kind were a bad idea; they were a handout that would discourage people from planning for their old age and the attitude of thrift that went with it.

The Liberals' plan looked dramatic: state-supported retirement. The Old Age Pensions Act's provisions were, however, quite modest and contained numerous qualifying hurdles as part of an effort to keep costs down. Pensions were non-contributory, meaning the aged did not need to have paid into a fund to claim one, but they were means tested – an intrusive administrative process that people hated because it involved a stranger prying into their financial affairs and private lives – and, in a bid to restrict them to people considered of sufficient moral standing, excluded the likes of paupers for the first two years. Moreover, while people had to earn less than £31 10s a year to be eligible for one, the maximum payment was a meagre five shillings a week, a maximum of £13 a year or about a quarter of the average labourer's wage. Indeed, the qualifying age of seventy had been deliberately set high. People who made it to the age of sixty-five could expect to live for another ten years, but average life expectancy was around forty-seven years for men and fifty years for women.

Take up was, nevertheless, huge. Half a million people drew a pension when the scheme launched in 1909 and the number had doubled two years later, making the scheme's real cost twice the £6 million the Liberals had estimated. The extra financial burden came at a bad time. Thanks to the 'two power standard' and pressure from the Tories and a jingoistic press, the Liberals had agreed to buy four Dreadnought-class ships – the biggest, best-equipped and most expensive battleships of the day – in early 1909 (and committed to purchasing more if they were needed), leaving them with a deficit in the region of £16 million.

The job of finding a way to plug this gap fell to the new Chancellor of the Exchequer, David Lloyd George (1863–1945), a self-made Welsh lawyer and shrewd political operator with a flare for public speaking. His answer was what he described, in a typical rhetorical flourish, as the 'People's Budget'. Standing at the House of Commons despatch box for more than four hours on the afternoon of 29 April 1909, Lloyd George explained that he was going to increase land and death duties, and income tax was now going to be graduated. The old income tax had kicked in on earnings above £150 a year. But as critics like the economist Leo Chiozza Money, who was elected for the Liberals in 1906, pointed out, less than 3 per cent of the population paid it, meaning the rich had a lower tax burden than middle-class professionals, proportionally speaking, because their incomes were derived from unearned sources rather than wages. Lloyd George announced three income tax bands. The rate for incomes up to £2,000 was kept at 9d; it increased to 1s for incomes between £2,000 and £3,000, and was put up to 1s 2d for earnings over £3,000. His populist flourish, however, was the 'super tax': 6d on incomes over £5,000 per year.

Yet Lloyd George's plan was not simply to redistribute the country's budgetary difficulties away. He also announced a new, though undetailed, policy: a system of 'national insurance', which would enable the Liberals to extend their social reform programme beyond the elderly. There was a rationale behind this. The new state pension scheme might have been more expensive than expected but that only demonstrated that the scale of poverty was beyond anything critics were prepared to accept. 'There are hundreds of thousands of men, women, and children in this country now enduring hardships for which the sternest judge would not hold them responsible,' Lloyd George told the Commons. And after years of dithering from the Unionist parties, the Liberals were taking decisive action. He was presenting a 'war budget': one for 'raising money to wage implacable warfare against poverty and squalidness'.

Lloyd George had made a pitch to the two groups the Liberals needed to keep onside if they wanted to stay in power: middle-class taxpayers who wanted more fairness than the nineteenth-century system had offered, and working-class voters who wanted social reform and might be tempted by the Labour Party. But a huge hurdle had to be cleared before he could celebrate. For all the talk of eroding the Tory bias in British politics, which dated back to the Lichfield Compact in 1835 and beyond, the Conservative-dominated House of Lords remained a bastion of Tory institutional advantage. In November 1909, for the first time in 150 years, the second chamber refused to pass a budget, arguing they were entitled to do so because none of Lloyd George's measures had been in the Liberals' 1906 election manifesto.

The standoff triggered two general elections. The first, held in January 1910, saw the Liberals returned as the biggest party but only by two seats, meaning an agreement had to be made with the Irish Nationalists and Labour to form a government. The second, which was held less than a year later and delivered an almost identical result, was focused on the Lords' ability to block bills passed by the Commons. The outcome, after Asquith threatened to swamp the Lords with a mass of new Liberal peers, was the Parliament Act of 1911, which permitted the Lords to turn back a bill a maximum of three times in a single parliamentary session – a supposedly temporary measure that remains in place more than a century later.

The official electoral mandate enabled the Liberals to set out the details of the system of national insurance that had been announced by Lloyd George in his People's Budget. As the two parts of the 1911 National Insurance Act made clear, the proposal was actually for two different schemes. The first, which was the Treasury's responsibility, introduced health insurance for all wage earners aged between sixteen and seventy and earning less than £160 per year. Following other countries' practices, insurance would be based on weekly contributions from three sources – 4d from male workers (3d from female workers), 3d from their employers, and 2d from the state – which Lloyd George, with his populist touch, told the public was 'ninepence for fourpence'. In return, insured workers would be entitled to a number of benefits. They would be able to claim sick pay for up to twenty-six weeks and treatment from a doctor on a list of government-approved practitioners, who would receive a set fee for their services. Men would also be able to claim a maternity allowance covering the cost of an attendant for their wives during childbirth.

The second part of the National Insurance Act was drafted by the Board of Trade, where a number of reforming civil servants, including William Beveridge, had supplied the new President, Winston Churchill, with ideas about how the state could tackle unemployment. The proposal was for something that had not been tried anywhere else before: compulsory unemployment insurance for workers who made their livings in vulnerable trades and industries, including construction and shipbuilding, where employment could be brought to a halt by something as simple as the weather. Like part one of the Act, unemployment insurance would involve contributions from workers, their employers and the state. It would also operate in conjunction with new labour exchanges, also the brainchild of Churchill's advisers, who borrowed the idea from Germany. These exchanges were meant to help workers find jobs by providing them with the most up-to-date information on where to look for employment. If that failed, insured workers could claim unemployment benefit of 7s a week for up to fifteen weeks a year.

People and institutions who already provided these services were not overly enamoured by the Liberals' proposals. While the British Medical Association complained about restraints of trade and the prospect of doctors being forced into government service, friendly societies and private insurance companies thought the state was trying to pull the rug out from under them. If an entity the size of the British state got involved in insurance, they argued, then it was likely to force everyone else out of business. Aware of these objections, Lloyd George looked for solutions that would create as few obstructions as possible. He consulted the medical profession and agreed that no doctor would be forced to treat patients under the scheme. He also considered buying out the insurance companies, but estimates of the cost – somewhere in the region of £30 million – meant he had to drop the idea. His compromise was to invite private providers to administer the government's schemes. Friendly societies, trade unions, private insurers and the post office would take care of the day-to-day business of national insurance, keeping track of people and employers who had to prove they had contributed by fixing stamps inside insurance books.

For the Liberals, there was a political price to pay, however, when it came to getting these proposals through Parliament. The Irish Nationalists wanted a new promise of Home Rule, and the Labour Party had demanded MPs be paid a wage – an issue that was particularly important for them at a moment when the Lords had decided trade union donations to the party were illegal. Although these decisions would have long-term consequences for the Liberals, their national insurance schemes were up and running quickly, with workers paying their first contributions in July 1913 and being entitled to draw benefits from January the following year. The impact was significant. While 2.25 million workers suddenly found themselves with unemployment insurance, access to doctors revealed that huge amounts of illness and disease had been going unreported by the labouring classes. Yet like the Liberals' pension scheme, it was not all good news for the British people. Coverage might not have been subject to the kind of geographical variations it had been before, when factors such as the size of the trade union operating in a local industry determined the kinds of benefits its members had access to, but there were still massive holes for people to fill. Unemployment insurance was mainly for skilled workers; health insurance was for wage earners only, leaving them to find the funds to cover spouses and children, and excluded hospital treatment. It was also inconsistent that someone aged seventy could claim a pension without ever having paid a penny into a pension fund, but workers had to have a history of contributions before they could claim time-limited benefits.

Unsurprisingly, these schemes faced significant opposition from both sides of the political spectrum. For those to the left of the Liberals, the proposals went nowhere near far enough in terms of what they offered and the fact they were contributory insurance, rather than benefits paid for out of general taxation and available to workers as of right. To the Liberals' right, commentators were just as critical as ever, even though the schemes looked more like compulsory self-help than sentimental collectivism. Drawing on tropes about red tape and business that would become fixtures in British politics during the twentieth century, Tories complained that national insurance was an unreasonable bureaucratic burden. It was unacceptable, they argued, that people who employed domestic servants would suddenly have to insure them too. But if these critics resented buying insurance stamps for their home help, they were even more infuriated by other, less celebrated developments that the likes of Beatrice Webb were cheering on.

4

The Health of the Nation

The 'People's Budget' introduced by Lloyd George in 1909 has long been seen as an emblem of a radical and reforming Liberal government. The stand-off with the House of Lords played a significant part in shaping this view. While some peers stuck to the line that the Liberals' proposals had to be put to the voters because they had not been in the party's 1906 manifesto, others spoke openly about what they thought was wrong with the government's plans. Speaking at a rally in Lincoln for the local tariff reform candidate in December 1909, Lord Willoughby de Broke, 'a peer, a Tory, a landowner, and an Englishman', explained that the 'People's Budget' required a fresh election, not simply for constitutional reasons but because it was 'saturated through and through with the poison of socialism'. The threat was amplified, he argued, by the fact that the Liberals were planning to co-operate with the Labour Party, agreeing not to stand against each other in strategically important seats at the next election. The government had silently accepted socialism 'as its driving force' and was 'attempting to carry a revolution without a mandate'.

The reason the Liberals' reforms of the tax system had people like Lord Willoughby hot under the collar was understandable. Graduated and differentiated rates of taxation meant a real, if somewhat overstated, increase in their financial liabilities. But the reality of pensions and national insurance – separate schemes with different rules and sometimes inconsistent principles – was a less obvious case of radical transformation. National insurance did not cover everyone or every eventuality and, like the new state pension, its payments were meagre. Funded through flat-rate contributions, rather than deductions from wages calculated according to an individual's ability to pay, national insurance was also a regressive tax. Sceptical observers might argue that the Liberals had only made available a limited version of private insurance, delivered by the private companies themselves, which was compulsory for just a section of the population. Although, thanks in large part to Lloyd George's rhetorical brilliance which saw him shamelessly raid the new liberal canon for ways to talk about poverty and social reform, it certainly looked like something much more radical had taken place.

Yet pensions, social insurance and tax reform were not the only social policy changes during the first decade of the twentieth century. Other often less celebrated, but sometimes much more radical, innovations had emerged in response to a number of long-term developments that influential politicians, social reformers and journalists considered deeply worrying. The focal point for these developments was the Boer War, in which Britain had finally prevailed in 1902 but only after spending significant sums of money and suffering huge reputational damage in the process. As commentators searched for the causes of the country's near-disastrous showing against what they thought was a rag-bag of poorly equipped guerrilla fighters, they ended up in intellectual and political territory where the idea of feeding the nation's schoolchildren for free seemed like a reasonable thing to do. Contrary to critics, including the Charity Organisation Society, who thought Britain was being turned into a Speenhamland system writ large, supporters of these policies believed they were simply continuing with the spirit of public health reform that had motivated the likes of Edwin Chadwick half a century earlier. In so doing, they believed they were addressing deep questions about British decline that were no longer seen in just economic or industrial terms, but as measurable physical problems too.

THE BRIGHTEST AND THE BEST

The year 1859 was a turning point in Victorian intellectual life. While John Stuart Mill's *On Liberty* was published, laying the foundations for what he was to call 'advanced Liberalism', the public also got their first look at Charles Darwin's *On the Origin of Species*. Darwin had become well known in scientific and literary circles twenty years earlier thanks to his writings about his five-year-long voyage around the globe, including his famous visit to the Galapagos Islands, on HMS *Beagle*. Now aged fifty and living a quiet life in Kent with his wife, Emma, his first cousin and a member of the Wedgwood pottery manufacturing family, with whom he had ten children, Darwin had spent more than twenty-five years thinking about evolution when a letter from a younger biologist, Alfred Russel Wallace, outlining ideas strikingly similar to his own, forced him to write up what was, by Darwin's own standards, a relatively concise summary – 490 pages – of the conclusions he had reached.

Darwin, who hated controversy, had marked the publication of his book by fleeing to Ilkley, a spa town in North Yorkshire, where he hoped he could avoid the attention that was sure to come his way. He knew there was an appetite for his ideas – indeed, the *Origin*'s first print run sold out on day one – but he also knew there were plenty of critics, from those who objected to his ideas on religious grounds to fellow scientists sceptical about the details of his argument, particularly his claim that natural selection could explain the wondrous complexity they observed in the world around them. Darwin's sense of the reception he might get was based, in part, on the fact he was far from the first thinker to propose a theory of evolution. Such ideas had been around for decades. His own grandfather, Erasmus, had written about progressive transformation in the organic world some seventy years earlier. Around the same time in France, the zoologist Jean-Baptiste Lamarck had formulated a theory about how species might evolve if parents could pass on to their offspring the improvements they made to themselves.

Most Victorians, though, had learned about evolution from one of the age's best-selling and most talked-about books, *Vestiges of the Natural History of Creation*, which had appeared anonymously in 1844 but was known to be by the Edinburgh publisher Robert Chambers. With a keen sense of what readers wanted, Chambers synthesized the latest scientific theories into an entertaining and sometimes scandalous narrative that took readers on a journey from the origins of the universe – described as an event like the Big Bang – to a possible future where mankind continued to evolve. A middle-class audience, which had grown wealthier during the industrial revolution and wanted to make sense of their place in the world, were fascinated by it. Indeed, the *Vestiges* was so popular it continued to outsell the *Origin of Species* for years after 1859.

The philosopher Herbert Spencer, who had grown up in the thriving Midlands industrial town of Derby that had been home to Erasmus Darwin too, was also among those trying to make sense of evolution for a middle-class audience in the years before the *Origin of Species* appeared. During the early 1850s, Spencer had proposed his own all-encompassing theory of evolution, which was central to his radical vision of liberalism. As he explained in *Synthetic Philosophy*, the multi-volume project that occupied him for the whole of the second half of the nineteenth century, he believed that everything, from individual organisms to human societies to the universe as a whole, exhibited a tendency to progress, passing from initially simple states to much more complex ones. The lesson for humans, Spencer argued, was that they should not stand in evolution's way and should instead let the progressive potential inside everyone and everything reveal itself. Individuals freed from paternalism and other artificial constraints would develop strong moral characters because they would respond to the challenges around them by striving to improve.

Although Darwin was certain humans had evolved, he made what he knew was likely to be a futile effort to direct his readers' attention away from the kinds of questions that Chambers and Spencer were happy to speculate on. He made just one comment – 'Light will be thrown on the origin of man and his history' – on page 488, hoping, against all reasonable hope, that people would believe he was undecided on the issue. But despite Darwin's best efforts, the debate about his book turned to humans almost immediately. People speculated about how everything – from psychology to literature to politics – could be understood in light of evolution. Notwithstanding the popularity of what later became known as 'social Darwinism', summed up by the phrase 'survival of the fittest', which Spencer coined as a description of natural selection, the contents of the *Origin of Species* seldom had much to do with what was being discussed.

One programme for social improvement that was based on the idea of evolution and unambiguously linked to Darwin's work, though, was eugenics – the brainchild of his younger cousin, Francis Galton

(1822–1911). A wealthy outdoors type, Galton had grown up in a strange environment: his grandfather was a Quaker but had been disowned by his local Friends' Meeting in Birmingham because he made his money from gun manufacturing. Although he seemed set for a career in medicine, Galton had taken a different direction after his father died while the young man was away studying at Cambridge, leaving him an inheritance he would live off for the next seventy years. Instead of becoming a doctor, Galton spent two years exploring south-west Africa and the Middle East and built himself a reputation as an expert on geography and travel. The author of a best-selling book called *The Art of Travel* (1855), he also discovered the anticyclone, invented the modern weather-forecasting map, and on one occasion was paid by the army to demonstrate his survival techniques to troops.

All this changed, however, when Galton read the *Origin of Species*. Marvelling at Darwin's command of a huge array of evidence, Galton was completely convinced by his cousin's case for evolution. What he found most interesting, however, was the analogy Darwin had used to explain natural selection. Look at how animal breeders were capable of preserving or improving particular traits, like fur colour or an ability to run fast, in dogs, cattle and pigeons, Darwin had argued, and then imagine what nature might be able to do over eons of time. What if that principle could be applied to humans, Galton wondered – and what if we did not need to wait millions of years for results?

Pondering his circle of acquaintances, all of whom seemed to have famous, rich and eminent fathers, Galton scoured society journals and biographical dictionaries for information about the men – and it was almost always men – who held the best professional jobs, respected roles and positions of note in Britain. As he did, he became convinced his hunch was right. People with prestige, wealth and power almost invariably seemed to be related to other people with prestige, wealth and power. He was sure this meant that intellectual ability was down to breeding. But, as critics of his book *Hereditary Genius* (1869) pointed out, he had a problem: how could he demonstrate that it was really down to nature rather than nurture?

Possessed of an endlessly inventive mind, enthusiasm for quantifying everything he could lay his eyes on, and a capacity for persuading the public to participate in his projects, Galton proved to be up for the challenge. He invented new instruments for measuring things like height and weight – including the first version of the dog whistle, which he used to assess people's hearing – and turned them into a kind of game which he demonstrated at the International Health Exhibition in South Kensington, London, in the mid-1880s. Almost 10,000 people paid 3d to complete a series of challenges that pitted them against their friends and family while supplying him with an unprecedented volume of information on things like reaction times and eyesight. Galton also developed the first versions of what we would now call the standardized psychological questionnaire, which he distributed to head teachers, scientists he knew through his family and social circle, and audiences at the public lectures he often gave, and sometimes offered cash prizes for the best and most complete responses.

For Galton, there was a specific point to all this activity, beyond intellectual curiosity. He believed that establishing the causes of intelligence had huge implications for government and politics. An increasingly complex world, where scientific and technological developments had wrought massive changes in less than a century, demanded 'abler commanders, statesmen, thinkers, inventors, and artists', he argued. If they were not created, identified and nurtured, then Britain risked losing its hard-won competitive advantages in trade, industry and international affairs. Galton urged the state to act on his research by intervening in public life to ensure the brightest and best made it to the top, as the government had made a start on doing in the civil service after the Northcote–Trevelyan Report of 1854, which had recommended an end to patronage and the beginning of recruitment by competitive examinations.

Galton wanted a system, however, that not only sifted the wheat from the chaff but also ensured there was as much wheat as possible. He argued that while promoting the best individuals immediately, the state had to consider what it could do to ensure that, in the long run, there were more intelligent people to choose from. Perhaps, Galton suggested, governments could issue people with health and intelligence certificates, and encourage the healthiest and cleverest to marry each other? Maybe there could be incentives for these people to have as many children as possible, such as grants that covered portions of the cost of their upbringing. If the past had been about the aristocracy keeping land and money in their hands through marriage and family, a eugenic future would be secured by the most intelligent members of society taking the most important jobs – including those of physician, statesman, lawyer and teacher – and then reproducing their talent through their offspring.

THE ROCK ON WHICH
THE STATE IS BUILT

Most of Galton's target audience were not sympathetic towards his ideas when he first proposed them during the 1860s. They were much more interested in the liberal philosophy espoused by the likes of Spencer and John Stuart Mill, who argued that progress came from individuals striving to be better people, rather than from what they inherited at birth. Towards the end of the nineteenth century, however, Galton found the situation had changed. The 'Great Victorian Boom', the period of economic growth that had been attributed to free trade after the repeal of the Corn Laws in 1846, had come to an end. Moreover, with a widening of the electoral franchise after the Second Reform Act in 1867, a series of well-publicized strikes and riots, such as the trouble that started in Trafalgar Square and spilled over into the West End in 1886, and Charles Booth's discovery that a third of Londoners lived in sometimes shocking poverty, there was a sense of unease among the middle classes, who worried that the working classes might be about to overthrow a system they had spent the previous fifty years reforming. Seemingly inevitable progress looked like it was over. Was the future going to be an era of decline?

These concerns were given impetus by statistics that were starting to pour out of the Office of the Registrar General, where people had been legally required to register births, marriages and deaths since 1837. As discussed earlier, at the beginning of the nineteenth century Thomas Malthus had made a series of gloomy forecasts about what he thought were the realities of population growth. The number of people would always increase at a much faster rate than their means of subsistence, he argued, meaning society would get bigger, sometimes quite sharply, but would always be pulled back by what he called 'checks': starvation, disease and death. Contrary to those predictions, the United Kingdom's population had grown rapidly and constantly over the previous century, with England's alone growing from just under 8 million when the first census was conducted in 1801, to a little over 30 million a century later, without any of the consequences Malthus had suggested. Thanks to improvements in public health, driven by things like free vaccination programmes and better sanitation in the country's cities, not to mention free trade, which increased the availability of cheap basic foodstuffs, death rates had gone down. As the Liberal government would discover when it made a state pension available in 1909, people were living longer than ever before. Notwithstanding the famine that wracked Ireland in the late 1840s and early 1850s, it looked like populations really could grow without threatening the stability of the social structure or the very future of the nation.

T. H. C. Stevenson, Superintendent of Statistics in the General Register Office, and other statisticians dug deeper into the great mass of information that had accumulated across the course of the nineteenth century, however, they started to notice something less obvious but no less significant. After a recorded high of 36.3 in 1876, the birthrate – the number of births per 1,000 members of the population – had started to go down, slowly but surely. By the beginning of the twentieth century, the rate had dropped to what looked like a quite alarming figure: 28.5. *The Lancet*, one of the world's oldest medical journals, was certain that this trend was 'a national calamity seriously threatening the future welfare of our race'. But why was it happening?

The answer was far from clear. On the one hand, there were difficulties when it came to comparing the past and the present, given that the volume and quality of statistical information had got so much better, so quickly. On the other, there was a good case for arguing that all the rapid decline showed was that the birthrate was not the best measure of whatever it was *The Lancet* and others thought it showed. Maybe the decline was largely an artefact of the overall growth in the number of people? Nevertheless, some statisticians thought they could detect causes. Karl Pearson (1857–1936) – a technocratic socialist, radical feminist and pioneering statistician who was also one of Galton's leading disciples – was among the first to suggest declining fertility among women. There seemed to be a trend towards smaller families, Pearson argued, with fewer women having five children or more.

The reasons for this trend were widely disputed. Was the problem contraception, information about which had become more widely available during the course of the nineteenth century? Were progressive politics and social reformers, who were largely responsible for the spread of literature on contraception, to blame? After all, the likes of Charles Bradlaugh, the atheist Liberal MP who had refused to take the parliamentary Oath of Allegiance, Annie Besant, the socialist leader of the matchgirl strikes in London during the late 1880s, and John Stuart Mill had all been in trouble with the law for distributing pamphlets about contraception that were considered indecent. Perhaps, as conservative critics believed, women were at fault because they were being persuaded by this information to abandon their duty to the future of the nation? Maybe the issue was that the cost of parenthood had become so high people were simply choosing not to shoulder it?

The closer statisticians and social investigators looked, the more the declining birthrate seemed a hugely complex problem. Geography seemed to matter: birthrates were lower in the crowded inner cities than in the agricultural areas workers had left behind during the industrial revolution. It looked like social class had a big impact too. While Charles Booth and his team of investigators showed that the birthrate was more than one and a half times higher in the poorest parts of London than in the richest, Seebohm Rowntree concluded that almost a quarter of people living in what he had called 'primary poverty' – when income failed to cover basic necessary expenditure – in York were in families containing more than five children. Surely people living in that kind of abject poverty could not afford to have such large families, while those above them in the social structure could afford more children than they had? As the more astute investigators explained, an important part of the explanation was quite clear. Children were actually wage earners in poor families – an issue Rowntree had identified in his account of the poverty cycle when he described how parents started to move above the poverty line the moment their offspring could go out to work.

Politicians and thinkers from across the political spectrum were unsure of what to make of all this. But they agreed that, if true, declining and differential birthrates had serious political and economic consequences. Commentators on the right, such as those at the *Daily Telegraph*, wrote about manpower as 'the rock on which the whole edifice of the State is built', and worked themselves up into an apocalyptic frenzy when they thought about the implications of the poor outbreeding the rich. Francis Galton was concerned that it would be even tougher for the state to recruit the kinds of first-class minds it needed if there were fewer of them around. Even Sidney Webb, who wrote a pamphlet called *The Decline in the Birth-Rate* (1907), argued that a country that could not renew itself from within would not be able to support the kinds of social reform he and his fellow socialists hoped to see.

Under pressure from the Office of the Registrar General, Prime Minister Asquith agreed that his government would put money into a project that promised to throw light on the darker corners of the problem. Everyone who filled out a census form in 1911 also had to complete a fertility survey, which asked them about the number of children they had produced and their family tree. Quiet and unassuming but dedicated to his work, Stevenson and his assistants immersed themselves in this information: a process that took years, even with the help of new card-computing machines that automated work that previously had to be done by hand. But simply calculating family sizes and trying to trace them through time was not enough, given the concerns people had about the birthrate. Stevenson needed to be able to explain what was going on in the mountains of data piled up in the General Register Office.

Stevenson's problem, however, was that the idea of trying to study social classes objectively – beyond the obvious claim that there was an upper and a lower class – was relatively new. As Booth and Rowntree had shown when they constructed their own classifications of society, putting people into categories was not simple. Economic issues like income were helpful but they did not tell the whole story. While social investigators had their prejudices about the value of different types of work and the impact of specific habits, such as drinking, on someone's fortunes, the people they studied had their own ideas. The skilled working class, for instance, had developed a strong sense of their independence, seeing their trades and professions as distinct from the menial drudgery of unskilled work – a superiority that was evident, they believed, in their trade unions and co-operatives, which offered them the kinds of benefits and security ordinary labourers could only dream of.

Yet, sat in his office in a wing of the grand neoclassical Somerset House on London's Strand, Stevenson was able to cut through these complexities and pass judgement on the more than 465 occupational categories, divided into orders and sub-orders, listed in the census data. As he did, he produced what subsequently came to be known as the 'professional model of social classes': a ranked hierarchy of groups, divided broadly between manual and non-manual, but subdivided between skilled and unskilled classes. His model made use of information about wages but it also involved his perception of different jobs' social and moral worth – with medicine, engineering and accountancy ranked above journalism – and had been designed in the belief that declining fertility was a trend that had spread downwards through British society. Tabulating the information about these groups' fertility rates and delivering conclusions took almost twelve years in total. When Stevenson finally published his findings in two reports, the first in 1917 and the second in 1923, he confirmed the suspicions that had underpinned some people's worst fears about the future. The fertility census showed that, from the 1860s through to 1911, the average number of children born to married couples had fallen by nearly half. It had also demonstrated that unskilled workers' families, at an average of four children, were twice the size of those of professionals. 'Our population has been recruited', Stevenson argued, 'under conditions fundamentally different' from the ones that had existed in the past.

But these hard facts were only ever part of what worried many of the politicians, social reformers and biologists, among others, who were involved in the discussions about population trends. They had not thought they could, or, indeed, needed to, wait that long for answers. The National Birth-Rate Commission was formed in 1913 by the National Council of Public Morals, an organization that had been founded nine years earlier by a disparate group of eugenicists, medics and churchmen who were worried about the general link between health and morals after a sharp, albeit brief, rise in the recorded cases of venereal disease. Mimicking a Royal Commission, the National Birth-Rate Commission carried out its own investigations, including one of the most extensive studies to date of women's contraceptive habits, and called witnesses for cross-examination at venues across London. Beatrice and Sidney Webb, the new liberal economist John Atkinson Hobson, the Labour MP Ramsay Mac-Donald, the birth-control campaigner Marie Stopes, and the writer and physician Arthur Conan Doyle were among the many eminent figures from the scientific, political and cultural worlds to take part in its proceedings. What worried them was not just that the population might be shrinking, but that the country, judged by the state of the individuals living in it, might be decaying in a very real, physical sense.

DEGENERATION AND DETERIORATION

One particular word came up with increasing frequency in discussions about the British population after 1900: degeneration. Popularized during the 1890s by a French journalist called Max Nordau, who used it to describe a condition he believed was afflicting the whole of Western civilization, from its philosophy and literature to its people and their homes, degeneration had a technical meaning – one that was the polar opposite of what Herbert Spencer had meant when he had started writing about evolution half a century earlier. As the zoologist E. Ray Lankester (1847–1929) put it in his book of the same name, degeneration was 'a loss of organisation making the descendant far *simpler* or *lower* in structure than its ancestor'. *The Lancet* was among the many influential voices arguing that this process had infiltrated modern Britain. Degeneration was 'undoubtedly at work among town-bred populations', the journal had told its readers in 1888, and it believed there were obvious reasons: namely 'unwholesome occupations, improper [diet], and juvenile vice'. The good news was the degeneration was reversible. But 'it would be wrong,' *The Lancet* urged its readers, 'to ignore the existence of widespread evils and serious dangers to the public health'.

One name that became synonymous with these discussions in Britain was Arnold White (1848–1925). The son of a Congregational minister, White was best known as a writer and journalist but his life before deciding to make a living from his pen had been eventful. He had worked for the P&O shipping company, been a coffee planter in Ceylon, a manager for the Edison Electric Light Company, and had travelled through Britain's colonial outposts searching for business opportunities. He had always been interested in politics, though, and aligned himself with the Liberal Unionists who had split from Gladstone's Liberal Party over Irish Home Rule in 1886. Indeed, White even stood for election to Parliament on three unsuccessful occasions from the mid-1880s to the mid-1890s, before one last failed attempt in 1906, when he ran as an independent. White's politics were an intriguing mix of individualism, typified by a passionate hatred of socialism, and xenophobic and racist fervour, symbolized by his enthusiasm for the British Empire and campaigns to restrict immigration, particularly Jews fleeing persecution in Eastern Europe. Yet he did not consider himself a conservative or reactionary. On the contrary, White thought he was a progressive; someone who was not only committed to building a better society for the aspiring common man but also a champion of the people who spoke truth to power.

White first tried his hand at writing for a living by reporting on the 'social problem' during the 1880s. Like other journalists, writers and social investigators, he was drawn to London's East End, where he observed the lives and habits of the people who lived there as part of the research for his first book, *The Problems of a Great City* (1886). Unlike the dry statistics and fine-grained classifications that filled the seventeen volumes of Booth's *Life and Labour of the People in London*, which started to appear three years later, White's book was an impressionistic and literary affair that did little to hide its author's prejudices. Discussing unemployment, immigration, wages, drinking habits and overcrowding, *The Problems of a Great City* was heavily moralistic and passed unremitting judgements on the people White had either met or observed from what he considered a safe distance. The people of the East End were simply a class apart from the rest of society, he argued, and the kinds of degenerate behaviour he had witnessed were caused by innate character failings, which were the product of flawed biology. For their part, the well-off were too com-passionate to do the right thing, meaning the state was constantly rescuing the least capable from the fate they would meet if nature took its course. Britain had become the world's 'rubbish-heap', he told his readers, where the dregs of humanity piled up in overcrowded slums, putting a huge strain on everyone else.

The Problems of a Great City sold well enough to earn White com-missions from a number of newspapers and periodicals, but he had to wait until 1899 and the start of the Boer War for his big break. Although Britain was ultimately successful, victory against the Dutch settlers in southern Africa was hugely problematic. Some observers were outraged by the brutal scorched-earth tactics and the regime of concentration camps that the British army had used in an effort to break their enemy. Others were less concerned with the rights and wrongs of the army's behaviour and more worried that even with such questionable tactics, and despite sending more than 400,000 troops – five times the number of people living in the Boer republics at the time – over the course of three years, they had struggled to defeat what were largely untrained militia forces. 'Black Week' in December 1899, when the army suffered three defeats and more than two thousand casualties, including one chaotic and humiliating loss after General Gatacre, who had been despatched to secure an area just south of Orange Free State, lost his way in the dark and became separated from six hundred of his troops, who were subsequently captured by the enemy, seemed to sum up Britain's problems. Such events were profound humiliations for the nationalistic elements and self-styled patriots of the press, who were quick to argue that bungling officers, who made poor decisions, and incompetent offi-cials, who failed to supply troops with the correct equipment, were to blame for the war dragging on.

As a patriotic imperialist, White looked on with horror. He was deeply worried about the apparent mismanagement of British soldiers and resources, but was also convinced that the failure to defeat the Boer forces quickly was a symptom of problems he had been trying to draw people's attention to for the previous fifteen years. The records of the Army Medical Corps, which had inspected potential recruits throughout the war, presented White with a golden opportunity to make his case. As he told his readers, it was no surprise Britain had struggled against the Boers, because the raw material the country had to work with was clearly not up to the job. In Manchester, for example, 11,000 men had offered themselves for war service by July 1900, eight months after hostilities had commenced. But it had become apparent quickly, he reported, that all was not well with these potential recruits: 8,000 of the men who had tried to sign up were considered 'physically unfit to carry a rifle and stand the fatigues of discipline'. Indeed, White went on, 'of the 3,000 who were accepted only 1,200 attained the moderate standard of muscular power and chest measurement required by the military authorities'. Simply put: 'two out of every three men willing to bear arms in the Manchester district are virtually invalids'. Given there was no reason to believe Manchester was worse than any other town or city in the country, White thought the consequences of this finding were terrifying.

White's story attracted a great deal of attention from across the political spectrum, and in the spring of 1903, the army's Inspector General of Recruiting was forced to confirm to Parliament that the general gist of what he had written was true. Indeed, with Seebohm Rowntree revealing that more than 25 per cent of men were turned away by the army in Leeds, York and Sheffield, and other military experts going public with worries about the quality of men the army had to choose from, White's suggestion that Britain was home to a large and possibly growing number of people who were physically inferior to their ancestors seemed to gather momentum. The Boer War had been won but, all things considered, it looked like the army had been fortunate not to experience more humiliation than it had. The real concern, critics like White argued, was that Britain had a huge empire with territories stretching across most of the globe, from Australia to India to Canada. But as Lord Rosebery of the Liberal Party opined: 'it is no use having an Empire without an Imperial race'.

The solution to these problems, however, was far from obvious. For White, whose politics were uncompromising and whose ideas often deeply unpleasant, the answer was to eliminate what he thought was the cause, root and branch. People who failed to meet the army's requirements should be stopped from having children, preferably with their consent but by forced sterilization if necessary. Although this view was extreme, it had support from across the political spectrum. Even figures such as the socialist Karl Pearson, and the novelist and fellow Fabian socialist H. G. Wells, were comfortable with the idea that controlling people's reproductive capabilities had a part to play in the social reforming projects of the future. For Pearson, in particular, the world had moved beyond the battle between individuals that philosophers like Herbert Spencer had seen as the defining aspect of evolution during the middle decades of the nineteenth century. Evolution was now being driven by competition between nation states in wars, economic affairs and ideas, Pearson argued; he believed governments were right to consider any option that might offer the country an advantage.

Arthur Balfour's Conservative–Unionist administration, however, was much less enthusiastic about such proposals. Aside from any moral concerns he and his colleagues might have had about the idea of restricting anybody's fertility, Balfour understood that people like White had their eyes firmly fixed on the working classes. With the Labour Representation Committee mobilizing in response to setbacks like the Taff Vale case, and the Liberal Party under Henry Campbell-Bannerman sensing the government was vulnerable on a whole range of issues, including free trade, Balfour had no interest in turning the working classes against the Tories. Nevertheless, the Prime Minister thought he had to be seen to do something.

MOUTHS TO FEED

The Interdepartmental Committee on Physical Deterioration was appointed in September 1903 and was intended as a compromise. On the one hand, it was a signal to people like White and Pearson that the government was taking concerns about the army recruitment scandal seriously. On the other, it was a response without teeth: as a simple committee it had not been empowered to make legally binding recommendations, meaning the government could brush its report aside should it decide its finding were not to its liking. This twin strategy was also reflected in the identities of the seven men chosen to sit on the committee. Colonel G. M. Fox, Inspector of Physical

Training at the Board of Education, H. M. Lindsell, Principal Assistant Secretary to the Board of Education, and J. F. W. Tatham, from the General Register Office, to name just three, were all serious men with relevant administrative experience. None, however, had a public profile that suggested they would stir up trouble or attract much attention from the outside world.

By opting for the word 'deterioration' rather than 'degeneration', Balfour also hoped he had taken the edge off some of the discussions into which the committee might be tempted to wade. Their initial instructions were to conduct a 'preliminary enquiry' into the allegations around army recruits with a view to setting out the terms for a Royal Commission, should they conclude that one was really necessary. But this remit was soon expanded to include permission to make recommendations about how the government might gather information on physical deterioration in future, as well as the ameliorative measures they might consider taking. From December 1903 through to June the following year, the committee trawled publicly available statistics and a number of usually off-limits collections, including the army's recruitment records, for data that would help build a picture of Britain's population. They also solicited written reports and held twenty-six days of hearings in the Privy Council Office in Whitehall, where they cross-examined a total of sixty-eight witnesses from government departments and fields like medicine, not to mention familiar faces from the era's debates about poverty, including Booth, Rowntree and Charles Loch, secretary of the Charity Organisation Society.

Perhaps to the government's relief, the committee concluded that, although the working classes were frequently in poor health, there was no evidence that the British people were experiencing long-term physical deterioration. In fact, the committee wrote, 'it would be as reasonable to argue from criminal statistics to the morals of the great mass of the people, as it would be to argue to their physical conditions from the feeble specimens that come under the notice of [army] recruiting officers'. As the Director General of the Army Medical Service, Sir William Taylor, explained, though, this finding was not necessarily good news for the government. 'Even if the proportion is no greater than in the past', it was still something that 'no thinking man can wish to see continue.' Indeed, he argued that the suggestion that the recent problems with recruiting men to the army in Manchester were no worse than anything that might have happened during the previous century should be no consolation at all. There were good reasons to be concerned about the physical condition of whole sections of the population.

An example of the kind of thing that had the committee worried was a seemingly innocuous measure: height. As part of their search for historical data that might help them to put the army recruitment scandal into perspective, they had stumbled upon a study Francis Galton had conducted during the late 1870s and early 1880s for the British Association for the Advancement of Science, founded to promote science and public engagement more than seventy years earlier. By co-operating with the army, schools and other public institutions as part of his efforts to prove his beliefs about eugenics, Galton had compiled information on 53,000 people, including a significant amount of data on boys aged eleven and twelve. Comparing the results for boys at two different types of educational establishments – public schools and industrial schools for juvenile delinquents, orphans and other children deemed difficult or special cases – he had discovered a number of shocking and under-reported facts. One was that the average height of public schoolboys was almost five inches greater than the average height of boys of the same age at industrial schools. Another was that this gap did not diminish with advancing age. The difference in height between adults at different ends of the class spectrum was not quite as large but, at three and a half inches, it was something that could not be ignored.

Exploring issues like inadequate diet, overcrowded and insanitary living conditions, the pressures on mothers who were forced to work late into pregnancy and then return quickly after giving birth, the decline in breast-feeding, the growth of habits like smoking among working-class children, and the impact of particular forms of employment on physique, the committee's report, published on 29 July 1904, actually told a positive story about modern Britain. Nevertheless, at the heart of the committee's analysis was a detailed dissection of the country that showed how progress and improvement were unevenly distributed. Those at the bottom of society might be living longer, but high rates of infant mortality, poor health and stunted physical development were still commonplace. The reason, the committee concluded, was not genetic – a term that had recently come into common parlance – as the likes of Arnold White argued. Rather, it was environmental. The explanation for these physical discrepancies between social classes lay in their lifestyles, habits and access to resources that enabled people to lead healthier lives.

The committee made a total of fifty-three recommendations. Many comprised an interrelated web of suggestions for better and more consistent information-gathering, so that the infrastructure was in place to spot problems early in future. An initiative of this kind would tackle the absence of reliable historical data by synthesizing the statistics that were already held by bodies such as the Poor Law Medical Officers and the Office of the Registrar General. It would also provide a forum for the investigation of issues that were still clouded with ignorance, such as the frequency of still-births, and provide a useful bulwark against the more extreme opinions that emanated from the political margins – something that Balfour had hoped the committee would do for him, of course.

Other recommendations involved solutions for problems whose roots, the committee argued, lay in the built environments of the country's cities. Few of their suggestions were revolutionary in either substance or method. For the most part, they argued in the Chadwickean tradition: environmental improvements would come from administrative sources. While existing rules, like those regarding pollution from factories, should be enforced more consistently, new ones should be created, including stricter domestic building regulations to help prevent overcrowding and the erosion of green public spaces. Buried away within the report, however, were a number of much more radical ideas that Balfour hoped to be able to ignore.

Reflecting on what they had learned from Galton's findings about height differences between social classes, the committee concluded that 'with scarcely an exception' there was a consensus that the 'time has come when the State should realize the necessity of ensuring adequate nourishment to children in attendance at school'. What was the point, the committee argued, in subjecting 'half-starved children to the processes of education'? In such circumstances, not only did the children themselves fail to benefit from the schooling they were being offered, but also the money that was being spent on it was effectively wasted.

The Conservative–Unionist government was not particularly enthusiastic about the idea of feeding the nation's children for free. Even before the committee's recommendations had been published in the summer of 1904, Balfour told William Anson, the parliamentary secretary to the Board of Education, who was handling the report for the government, that local rates – levied against property and the source of most funding for schools – would not be increased to pay for anything. Balfour's problem, however, was that refusing to commit any extra resources meant he now looked like he did not care about malnourished schoolchildren. Rather than appear to make a U-turn on his earlier hard-line stance, he decided to devolve responsibility for the school meals issue by forming another committee to look into it. Then in December 1905, less than a month after this committee reported, he resigned. Balfour had done so in order to force the Liberals to form an administration immediately. He hoped that a short spell in power before a general election would reveal their internal divisions and allow the Tories to secure a majority.

Balfour, of course, lost his wager in January 1906. And when Henry Campbell-Bannerman became Prime Minister with a thumping Liberal majority of 130, supplemented by 30 Labour MPs, after a campaign dominated by the issue of tariff reform, the school meals' question became the Liberal Party's responsibility. The Education (Provision of Meals) Act, which was passed into law in December 1906, was typical of the new administration – still rooted in old liberal concerns about free trade, balanced budgets and constitutional reform, but feeling the impact of new liberal ideas about social reform – and its approach to welfare issues at a moment when it was struggling to get on top of its fiscal inheritance from Balfour's Unionist government. Like legislation around public works since the 1860s, the school meals act was permissive rather than prescriptive, in that it did not oblige anyone to do anything and promised no extra funds from Whitehall for anyone who did. Unlike Balfour, however, the Liberals did allow local authorities to increase rates by up to a halfpenny for the purpose of feeding any child whose family they considered unable to do so themselves.

The result was a wide array of different practices across the country. Meals could be provided to children whose families were able to prove economic hardship or, less commonly, when a local authority simply decided they were malnourished. But decisions were ultimately at the discretion of local authorities. By 1911, five years after the legislation had been passed, only 40 per cent of Local Education Authorities offered meals. Even during the traumas of the Great Depression two decades later, when unemployment was catastrophically high and many working-class families struggled to put food on the table, meals were served to around only 4 per cent of the school population, with 15 per cent of schools still offering no meals at all. Indeed, local authorities that did make meals available were hardly offering extravagant or costly menus. While bread, dripping, butter and porridge were breakfast staples, hastily assembled broths, stews and pies were the most common lunch dishes. According to some commentators, a child's willingness to eat the food was the ultimate means test.

Regardless of take up and the quality of the food on offer, not everyone was happy with these developments. Recognizing the scale of the problems that had been revealed by the Boer War and the Interdepartmental Committee on Physical Deterioration, Charles Loch, the Charity Organisation Society's usually uncompromising opponent of the 'degraded pauperism' he thought state intervention encouraged, conceded there might be some situations in which the state could justify feeding children. He argued, however, that school meals were still outdoor relief: a payment in kind to parents who should really be heading to the workhouse if they did not have enough money to provide for their own family. Loch could only bring himself to accept the practice on the condition it involved a means test of the strictest kind and if meals were served in complete secrecy, lest anyone get the impression that they too could acquire food for free.

Such concerns highlighted the complexities of the problems that had been revealed during the fall-out from the Boer War. While Loch and his colleagues at the Charity Organisation Society were happy with the Interdepartmental Committee on Physical Deterioration's suggestion that handing out food to poor children was likely to make people taller in the future, they had a number of reservations about what doing so might mean. One was their long-standing concern about the impact of such actions on the values of independence and self-reliance across society. Another, though, was the sense that school meals were the thin end of a very thick wedge when it came to local and national government involvement in affairs that the Charity Organisation Society thought were matters for individuals. As politicians and social reformers considered what else might be required to achieve the aims that their actions on school meals had set, it looked like Loch and his allies just might be right.

5

The Well-being of the Whole

The Boer War had been the spur for searching questions about the state of the nation. The working classes had been the target for many of the most panicked speculations, with doctors, army officers, politicians, journalists and social reformers quick to suggest their physical condition posed a threat to the country as a whole. New policies, such as feeding hungry schoolchildren, had emerged as possible, though contested, parts of the solution. But the most persistent and committed reformers had not limited themselves to worries about whether the poor were consuming a sufficient number of calories every day. On the contrary, they had been just as interested in the failings of Britain's ruling classes as they had in the men who appeared to be too unfit for army service.

Francis Galton, of course, had made a concerted effort to raise the alarm about Britain's social and economic elite when he first started writing about eugenics in the late 1860s. Reflecting on the country's situation two-thirds of the way into the nineteenth century, he had expressed concerns about the likelihood of its startling progress continuing. The world was a complicated and competitive place, Galton had argued, and it would require a 'galaxy of genius', deployed throughout society, for Britain to carry on leading the pack. Although few people initially shared his pessimistic take on the country's situation, and even fewer his radical proposals for improving it, a growing number of politicians and social reformers had come to agree with his assessment by the early twentieth century. The army's recruitment crisis during the Boer War looked increasingly like a symptom of a much deeper set of problems with the way the country was organized and run.

Engaging with these issues involved asking difficult questions about the nature of modern industrial societies, and whether the ideas that Britain's politicians had put their trust in for so long had run their course. Social reform and free trade seemed to have been at the root of Britain's success, from technological innovations like the railways to the country's dominance of world trade to lengthening life expectancy for its people, during the previous century. But success had brought great and sometimes disorientating change. People had moved from the countryside to the cities, the electoral franchise had expanded significantly, and, after the general election of 1892, there were workers' representatives in Parliament, visibly challenging the old order's norms and conventions – as Keir Hardie, Labour's first MP, did when he sported a deerstalker hat and tweed suit, rather than the top hat and frock coat that Conservatives and Liberals had long worn around Westminster. The big concern for some politicians and social reformers was whether this new and increasingly democratic society was capable of tackling the new problems that had emerged alongside it by the early twentieth century. Highly specialist and expert knowledge was necessary if Britain was going to avoid a repeat of the Boer War humiliations, critics argued. But surely the inclination of many people was to stand in the way of not only the creation of that knowledge but its application too?

NATIONAL EFFICIENCY

The Political Economy Club of London had been created in 1821 by James Mill, David Ricardo and a number of their allies as part of their effort to promote and disseminate their ideas about politics, the economy and society. Every major figure in nineteenth- and twentieth-century political economy, from Malthus to Keynes, was a member, and many of the leading and most distinguished liberal politicians, public officials and businessmen, including Edwin Chadwick and William Gladstone, were among those who mingled over dinners in expensive and fashionable London restaurants and listened to talks about the latest work in political economy at wood-panelled gentlemen's clubs and societies. The club may not have been in government but, judged by the direction British politics took during the fifty years after its founding, it had been successful in bringing together the great and the good and spreading the free trade message among them.

The lessons that the Political Economy Club had to teach people about the way ideas generated by intellectuals and academics could be turned into government policy were not lost on the likes of the Fabian socialist Sidney Webb. Webb thought grassroots movements were an essential element of social change, but he was convinced that it was much more important to capture the political and bureaucratic elites who put ideas into practice. He founded his own, albeit much smaller, version of the Political Economy Club in 1902. The Co-Efficients was an informal monthly dining group with twelve members, including the Liberal MP R. B. Haldane, the novelist H. G. Wells, the philosopher Bertrand Russell, the economist W. A. S. Hewins and the geographer Halford Mackinder, who took over from Hewins as director of the London School of Economics in 1903. The group met once a month for almost seven years at venues around the capital, including the Ship Tavern in Whitehall Court and the St Ermin's Hotel near St James's Park. Over dinner and drinks, they would talk about politics, economics and international affairs, with the intention of sharing ideas and identifying opportunities to disseminate them.

The name 'Co-Efficients' came from two sources. One was Webb's hope that co-operation would mean more progress towards their political goals than individual members could achieve on their own. The other was the group's common interest (at least after Bertrand Russell, a fervent anti-imperialist and free trader, had resigned after a year), in what became known as 'national efficiency'. There is no certainty on when the phrase 'national efficiency' was first used. Journalists, however, first noted that their colleagues were writing about it during the intense discussions about why it had taken the full might of the British army until 1902 – around three years – to defeat the Boers in southern Africa. National efficiency, or 'efficiency' as it was sometimes called for short, meant different things to different people. Nevertheless, it was rooted in the belief that, from the third of men who had been rejected by the army in Manchester because they were in such poor physical condition to generals who had lost their way in the dark during a march on enemy positions, the war demonstrated an urgent need for modernization.

Fabian socialists such as Wells and his fellow writer George Bernard Shaw were among national efficiency's most prominent voices. National efficiency's connection with modernization not only resonated with their progressive impulses, it also provided them with a useful focal point, one that made it easier to frame their ideas as being in the national interest, for most of the decade leading up to the First World War. Yet national efficiency was always a politically heterogeneous and cross-party movement. The loose collection of Liberal Imperialists (known as 'limps' to their opponents), including Lord Rosebery, Prime Minister for three months after Gladstone retired in 1894, R. B. Haldane, who ran the War Office under Campbell-Bannerman and would later serve as Lord Chancellor, and Herbert Asquith, Campbell-Bannerman's successor as Prime Minister, were also among those whose speeches and writings were littered with references to efficiency as Britain's new primary political and social goal. Indeed, some Tories found the idea appealing too. Winston Churchill, who sat on the Tory benches until 1904 (when he joined the Liberals over Balfour's wavering stance on free trade) was drawn into national efficiency's orbit thanks to his belief that British politics had simply become stale and incapable of solving the major problems that confronted the country.

While these observers' concerns were frequently about domestic matters, their attention was drawn to particular issues thanks to international affairs. Aside from the impetus provided by the conflict with the Boers, rapid economic and industrial development in the USA and Europe during the final third of the nineteenth century had caused politicians and economists to worry about Britain's apparently flagging performance in comparison, something that was symbolized by its share of the total world exports of manufactured goods shrinking by a third – to the still-not-insubstantial 31 per cent – by 1900. The threat from Germany, Britain's leading industrial competitor since its unification in 1871, was felt particularly acutely, not least because Germany had embraced the idea that government could be a powerful force for economic and social development. The national efficiency movement looked on with envy at many of the things Germany's much more significant bureaucratic and administrative infrastructure seemed to have delivered: world-leading science-based industries (in particular chemical engineering and, later, pharmaceuticals), which produced companies like Bayer; universities with pioneering postgraduate degrees and training that attracted aspiring scientists from across the globe; powerful and well-organized armed forces, including a navy that had trapped Britain into a naval arms race; and a system of social insurance, beginning with Bismarck's scheme for injured workers, that looked like a very modern way of warding off the threat of revolutionary socialism and general unrest among the working classes.

Other writers, such as Alfred Stead, son of the pioneering investigative journalist and editor of the liberal *Pall Mall Gazette* W. T. Stead, who would later die on board the *Titanic*, looked beyond Europe and with great enthusiasm to Japan. An admirer of *bushido*, the moral code of Japan's military elite, and proponent of the Anglo-Japanese Alliance signed in 1902, Stead wrote extensively about the country, including *Japan: Our New Ally* (1902) and the 476-page tome *Great Japan: A Study of National Efficiency* (1905), which featured a foreword from Lord Rosebery. The reasons for Stead's fascination were simple. While Britain had struggled against the Boers during the opening years of the twentieth century, Japan had defeated Tsarist Russia in 1905 after an eighteen-month war, in the process challenging long-held assumptions about European superiority over Asia. Unlike nations such as Germany and the USA, however, Japan was not a recent invention: it was an ancient country that had been highly insular – going so far as to ban its citizens from travelling abroad until the 1860s – but had transformed itself into a significant presence on the world stage by importing science and technology from the West. Despite modernizing, Japan had retained most of its traditions, including a collective social philosophy – much admired by Stead and others – which demanded that individuals sacrifice their narrow self-interests to a greater good. The idea that similar changes could be wrought in Britain was highly seductive. While H. G. Wells's hugely popular novel *A Modern Utopia* (1905) imagined a world with a ruling elite drawn from across society and known as 'samurai', Robert Baden-Powell saw his Boy Scouts movement as a way of adapting and teaching *bushido*'s chivalrous codes of loyalty for British children.

The lesson to be drawn from these international competitors and allies, national efficiency enthusiasts argued, was that Britain's way of doing things, which had served it well for most of the nineteenth century, was finished. Free trade and the wisdom of the crowd could no longer be the cornerstones of politics, the economy and society; experts and rational planning should have a much bigger role to play in the future. A number of old ideas received a boost from these arguments. The sudden explosion of popular interest in issues like degeneration and physical deterioration at the beginning of the twentieth century led to the formation of the Eugenics Education Society (later simply the Eugenics Society) in 1907. Although Francis Galton was sceptical at first, believing the society's populism threatened the movement's reputation among scientists, who would be needed to develop the knowledge base underpinning his proposals, a wide range of public figures joined the organization, including Loch and Helen Bosanquet of the Charity Organisation Society, not to mention Arnold White, the journalist who exposed the army recruitment scandal in Manchester and who was a member of the society's first council. Even economists such as William Beveridge and John Maynard Keynes would sign up later on. The society worked to promote eugenics to the British public, whom they wanted to practise eugenic principles such as limiting or increasing the size of their family, depending on their economic circumstances. But they also aimed to capture the attention of the political class, which they hoped would introduce eugenics legislation such as sterilization of the mentally ill.

As Galton's concerns about the Eugenics Education Society suggested, a common concern among those interested in national efficiency was whether the kind of expertise they valued was compatible with Britain's new and increasingly democratic state. Few national efficiency enthusiasts would openly admit to thinking the widening of the franchise during the nineteenth century, which meant the majority of adult men had the vote by 1900, was a bad thing. They nevertheless doubted democracy's capacity for delivering the kinds of reforms they thought were necessary. Hugely complex modern industrial societies seemed to be plagued by problems that required a deep understanding of sophisticated and technical issues – from the flows of international trade to the basis of a healthy diet. Expert knowledge could come to nothing, however, if the populous opted for immediate gratification over their long-term interests, either by voting for what the efficiency enthusiasts thought was the wrong political party or simply by refusing to change their behaviour. Poverty, for example, could be relieved by handing over money to everyone who asked for it; but would that be the best use of resources or, ultimately, do much towards the goal of eliminating poverty across society? As Sidney Webb explained in 1908 in an article entitled 'The Necessary Basis of Society', good government and social progress were really a matter for 'elaborately trained' experts rather than an obvious or inevitable 'outcome of popular feeling'.

'THE BOFFINOCRACY'

The national efficiency movement bought fully into the idea, increasingly popular after Darwin, that competition was the root of all progress. However, whereas early evolutionists like Herbert Spencer had identified competition between individuals as the source of improvement, national efficiency enthusiasts tended to agree with Galton's disciple and Fabian socialist Karl Pearson, who argued that competition between countries was what really mattered at the dawn of the twentieth century. Nations were at war with each other, they argued. Sometimes this meant a conventional armed conflict, but most of the time, they explained, it involved a struggle for superiority conducted by economic, cultural and political means. And Britain, it seemed, was not doing as well in that struggle as its social elites and political leaders thought it should be. When it came to the question of why, education was a popular answer. While Germany had an impressive system of government-funded technical schools offering instruction in science, technology and engineering, not to mention the most advanced and best-equipped university laboratories in the world, the British state had relatively little involvement with its educational establishments. What hope was there for the country's people and its institutions, the likes of Lord Rosebery and Joseph Chamberlain asked, if it was incapable of producing 'first rate' men?

The first meagre government grants had been given to schools during the early 1830s. However, it was not until the Taunton

Commission, on which T. H. Green, the Idealist philosopher and inspiration for many new liberals, had sat during the mid-1860s, and a small flurry of legislation, including the Endowed Schools Act of 1869 and the Education Act of the following year, that governments had started to think seriously about schooling as anything more than a commodity to be purchased by those who could afford it – especially at the secondary level. Education had become compulsory from the ages of five until twelve but, learning some of the lessons from Poor Law reform during the first half of the nineteenth century, efforts had been made to inject local democracy into the process. Elected school boards were given the power to raise money through local rates, which they were supposed to use to develop schools that their communities needed, either by building their own non-denominational schools or by funding places in existing, usually church-run, establishments. There had also been tentative moves towards opening up secondary education to the poor, particularly by providing endowments for grammar schools, which were intended to address the increased demand for further schooling after free elementary education had increased the supply of capable students.

Yet reforming and extending education in Britain was no easy task, not least because those who ran the country's existing schools were suspicious of the state's intentions. Although public schools like Eton and Harrow had been made formally independent during the 1860s, after a government investigation into financial abuses of their charitable status and general mismanagement, churches, which had provided education in their local communities for centuries, became alarmed by the idea that the government might step in. Church schools could apply for public funds, and frequently took advantage of government grants for new school buildings, but they were wary of the strings that were attached such as the requirement they teach a non-denominational curriculum in exchange for local school board funds. Indeed, it was common for church school representatives to seek election to their local school boards in order to divert money away from non-denominational board schools and towards their own establishments. Religious dissenters, who struggled to exert the same influence over local democracy, and their sympathizers in the Liberal Party who were uneasy with what they saw as infringements on matters of freedom of conscience, complained bitterly about such subterfuge. When religious schools were dominated by the Catholic Church and the Church of England, they argued, it was effectively Rome and Canterbury shaping the minds of new generations of parishioners 'on the rates'.

Public officials and social reformers looked on in bemusement. As far as they could see, while some areas had little in the way of educational provision at all, huge numbers of cash-strapped, overflowing and crumbling church schools were run by poorly paid staff, including pupil-teachers who taught younger children in exchange for being able to stay on after the age of thirteen. A number of incentives had been tried in a bid to encourage schools to improve without feeling the government was imposing on them. A payment-by-results scheme had been introduced during the 1860s, with grants given to schools for each child who attended regularly and larger sums for those who demonstrated proficiency in the 'three Rs'. But there was nothing like a single national system of education and no widespread sense that education either was or should be a ladder, with steps leading from elementary school through to university. There were scholarships for the poor but talented. As was the case with unemployment insurance before the Liberal government's reforms, however, availability was patchy and dependent on where people lived. Children went to different types of school, for different lengths of time, depending on their social class.

By the start of the twentieth century, however, the situation had changed. In 1895, a Royal Commission on secondary schools, headed by the Liberal Lord Bryce, had recommended that secondary school capacity be expanded, with additional scholarships to supplement the ones that were available through grammar schools. A number of local school boards, including in London, had already been putting some of the money they collected through the rates into improving their educational provision beyond the official school-leaving age of twelve. But significant numbers of politicians, including Tories such as Sir John Gorst, who would later be a leading advocate for providing free meals in schools, were strongly against such extensions, not least because they threatened to crowd churches out of the education market. They attempted to put a stop to them by mounting a legal case against rate-funded adult education classes run by the London School Board. The Cockerton case, named after the district auditor whose decision two courts subsequently upheld on appeal, made it illegal for school boards to spend public money on anything beyond their statutory duties to provide elementary education.

Mindful of the ammunition the Boer War had given the government's critics, the Conservative Prime Minister Arthur Balfour responded with an Education Act in 1902, which formally endorsed efforts to extend schooling beyond the elementary level and provided a new administrative framework for it. More than 2,500 local school boards, created after the Elementary Education Act of 1870, were abolished and replaced with around 330 Local Education Authorities, which were handed the responsibility for running education at all levels within county and district council areas. The impact was immense: more than a thousand new secondary schools were created in the twelve years that followed, and around a third of places at grammars became free places. But Balfour paid a political cost. On the one hand, the Conservatives had little choice but to continue funding religious schools, albeit with catches and conditions for those that wished to continue with denominational religious instruction (including that they pay for their own buildings). This angered dissenters, not to mention Joseph Chamberlain's Liberal Unionists, who retained traditional liberal objections to the state funding of religious education. On the other hand, a Treasury already under pressure from the still unpaid Boer War debts was subject to more financial strain. All of this fed into the atmosphere of discontent that led to Balfour's crushing defeat at the ballot box in 1906.

The Webbs and their allies approved wholeheartedly of the moves, and not only because the Education Act signalled a determination to consider schooling a matter of serious national importance. The move from school boards to Local Education Authorities meant central government was trying to impose some order on education across the country and, by reducing the number of administrative units responsible for it, offsetting at least some of the extra expenditure on secondary schooling with efficiency savings. More importantly, however, Local Education Authorities were not subject to the whims of the local community in the way elected local school boards were, meaning they could be populated by experts. With a little guile and patience, the Webbs reasoned, institutions like Local Education Authorities could be infiltrated by people sympathetic to their ideas, who could get to work without worrying about what they thought were the trivial concerns and distractions that elected laymen brought to discussions. The Webbs were happy to defend the Conservative government, and set about promoting the Education Act's virtues in the press.

Yet the administrative structure of schooling and its availability were just two aspects of what the national efficiency movement wanted to change about education in Britain: they believed the content of school curriculums needed to be transformed too. As the likes of Oliver Lodge, a physicist and pioneer of radio technology, and Joseph Chamberlain argued, their aim was not to reproduce for the masses the diet of arts and classics that dominated the public schools and universities populated by aristocrats and the elite. That was not so much an education, they explained, as an induction into a particular culture – one in which merit and achievement were less important than things like character. For the consequences of such amateurism, they argued, people need look no further than the army, which recruited its officers from the public schools and had endured such a torrid time of late.

Schools should instead deliver a broader curriculum, national efficiency advocates explained, one that included science, technology and engineering. Not only did these fields require a different skill set, they were necessary for Britain to arrest the industrial and economic decline that seemed to have taken hold during the previous thirty years. The precise details of such an expansion were, nevertheless, matters of much disagreement. For Lord Rosebery, universities were the most important sites of innovation. He imagined more of them following the examples of 'redbrick' universities in cities like Leeds and Birmingham, which had forged close reciprocal relationships with local businesses that helped produce money for research and relevant training for students. Others, including Sidney Webb, believed more specialization was required earlier on, with more science taught to everyone at a younger age – at the expense of arts and humanities subjects, if need be.

A matter on which all could agree, however, was that this new form of education was not for everyone. The masses certainly required good basic schooling, and it was important that they got it. But national efficiency was focused on a different goal: creating a new, bigger and better-educated elite – a 'boffinocracy', as it was sometimes jokingly called. This new elite was absolutely essential to securing Britain's future because it would develop and apply new scientific ideas, not to mention run the country's administrative and government machinery. The boffinocracy would be well rewarded, both financially and in terms of their social and cultural status. But, people like Sidney Webb argued, this new class of experts would be created with the intention of making life better for everyone.

A NATIONAL MINIMUM

The boffinocracy was a means to achieve a particular end: raising living standards across every social class, and particularly at the bottom. Fabian socialists went furthest in explaining what they thought the government might achieve if it poured resources into science, technology and engineering in pursuit of this goal. They argued that it should be possible to guarantee every citizen a 'national minimum'. As Sidney Webb explained, a national minimum – a basic level of entitlement to goods and services that were available in a modern industrial society – was a matter of social justice in a country that was capable of producing so much wealth. But he also believed it made good economic and political sense. Enforcing a national minimum was, Webb argued, 'in the interests of the well-being of the whole', with even the richest benefitting from improvements in the condition of the poor.

In following this line of reasoning, the national minimum was an extension of the kinds of ideas that had inspired public health reformers like Edwin Chadwick during the nineteenth century. Although critics had initially resisted proposals for the state to pay for things such as sewers, citing not only the allegedly prohibitive costs but also the idea that the degradation of an environment was an indicator of the moral worth of the people that lived there, public authorities had taken responsibility for a whole range of preventative aspects of illness and disease, from vaccination programmes to waste collection. An important part of the rationale was simple and self-interested: disease did not respect class boundaries, and the wealthy had come to appreciate that what started in the slums might easily end up where they lived. The national minimum was this principle writ large. If society was to be fit and healthy, then the state would need to be more active in other areas of people's lives. The fact was, the Webbs argued in 1911, 'we have both the knowledge and the power to cope with' destitution and poverty 'as we have coped with cholera and typhus, highway robbery and the slave trade, if only we have the will'.

As Beatrice Webb showed on the Royal Commission on the Poor Laws and Relief of Distress in 1909, when she and her three fellow commissioners produced their minority report setting out a comprehensive alternative to self-help as the route out of poverty, the Fabians' vision for a national minimum was extensive. They wanted government to create the new elite by ensuring clear and free routes to continued education, right up to university level, for anyone who was capable of making use of the opportunities. Building on the already accepted areas of regulation, such as the Factory Acts which had put limits on the number of hours that workers could be employed each week, they also wanted the state to enforce a minimum wage and instruct businesses to allow people on their payroll a set number of holidays per year.

As they explained in newspaper and periodical articles, as well as their one-shilling pamphlets containing transcripts of lectures or short articles on topical subjects, the Fabians believed there was little evidence that things such as a minimum wage would interfere with markets, erode labourers' work ethic or take a huge bite out of capitalists' profits, as advocates of laissez-faire economics claimed they would. Nevertheless, the Fabians and their allies in the efficiency movement knew that the viability of the national minimum idea was not simply about whether it interfered with market forces: money was needed too. The Webbs estimated that reforms in education alone would require three times what was being spent on it at the start of the twentieth century. But they believed that less comprehensive approaches were riddled with false economies. Some individual policies might have what looked like eye-watering costs, but the sums would be recouped elsewhere. In this respect, the Webbs believed that politicians of quite different ideological bents should be able to agree on the benefits of raising basic living standards, as Fred Jowett, a founding member of the Independent Labour Party in Bradford, and Sir John Gorst, a self-styled Tory democrat and author of *The Children of the Nation: How their Health and Vigour Should be Promoted by the State* (1906), had done on the question of whether or not to provide schoolchildren with free meals.

An important component of the national minimum's extra costs was the money that would need to be invested in rethinking and dramatically expanding the administrative machinery required to deliver it. By 1900, and despite all the emphasis in liberal circles on the importance of limited government, social reform had seen the size and shape of the British state change significantly – sometimes in a fashion the efficiency movement approved of. The state collected all manner of information on its citizens, including about births, marriages and deaths, and employed masses of people to enforce laws and regulations covering a range of different things, from school attendance to working hours to the prevention of adulteration of food. Crucial improvements to the overall standards of administration had been made in a number of areas, such as when competitive examinations had been introduced for recruitment to the civil service. Moreover, Britain's empire showed the country was capable of running a large organization with a relatively small number of people. Yet the efficiency movement thought the government in charge of pulling the administrative levers had expanded haphazardly. The Cabinet, for instance, had grown from fifteen to twenty members, but exact areas of responsibility were frequently unclear, bringing gridlock to decision-making. Local government was no better. County, borough, urban and rural district councils, Poor Law Boards and Local Education Authorities all overlapped and often replicated services and functions. A full-scale rationalization of national and local government was required, one in which responsibilities were divided sensibly between experts and elected officials.

National efficiency enthusiasts were under no illusions that wide-scale changes could be imposed quickly. They were convinced, however, that by the end of the first decade of the twentieth century there was a convergence of issues and events, most of which were connected with the fall-out from the Boer War, that meant not only were the kinds of policies they approved of being more widely discussed, the expertise they were interested in was starting to take root across the country too. The extension of education, the provision of free school meals and the advent of national insurance after 1909 all created new bureaucracies and enabled the acquisition of new knowledge about the people who encountered them. These developments promised the new kind of scientific rationality that the national efficiency movement endorsed, but it also became apparent that it was not that easy to impose expertise on people from above. Old questions about personal responsibility continued to matter, as did the poor's suspicion of those who claimed to want to help them. At the same time, however, the uncoordinated extension of expertise into everyday life in Britain before the First World War created new opportunities, especially for a group who had been largely silent in all the official discussions about national efficiency – women.

EFFICIENCY BEGINS AT HOME

Although some social reformers had been driven by the sight of malnourished children trudging through school gates to ask what public authorities could do to help, others had been more concerned with the question of whom to blame. Money might be short in some places, people like Arnold White had argued, but that was no excuse for the evidently woeful, sometimes negligent job some women were doing of running their home. Even mothers who provided their families with meals each day were at fault, White told readers in *Efficiency and Empire* (1901), because he thought many of them showed scant interest in feeding them things that would make them fit and healthy. While the Scots had discarded hearty oatmeal in favour of white bread, from which most of the nutrients had been milled out, the United Kingdom was awash with 'tinned fish and frozen meat' rather than wholesome home-cooked meals.

White was not the only observer to lay the blame at the feet of the women he thought were responsible for running British homes. Major General Frederick Maurice, another early voice of fears about army recruitment during the Boer War, blamed 'the ignorance of the mothers' too. 'The almost appalling and inconceivable mistakes that they make in the food of their children would make a humorous subject for much writing, if it were not so pathetic and fatal,' he claimed. The Interdepartmental Committee on Physical Deterioration also heard this from a number of the social investigators, doctors and public officials they interviewed, who were quick to accuse 'a large proportion of British housewives . . . tainted with incurable laziness and distaste for the obligations of domestic life . . . [who] naturally have recourse to such expedients in providing food for their families as involve them in least trouble'. Indeed, when free school meals were introduced in 1906, the matter was given an extra dimension when some middle-class commentators learned that many poor children had to be taught how to sit at a table to eat, not to mention how to use a knife and fork.

These accusations were indicative of the complex and judgemental situation women faced in early twentieth-century Britain. On the one hand, they were excluded from public life in all kinds of ways, most notably by being denied the vote. On the other, they were seen as responsible for other, mainly domestic, spheres, which, aside from any concerns about the legitimacy of such a division, was a huge challenge for working-class women who could not afford the servants their middle-classes critics employed. To be sure, White, Maurice and their fellow critics were not so naïve as to think women did not do things like take paid employment outside their homes. As Charles Booth and Seebohm Rowntree had shown in their surveys, many families could not meet their basic needs with just one wage, so it was no surprise that low-paid and uninsured work was a reality for many working-class women. Yet as the Royal Commission on the Poor Laws and Relief of Distress had highlighted, women also made up 60 per cent of the Poor Law claimant count. Navigating the patchwork of help that was on offer, from grants in aid of wages to medical assistance, was simply part of what many mothers did to help their families get by. But the clash between the ideal of a nuclear family with clear and gendered responsibilities and the reality of life for poor families made things difficult when it came to national efficiency. Did future progress depend on women taking on new roles, or returning to one that some commentators imagined they had played in the past?

Some women, particularly among the middle class, reacted by embracing the idea that the well-being of the British population was their unique responsibility. One example of this phenomenon was 'civic motherhood', sometimes known as 'eugenic motherhood', which was popular during the first two decades of the twentieth century. According to proponents of this idea, the lesson to be learned from all the empirical evidence gathered about physical deterioration, as well as the more impressionistic observations of life in Britain's slums, was that the domestic sphere needed to be taken more seriously. Children would only become fit, strong, healthy and intellectually capable adults who avoided degenerating vices if they grew up in the kind of environment where mothers could nurture and care for them, utilizing the instincts and skills nature had endowed them with. As Ellice Hopkins, a deeply religious social purity campaigner who spent nearly fifty years working with former prostitutes and campaigning against the sexual double standards on which they were judged, put it in *The Power of Womanhood* (1899), 'the welfare and very life of a nation is determined by moral causes . . . it is the pure races that respect their women and guard them jealously from defilement that are tough, prolific, ascendant races, the noblest in type and the most fruitful in propagating themselves'.

Radical 'eugenic feminists' such as Sarah Grand and Mona Caird used these ideas as the basis for arguments about the need for women to be given greater freedom and power. If women had an important role to play in shaping the country's future surely they should be given the autonomy such responsibility demanded? Women should not be so dependent on men that they were forced to make decisions, such as marrying physically or intellectually unfit but economically well-off partners, which contributed to the deterioration crisis. Others drew less radical conclusions, though. While agreeing that women had unique skills and responsibilities that were central to the task of creating a healthy future population, they focused on promoting a narrow vision of motherhood, over which women would have complete autonomy.

A number of different ideas for government policies emerged at the intersection of these movements and concerns. One of the most important was family allowances. Men were able to claim abatements for each of their children under the income tax system – a situation that helped the Liberals sell differentiation and graduation of income tax to the middle classes when they also planned to increase public spending on things like pensions. Yet many people across the political spectrum thought these arrangements were inadequate. Abatements were only useful to people who paid income tax, meaning that the poor families social reformers were most interested in helping were excluded. Perhaps, some commentators wondered, there could be a payment for each child that went to everyone? Some organizations, including the London School of Economics under William Beveridge during the 1920s, decided to make payments of this kind to their employees. But the idea of asking the government to offer such allowances to everyone was controversial. Leading trade unionists predicted that less scrupulous employers would try to save money by cutting wages for men with families and, in the process, eliminate any impact the payments were supposed to have on economic hardship.

Eugenic feminists, thinkers connected with the suffragette movement and others had clear ideas about how to solve these problems. They believed that, rather than channel help for children and families through men, the state should focus on women, providing an 'endowment' for both mothers and families. The most prominent voice in this movement by the 1920s was Eleanor Rathbone (1872–1946), the daughter of an eminent Liberal MP who had thrown herself into politics and charity work in Liverpool, becoming the first woman to be elected to the city's council in 1909. A campaigner for women's suffrage, Rathbone had turned her attention to the wider economic challenges women faced once the vote had been won. Unlike Rowntree and other social reformers, she thought it was a mistake to believe problems relating to families and poverty could be solved by raising the wages earned by men. In books like *Disinherited Family* (1924) and from her platform as chair of the Family Endowment Society, she argued that women could only become the equals of men, and the British population would only improve in the ways campaigners wanted, if women were paid directly for being mothers. As critics pointed out, Rathbone's policy risked turning women into employees of the state. But, as she and her supporters often responded, it had the benefit of both tackling poverty and taking the needs of women of all classes seriously.

Family allowances aside, this idea of addressing a broader range of women's needs, both actual and perceived, had wide support among public health officials and campaigners during the early twentieth century. Arthur Newsholme (1857–1943), who made his name as the medical officer for health in Brighton before becoming Chief Medical Officer of the Local Government Board in 1908, believed strongly that the state should be prepared to spend money on broad-ranging preventative health programmes. A veteran of the late nineteenth-century campaigns for better sanitary conditions, he appreciated the Chadwickean approach to public health and believed it could be extended to a wider range of behaviours and habits.

Some of the services Newsholme had in mind had been provided in the past, albeit sporadically and unevenly, by local charitable and voluntary organizations, particularly since the 1860s. Members of these groups went out into working-class districts and tried to make contact with people and families they thought were at risk of contracting diseases such as tuberculosis or, during periods of moral panic, venereal disease, and provide them with health and lifestyle advice. They did so through lectures, pamphlets and community meetings in church halls and premises connected to trade unions and co-operatives. But they also went to places like bathhouses, which were important social spaces for working-class women who were excluded from the male-dominated public house and too poor to shop in the new department stores where middle-class women liked to spend their leisure time. As local authorities and hospitals developed plans for what would later be called health outreach programmes, those organizations' workers became an increasingly useful resource. One result was the emergence of a new figure: the health visitor – a volunteer who promoted domestic hygiene to poor mothers in the belief that doing so would cut high rates of infant mortality, which had actually increased – from 146 to 156 per 1,000 births – during the final quarter of the nineteenth century.

Despite having good intentions, health visitors were problematic. Their target was working-class women but they themselves were often middle class, as one would expect of people who had enough spare money and time to do the job for free. The women being inspected were frequently suspicious of health visitors, who entered their homes and told them (in what they felt were patronizing tones) about the importance of opening windows, unblocking chimneys, staying away from alcohol and sending their children to school. Rather than welcome health visitors enthusiastically into their homes, as many social reformers and middle-class commentators thought they should, working-class mothers kept them at arms' length. Over time, however, this situation changed. In part, this was because health visiting took a different tack to other public health movements, such as the sanitary reformers. Rather than asking government to compel people to let visitors in and follow their instructions, health visitors worked at winning the trust of those they wanted to reach. In Manchester there were efforts to appoint more women of the same social class and who lived in the same neighbourhoods as the families they would be asked to inspect; other authorities impressed on their middle-class visitors the importance of learning about the challenges working-class families faced, such as the financial hurdles that stopped them from buying both the healthy foods they were being told to eat and the kitchen utensils they would need to prepare them. In the process, working-class mothers become more willing to let health visitors into their lives – not least because most health visitors were instructed to tell them about where they could lay their hands on the things they and their families needed desperately, including medicines.

After the 1907 Notification of Births Act made it compulsory to inform the local medical officer of health that a child had been born, these visits started to become a universal system. Local government boards also set up baby and maternal welfare clinics staffed by volunteers and medical professionals, usually a female doctor who visited at set times each week. These clinics offered a range of services, from cookery classes to baby weighing, and even offered cheap meals for those who needed them. There were 300 of these clinics and 600 health visitors in Britain by the outbreak of the First World

War; four years later the numbers had grown to 700 and 2,577 respectively, partly because the government poured extra money into maternity services during a panic about the war's impact on population numbers. Not every initiative worked. The milk sold by milk depots – sites where mothers could buy properly pasteurized milk – turned out to be too expensive for the people for whom it was intended. However, the idea that public health schemes should engage with, rather than lecture, the people who used them was becoming more widely accepted among the authorities and experts.

The expansion of services such as maternity clinics and health visiting also had the effect of carving out new opportunities for women. Areas of public administration had been opened up to women during the late nineteenth century, such as when the property qualification for the office of Poor Law Guardian was abolished in 1894. It was often the case, though, that women were joining male-dominated institutions with well-established rules and practices, not to mention marriage bars, which they were not expected to change. In contrast, public health offered women the chance to shape new agendas. Welfare services provided genuine employment opportunities in high status professional positions, rather than just the volunteering roles that had been commonplace for the previous fifty years. This was particularly important at a time when all the major medical bodies, including the British Medical Association, either explicitly barred or refused to admit women, making the medical profession what the women's rights campaigner Frances Power Cobbe described as a trade union designed to 'keep ladies out of the lucrative profession of physicians and crowd them into the ill-paid one of nurses'.

These developments were consolidated by the Maternity and Child Welfare Act in 1918, which gave official recognition and approval to the services local government boards had developed since the late nineteenth century. The act permitted local government boards to establish committees for maternal and child welfare, which were funded partly by central government and partly by local rates. These committees were an important part of an expanding base of health and social care provision in Britain in the decade after the Liberals' introduction of pensions and national insurance. In towns and cities like Leeds, where light industry meant women made up a significant proportion of the workforce and therefore had access to health insurance, hospitals started to develop specialist and general care services catering for their needs. But there were plenty of women who were excluded from these schemes and unable to obtain sufficient cover from private sources. Community-based services indicated that a preventative approach could be embedded through sympathetic engagement with the people medical professionals and politicians wanted to reach. In some cases, the new committees were even able to provide services like crèches for mothers who needed to work. With maternal and infant health services also giving women a small foothold in the medical profession, the history of welfare services and the struggle for women to obtain equal rights and status were fused.

These developments, however, were the subject of different kinds of reflections once the country entered the First World War in 1914. For those who had opposed them, these services were evidence that the gradual drift towards their provision by local authorities, not to mention the Liberal government's decision to fund things such as non-contributory state pensions, had been the start of a much bigger project of welfare provision. To be sure, there was no grand plan and policies had often developed in unintended directions. But there was a definite sense that something like the comprehensive cover described in the minority report of the Royal Commission on the Poor Laws and Relief of Distress was possible. Those who had helped drive things like free school meals, maternity services and social insurance forward were not quite so sure. Although they were satisfied with the progress they had made towards visions like national efficiency, they wondered how many of those policies and ideas would survive in country changed irrevocably by war.

6

The Greatest Argument for Socialism Ever Produced

In January 1919, a little over two months after the end of the First World War, the Liberal MP Winston Churchill was treated to dinner in London by the top brass at the Ministry of Munitions, the government department he had run for almost two years and was now leaving for a new appointment as Secretary of State for War and Air. Churchill's war had been a remarkable one compared with the roles played by many of his Westminster colleagues. In his early forties and First Lord of the Admiralty when the conflict started, his distinctive bulldog features and walking cane made him a press favourite and a popular choice for manufacturers who emblazoned tea towels and trinkets with patriotic images. Yet his reputation had taken a huge hit in 1915 after he had shouldered the blame for the disastrous campaign at Gallipoli, where badly prepared Allied forces, including large numbers of troops from Australia and New Zealand, suffered massive casualties trying to take Constantinople, the capital of the Ottoman Empire. Having been forced to resign from the Cabinet, Churchill decided to spend some time away from Westminster and served as a commanding officer on the Western Front. He believed he had learned a great deal about politics and government from these experiences. His conclusions, however, were not exactly what many people in the room or across the country might have expected. The Ministry of Munitions' contribution to Britain's victory was, he told them, the 'greatest argument for State Socialism ever produced'.

Churchill's assessment echoed what other liberals were saying. During the war, whole swathes of society and the economy had been bent to the state's will, with restrictions imposed on everything from pub opening hours to the rents landlords could charge their tenants. Moreover, state spending had reached eye-watering levels, with government debt standing at £8,000 million, more than thirty times what it had been four years earlier. The *Manchester Guardian* – once the representative of the reformism that had brought an end to the protectionist Corn Laws but now the voice of Leonard Hobhouse's active and interventionist 'new liberalism' – called this 'war socialism'. Churchill admitted he was wavering over what this meant for the future; 'trembling', as he put it to his friends in the Munitions Ministry,

> on the border-line between individual enterprise proceeding in fierce competition in all industries and walks of life and a vast organised machinery of production supported and equipped by all that was best in the nation and proceeding on calculation and design to multiply enormously the prosperity of the whole people.

Others, though, were much more certain that direct state organization of society and the economy should be a feature of peace.

There were numerous layers to these discussions. The idea that Britain could exert more control over its economic and social affairs was one thing; the purpose that control should serve and the form it should take were quite another. With 4 million men – many battered, bruised and psychologically scarred from an experience in the trenches that had been far more brutal than anything that had been anticipated – due to return home, politicians promised substantial reforms (such as a massive house-building programme) would make life better for ordinary people. It was possible to envisage a Britain in which the state did more for its people than simply co-ordinate social insurance schemes covering some of them in times of sickness and unemployment. But was the government really committed to the kind of significant change that this transformation would require?

WAR, ECONOMY AND SOCIETY

The outbreak of war in Europe in 1914 had presented the British government with a number of different challenges. The Liberal Prime Minister Herbert Asquith, who only committed the country's armed forces to combat after being boxed in by the outcome of diplomatic processes, had to convince sections of his party, as well as progressive opinion more generally, that the conflict was justified. Many Liberals saw Britain's decision to go to war with Germany, ostensibly in support of Belgium, which Britain had asked to be kept neutral, as a moral issue – an appropriate response to Germany's aggression in invading Belgium to get to France – much as they had the Boer War fifteen years earlier. Although the debate over the rights and wrongs of going to war was drowned out by patriotic fervour once it was under way, Asquith had more practical concerns. There was a widely held belief that the conflict would be over quickly and conducted mostly at arm's length, with navies, including the expensive Dreadnought battleships the Liberals had been forced to buy almost a decade earlier, duelling it out at sea. It soon became clear, however, that such hopes were misplaced.

On the face of it, party political differences had been put aside in an effort to focus on the war. There was an electoral truce, and Asquith made what looked like gestures towards impartiality. These included his decision, albeit under pressure from the press, to appoint Lord Kitchener – a Tory responsible for the army's controversial scorched-earth tactics and concentration camps during the Boer War – as War Secretary. Nevertheless, there was tension below the surface. After three-quarters of a century of promises dating back to the Lichfield Compact of 1835, the Liberals had used the Parliament Act, which had been drawn up after the Lords had blocked the passage of the 'People's Budget', to push through Home Rule for Ireland in early 1914. Furious, the Conservatives and their Unionist allies tried to hold up proceedings by focusing on what to do about Ulster in the north, where there was a Protestant and Unionist majority. Home Rule was deferred until after the war was won but, thanks to the Easter Rising in 1916, Ireland was a difficult and divisive domestic issue that would not go away.

There were also serious differences of opinion about how to run the war. While Churchill had initially described the situation as 'business as usual', Asquith had thought government would require just a few tweaks, such as the addition of a new War Secretary to take care of what was happening across the Channel. However, Kitchener, who was in his sixties now and had military experience dating back to the

1870s, sensed the war might be much longer and a bigger drain on the country's resources than many of his Cabinet colleagues believed. The army's ranks swelled, with more than 400,000 volunteering during the first month, thanks in large part to the idea the war would be both glorious and over by Christmas. These enthusiastic but novice recruits had to be trained and equipped. Kitchener drafted in experienced soldiers from across the Empire in anticipation of a drawn out conflict that would require calm minds, co-ordinated efforts across land and sea, and co-operation with allies. Notwithstanding these insights, Kitchener lacked the managerial skills, not to mention the administrative capacity, that were required to run a war of the kind that took shape across mainland Europe and beyond.

After strategic disasters, including Gallipoli, and a scandal about a shortage of munitions broken by *The Times* in May 1915, the government faced accusations of incompetence. Asquith felt compelled to ring the changes and, wishing to avoid the disruption of a general election, offered to form a coalition with the Conservatives. The Prime Minister ensured his Liberal Party held the key positions, and kept the Tory leader, Andrew Bonar Law, out of the way by sending him to the Colonial Office. But there was still massive upheaval as half the Cabinet made way for their Tory opponents, including Churchill, who was moved from the Admiralty to be Chancellor of the Duchy of Lancaster – a job that had as many meaningful wartime duties as its title suggests.

A sign of bigger changes to come was Asquith's decision to embrace the left as well as the right in his new coalition. The Labour Party had initially opposed the war, arguing that workers would be killing workers in the interests of the ruling classes. But it quickly dawned on trade unions that the armed conflict put them in a strong position. They helped the government address labour shortages by brokering 'no strike' agreements and temporarily suspending practices such as the 'closed shop', which required workers to join specific unions if they were to be employed in particular workplaces. One outcome of these developments was an influx of women into jobs, including in munitions factories, from which they had been excluded before the war but in which they were now needed because so many men were away on military service. In return, Asquith made the first ever

Labour Party Cabinet appointments: a total of three MPs, including the Labour leader Arthur Henderson (1863–1935), a Glasgow-born, teetotal, former iron moulder who had left school aged twelve, who was made President of the Board of Education.

By late 1916, however, Asquith was under severe pressure. Influential Conservatives had decided the Prime Minister should resign. More damagingly, the War Secretary Lloyd George, who had embraced the idea that war required a complete restructuring of government, looked to be involved in secretive negotiations to undermine his party leader. Although he was not proposing the Prime Minister should step down, Lloyd George had suggested a separate war committee be formed and that Asquith should be excluded from it. Acrimonious backroom wrangling followed, leading to Lloyd George replacing Asquith as Prime Minister. Some Liberals refused to serve under someone they thought had helped the Tories stab Asquith in the back, splitting the party between front- and backbenchers, with one faction remaining loyal to Asquith and the other following the new Prime Minister. But Lloyd George's unrivalled political skills enabled him to negotiate this tricky terrain. And where others might have let Churchill, a close friend, back in from the cold, he was happy to continue to exclude a man towards whom many Tories were still deeply hostile, thanks to his decision to defect to the Liberals almost thirteen years earlier when the Tories were wavering over their commitment to free trade.

Each of these developments led to a step-change in the war effort, particularly once Lloyd George declared himself ready to fight 'to a knock out'. When Britain had gone to war against the Boers at the turn of the century, it sent approximately 400,000 men over the course of three years – a number that had put considerable pressure on the state's coffers. At the time of Asquith's reshuffle in 1915 the number despatched to the theatre of war was close to 2.5 million. Three years later, after conscription had compelled all unmarried men and childless widowers aged between eighteen and forty-one and not working in an occupation classified as essential to report for military service, the ranks had been swollen by a further 2 million. Moreover, in addition to a navy that had benefitted from a three-decade-long arms race with Germany, the country had a burgeoning air force whose pilots fought daring, spectacular but incredibly dangerous mid-air duels against celebrated adversaries such as the 'Red Baron'. By the end of the war more than 700,000 men had been killed, getting on for double the size of the British army in early 1914.

Yet change involved more than new faces in the Cabinet and additional bodies in the army. The shape and size of government changed too, as Britain embraced 'total war': a condition in which every action, decision and movement was guided by assessments of its likely contribution to victory. Entities called 'ministries', rather than boards, were established as the government tried to get to grips with problems that either did not exist during peacetime or were previously not seen as matters requiring sustained administrative attention. The Ministry of Munitions, initially assigned to Lloyd George, was the first of these organizations. But others, including the Ministry of Labour and the Ministry of Shipping, quickly followed.

This new form of war government required all kinds of additional support. The civil service expanded to more than 400,000 people – double its peacetime number. The government also discovered it needed help from all kinds of non-army personnel to make the military operation and domestic economy work as they wanted them to. Economists such as William Beveridge were drafted into the Ministry of Food, where he devised a system of rationing and price control. Businessmen like Joseph Maclay, co-owner of one of Glasgow's biggest shipping firms, were recruited in the belief they had organizational skills and know-how that were lacking in Whitehall. Scientists were called on to help British industry produce goods the country had been importing, such as dyes, and modernize its infrastructure via new mass-production techniques and electrification. Chemists, who helped develop explosives – not to mention defences against chemical agents that factory workers had to handle and the enemy might use in weapons – were particularly popular. By the end of the war, after sustained lobbying from the scientific community, the government had established a Department of Scientific and Industrial Research.

All these things needed to be paid for. In the past, Britain had funded wars by increasing taxes and then taking out loans to make up the shortfall. This approach had been successful because the country had a robust system for collecting taxes, which not only provided a reliable revenue stream, meeting around half the up-front costs, but also ensured that lenders were confident debts would be repaid. Although the differentiated and graduated income taxes introduced by the Liberals a decade earlier had increased the state's tax-raising power, the government was forced to broaden its reach still further. While the income tax threshold was lowered, trebling the number of people who paid it to 6 million, the standard tax rate was pushed up to 30 per cent, duties were put on products such as sugar, beer and tobacco, and a special tax for excess profits earned in the production of war goods was introduced (set initially at 50 per cent of pre-war profit levels, but later increased to 80 per cent). Individuals earning enough to pay Lloyd George's 'supertax' – levied on incomes over £5,000 per year – were being taxed directly at a rate of 52 per cent. Yet with the war costing £3 million a day and rising in 1915, the sums raised through tax were nowhere near enough. By 1919, the country had a deficit – the gap between its income and outgoings – of £1,500 million, around eight times what it had been five years earlier.

The war had hammered everything out of shape. But one of the biggest changes in Britain was the size of the state compared to everything else. With factories pumping out goods to meet government orders, by the end of the war government spending was around 50 per cent of Gross National Product, the market value of the goods and services produced at home and abroad by British citizens – more than four times what it had been before 1914 and double its share during the Napoleonic Wars a century earlier. With the government deciding that trade union rights had to be curtailed and some workers treated like soldiers, rather than as employees, if production was going to be maximized, the consequences of these developments were huge – especially for those who had spent a century extolling the virtues of economic liberalism and a small state.

COUPONS AND COALITION

Churchill's declaration of 'business as usual' had been a signal of the Liberal government's belief that, for the most part, it would be able to fight a war abroad without changing much on the home front. Even when Asquith was forced to form a new coalition in May 1915, he still refused to appoint the Tory leader Bonar Law to the Treasury, where the leader of the main coalition partner would have expected to end up, because he was a tariff reformer and therefore, as Asquith saw it, on the wrong side of one of the most important issues in British politics. As the country had sunk deeper into total war, however, even formerly totemic principles such as free trade had been sacrificed as the government channelled everything into the war effort. The result for the Liberal Party was strange. They held the office of Prime Minister but had unpicked many of the threads that held the pre-war economy together and imposed controls on every aspect of economic and social life.

The gold standard – the principle that anyone who held sterling could convert it into gold at a fixed price and an emblem of liberal capitalism since the 1870s – was an early casualty of the pragmatism deemed necessary to secure victory in war. Convertibility to gold guaranteed a currency's value and, in the process, fixed exchange rates and made borrowing cheap. It was a watchword for stability, largely because it constrained governments, which could do little about whole swathes of the domestic economy, in significant ways. A currency tied to gold kept inflation down, but, as a consequence, governments could not borrow or print money as they pleased because, in theory, they needed to hold enough gold to cover the currency conversion. To use the preferred language of the gold standard's advocates, governments had to be disciplined. With war requiring extra spending, Britain, like Germany, came off the gold standard in 1914.

Trade and manufacturing also had to be rethought. Importing and exporting could not carry on as normal, especially when the German navy started targeting shipping routes across the Atlantic Ocean. In September 1915 the Liberal Chancellor of the Exchequer, Reginald McKenna, tried to free space in shipping lanes for essential goods by taxing luxury imports, such as cars and musical instruments. A Capital Issues Committee was also established to restrict the flow of capital out of the country, which the government argued made borrowing more difficult because lenders worried about the possible impact of capital flight on debt repayments. Such coaxing, however, fell well short of what was required to ensure the economy produced what the country needed when it needed it. The government stepped up its interventions, sometimes through legislation, at other times through its immense purchasing power, on occasion by placing controls on the supply and distribution of goods. Among other things, the government bought up all available sugar, capped rents on agricultural land and working-class housing, made food hoarding an offence, introduced rationing, placed restrictions on the sale of alcohol, and made some businesses and factories prioritize government orders – before going the whole hog and opening its own munitions factories.

These actions annoyed different groups of people at different points in time. Workers grumbled about pubs closing early, landowners complained about static returns on their assets, and some industrialists argued their businesses had been made subservient to the state. High rates of inflation, partly a consequence of the government's refusal to deploy controls such as rationing earlier, also put a huge dent in standards of living, especially for anyone on a fixed income. But sections of the middle class, whose businesses produced the kinds of things the government needed, had a very good war. While companies that supplied materials such as coal and iron saw a predictable increase in demand, engineering firms also took advantage, especially once the Ministry of Munitions decided to help non-munitions companies adapt their production plants and processes so they could make artillery shells and other things the army desperately needed. Profiteering was a worry but, faced with pressing needs and having the blunt tool of the tax on excess profits, the government thought it was making the best out of a difficult situation.

Yet if free trade was considered incompatible with fighting a modern war, another of the Liberals' traditional reforming causes received a significant boost. The conflict had involved four years of sacrifice on the part of ordinary people, who had borne the brunt of violence in the trenches abroad and submitted to state controls on everyday life at home. Indeed, while volunteers had flooded into the army during the early stages of the war, conscription had been necessary to keep the war machine moving later on. What would people who had been compelled to bend to the state's will, going so far as to give up their lives for the cause, receive in return?

An obvious problem was the electoral franchise. Voting was still limited to men who owned property worth £10 or more, or who paid an annual rent of that value – a legacy of the old belief that the electorate should be composed of men of the right character, and late nineteenth-century concerns about the possibly negative consequences of allowing the whole working class to participate in elections. This situation meant that many soldiers (and all women) would not be able to cast a ballot in the general election that was expected to follow the war's end. Some politicians suggested that military service be introduced as a qualification, though there was some confusion about whether discharged soldiers would then be excluded. Others, such as the moderate women's rights campaigner Millicent Fawcett, pointed out that the war could not have been won without the contributions of those on the home front, specifically women. The eventual conclusion of those debates was the Representation of the People Act, which passed through the House of Commons in June 1917 and which enfranchised all men aged twenty-one and over, and women aged thirty and over who either occupied a house, owned land worth more than £5 or were married to a man who was entitled to vote. Although the inequality between men and women would remain for another decade, the act extended the vote not only to the working classes but also to members of the middle and upper classes who had been unenfranchised until that point, such as young men who lived with their parents. Overnight, the electorate expanded to more than 21 million people – an increase of more than 13 million.

With British politicians spooked by the Russian Revolution, which saw the overthrow of the Romanov monarchy in early 1917 and the Bolsheviks seize power in the name of the country's workers in October that year, there was a sense that something more than extending the franchise was required. A Ministry of Reconstruction had been set up in August 1917 to start the process of rebuilding the economy and society once Germany had been defeated. All manner of issues required close attention. Resources and production capacity had been directed to military ends and British industries and companies, particularly those working with and trading in goods like cotton and coal, had lost important overseas markets thanks to the global disruption. There were also 4 million men overseas. How would they get back home, and what would they do for work when they finally did return? If the wartime controls were lifted straight away in these conditions then there was a strong chance that there would be shortages of basic goods, such as food, resulting in spiralling prices and potentially destabilizing the country in the uncertain early stages of peace.

Most of these problems could not be tackled until the war was over. But there were a number of broader issues that could be considered in the meantime. An Education Act, the brainchild of H. A. L. Fisher, vice chancellor of the University of Sheffield and President of the Board of Education under Lloyd George, became law in March 1918. Building on the Conservative Balfour's Education Act of 1902, which had created Local Education Authorities and more than a thousand new schools in the decade before 1914, Fisher's act raised the school-leaving age to fourteen, abolished fees in elementary school, committed government funds to increasing local authority grants and teachers' salaries, and established the principle, though not the practice, that lack of money should not prevent children from receiving an education from which they were capable of benefitting. The act was a gesture towards the better society returning soldiers could expect to find. Fisher, though, dreamt of a much more ambitious programme being built on these foundations: one in which education was a much more important and conventional part of everyday life, with colleges that young people could attend part time after they had left school at fourteen an example of the kind of institution he had in mind.

However, with the last general election having been held in 1910, the second of the two elections Asquith's Liberals had been forced to hold that year thanks to the House of Lords' decision to block the 'People's Budget', the British people had to be consulted before more substantial reforms could be pursued. The triumph over Germany had not healed the Liberal Party's wounds, so Lloyd George went to the country as the head of the wartime coalition, minus the Labour MPs, who had resigned as soon as victory was declared. Coalition suited both the Prime Minister and the Conservative Party. Lloyd George knew that, even before leading the country to victory, he was one of the most popular politicians in the country but that the split with Asquith meant he stood little chance of winning a majority on his own. Bonar Law, on the other hand, was regarded by many Tories as a second-choice leader who had played a predictably marginal role in beating the Germans, having spent most of the war at the Colonial Office. Lacking Lloyd George's charisma, and still with hints of the accent he had acquired during the first twelve years of his life in Canada, Bonar Law had the slight, if somewhat intangible, air of an outsider. A Tory-dominated coalition was convenient, especially if Lloyd George's popularity and social reform credentials rubbed off on them.

The 'coupon election' – a reference to Asquith's disparaging comments about the letter 159 Liberals and 364 Conservatives received from Lloyd George and Bonar Law as confirmation of their status as coalition candidates – was the biggest in British history, with nearly 10½ million votes cast eleven days before Christmas in 1918, a month after fighting had ended. The coalition won more than 50 per cent of the popular vote and a majority of 249, but the result was complicated for the Liberal Party. While Lloyd George's supporters numbered 133 MPs, just 36 others had made it back to Westminster. Even Asquith lost his seat in East Fife, a constituency he had represented for more than thirty years. The Conservative Party, however, had captured 332 seats. Lloyd George might have been Prime Minister, but there was no getting away from the Tories' numerical advantage in Parliament.

The most pressing tasks for the new government were to bring the war to an official end and establish some semblance of domestic order. While Churchill, who had taken the post of Secretary of War and Air as part of his political rehabilitation, was preoccupied with devising a fair way to demobilize 4.5 million men who had served for varying lengths of time, Lloyd George was focused on the Versailles peace conference, which took place during the first half of 1919. However, it looked like some of the worst fears about what would happen to the economy once war production was scaled back were misplaced. Demand for consumer goods soared as the shackles of government controls on the economy were thrown off. The coalition had committed to doing much more than restoring ordinary peace-time production, though. Most strikingly, Lloyd George had declared that Britain would become a country with 'habitations fit for the heroes who have won the war' – a promise that is usually shortened to the more memorable 'homes fit for heroes'. With one of the sharpest economic booms in history under way, there seemed little reason to doubt this would happen.

HOMES FIT FOR HEROES

The responsibility for delivering Lloyd George's promise fell to the new Minister of Health, Christopher Addison (1869–1951), whose quiet and unassuming manner, bordering on boring, revealed little of the brilliance that had led the University of Sheffield to make him their first Professor of Anatomy. Departing from the views of his Tory-supporting father, a Lincolnshire farmer, Addison had embraced Lloyd George's version of new liberalism, including radical causes like land nationalization, after working in Charing Cross Hospital and seeing grinding urban poverty at first hand. Elected to Parliament as a Liberal MP for Hoxton in east London in 1910, Addison had earned his reforming spurs by helping the government negotiate with the British Medical Association over its national insurance plans, which some doctors had opposed on the grounds they would be a restraint on trade that turned them into state employees. He was rewarded for his loyalty to Lloyd George, not to mention his role in developing the capitation fee solution to doctors' objections, with a series of plum jobs, first at the Munitions Ministry and then the Ministry of Reconstruction. Health, however, was always Addison's forte.

As the act of Parliament that established it in 1919 made clear, the new Ministry of Health had a remarkably wide remit that cut across territory occupied by a number of other institutions and branches of government. Following in the Chadwickean tradition of nineteenth-century public health reformers, including the division of labour between Westminster and the local authorities that were often the sources of administrative innovation, the ministry was intended to 'take all such steps as may be desirable to secure the preparation, effective carrying out and the co-ordination of measures conducive to the health of the people'. In so doing, the Ministry of Health was meant to shift efforts from the day-to-day fire-fighting that was associated with hard-pressed Poor Law administrators and give health, broadly construed, the attention it required. The vision was forward looking – prevention rather than cure – and radical social reformers were excited by what might be done through an agency that was responsible for things such as collecting and disseminating public health statistics and aspects of medical training, as well as maternity and child health services.

House building was a logical part of this remit. Aside from the long-standing links between habitation and health which had driven Poor Law Unions in the East End of London to use the rates to collect waste back in the 1830s, public health was understood to have an important role to play in the broader political economy of the modern liberal state. As Chadwick had realized more than three-quarters of a century earlier, poor health had potentially bad consequences for not only the public purse but also the economy as a whole. At the turn of the twentieth century, local authorities seemed to have embarked on the final chapter in dealing with those problems. Acts of Parliament in 1890 and 1909 had given them the power to clear slums and replace them with new homes, often on greenfield sites – undeveloped and unused plots of land, often on the outskirts of cities. Some local authorities had included house building among the small-scale public works projects they had been permitted to run since the 1860s. However, most councils proved to be much more enthusiastic about demolishing slums than they were about replacing them, with just 18,000 houses built nationwide during the twenty-five years before the First World War.

The Ministry of Health estimated that 500,000 new properties would be required by the end of 1921 to house the millions of men who were returning from the front. Given that the country had managed an average of 80,000 a year in the years immediately before 1914, this was a huge number, especially as labour and materials' shortages meant construction had ground to a halt during the war. Politicians including Churchill, who was perpetually worried about the working classes being seduced by socialism, thought the situation was highly combustible. And they looked to be right when rent strikes happened in places such as Coventry and Woolwich in south-east London, where increased demand for workers in munitions factories had seen local populations swell. The coalition decided to placate the public with an extension of wartime rent controls. Few people, however, thought such measures could be applied indefinitely.

Building half a million homes was much easier said than done. For one thing, the British state had never conducted a mass house-building programme before. When it came to what would come to be known as 'social housing', governments had been happy to leave matters to philanthropists and charitable ventures. Octavia Hill, a member of the Royal Commission on the Poor Laws and Relief of Distress, was one of the best-known social reformers to make their name in this sphere. The daughter of a corn merchant who had been declared bankrupt, Hill had been introduced to social reformers who had imbibed all the lessons Robert Owen wanted people to learn from his utopian community at New Lanark when her mother took an administrative job with a co-operative crafts group in central London. Inspired by the likes of the art critic John Ruskin, whose writings about the adverse impact of capitalism on morals and the environment were widely influential, Hill was convinced that the state of Britain's slums and the people who lived in them were connected. She and her collaborators bought and restored run-down properties, including one in what is now Garbutt Place, near Baker Street in Marylebone, and imposed strict terms and conditions on the tenant families who had previously been crammed into single dank rooms. Like other famous philanthropic organizations such as the Peabody Trust, which was founded by the American banker George Peabody in 1862 and which built new housing blocks in Spitalfields, Blackfriars, Clerkenwell and Islington, Hill created vastly improved living conditions but expected residents to abide by strict terms covering everything from the upkeep of their properties to the timely payment of rent. Anyone who broke the rules faced eviction – an important element of Hill's pitch to potential investors, who thought working-class housing was too risky to deliver a regular return.

The small-scale projects run by Hill were no match for the size of the problem that confronted the Ministry of Health after the war. Aside from the practical challenges that construction companies faced when it came to obtaining basic materials like brick and slate, many of the skilled workers they needed to build the houses were still in the army. Moreover, with Britain off the gold standard and having borrowed heavily throughout the war, inflation was high, meaning working-class housing, which would command low rents and take years to deliver profits, was an unattractive prospect for investors. It looked like the state would have to step in. Such a course of action would be expensive, but if the alternative was hundreds of thousands of dislocated people, including demobbed soldiers, living in over-crowded and demoralizing conditions, there seemed to be no other choice. As Lloyd George told the coalition Cabinet, 'even if it cost a hundred million pounds, what was that compared to the stability of the State?'

Addison's answer was the Housing, Town Planning, etc. Act of 1919. Rather than see the state suddenly take full control of house building across the country, the act outlined a more cautious carrot-and-stick approach to stimulate the supply of good quality homes in Britain. Following the lessons learned about Poor Law relief during the nineteenth century, local authorities, rather than central govern-ment, were handed responsibility for identifying housing needs and formulating plans to meet them. While places like inner London were overcrowded, especially since railways and other aspects of modern industrial infrastructure had cut large chunks out of the urban landscape, other cities, including Glasgow, had housing surpluses fol-lowing recent property speculation bubbles. Addison's plan was to offer local authorities subsidies that plugged the gap between the ini-tial costs of building the houses they needed and the point at which they could expect to generate a return from rents. Within a year, private builders had access to these subsidies too.

Quantity was the major motivating factor behind these policies but, thanks to the work of the national efficiency and eugenics move-ments in the decade before the war, quality mattered too. As Waldorf Astor, a Conservative MP and Lloyd George's parliamentary private secretary during the final years of the war, explained during the par-liamentary debate on the 1919 bill, good environments begat good people. Referring to the categories that the military put potential recruits into, he argued that, 'If we can only assess the value to this country of an A1 population and assess the loss of having C3 men and women and children, I believe the House will agree that our housing proposals are cheap.'

One of the most important influences on the efforts to translate these ideals into practice was Raymond Unwin (1863–1940). A trained engineering draftsman, Unwin had come to architecture in his early twenties thanks to his interest in progressive politics and, in particular, the writer and designer William Morris's Socialist League. Committed to the principle that good design was the gateway to social progress, Unwin had started an architecture firm with his brother-in-law, Barry Parker, during the mid-1890s and set about trying to convince people that low-density housing was the solution to Britain's problems. His firm won a number of prestigious contracts, including to build workers' housing in New Earswick, the town created by Joseph Rowntree for his company's workers in York, and another for Letchworth, a new 'garden city' about forty miles north of London. Shortly after the start of the war, Unwin had abandoned private practice to become the chief planning officer to the Local Government Board. Six months later he moved to the Ministry of Munitions, where he struck up a friendship with Addison.

Under Unwin's influence, the Ministry of Health's Housing and Town Planning Act laid the foundations for a particular vision of life in post-war Britain. Gone would be the slums full of run-down buildings where entire families lived in single rooms. In their place would be homes on their own plot of land, with plenty of clear space between them. These houses would have to be built on the outskirts of cities, but people would be happy to move to them because rapidly improving transport infrastructure, such as the underground train network in London, would make travel much easier than it had been in the past. Indeed, subsidized rents would more than make up for the money people would have to spend commuting back and forth to their jobs. The Conservative MP Ernest Pretyman was no fan of the overall housing programme but he found himself completely sold on this therapeutic vision. Like others, he was seduced by the idea of houses 'in semi-rural conditions with good garden plots and with good transport access'. A man would be able to do his 'work in the factory while his family can live in fresh air under semi-rural conditions'. The result, Pretyman explained, would be 'not only a healthy family, but healthy occupation outside where they can go and work together in the garden'.

Around 176,000 homes were built under the 1919 act. Entirely new towns sprang up, including Wythenshawe near Manchester and Becontree on the outskirts of London, where, by the Second World War, 116,000 people lived on what was then the largest council estate in the world. Yet the process was far from painless for either local authorities, who soon discovered that inflation since the start of the war meant the homes cost almost double original estimates, or the people who expected to get the opportunity to live in them. Despite being billed as a solution to a general housing crisis, it was apparent the new homes were not intended for the poorest Britons. Wide-open spaces and modern amenities like private indoor toilets were a significant improvement on the cramped conditions people had been used to. But only skilled workers on decent and regular wages could afford the rents that had to be charged to cover the costs of maintaining what was on offer. At the Old Oak estate in Hammersmith, for instance, a three-bedroom house built before the war was 7s 4d a week to rent, while a new house built under Addison's scheme was 11s.

Indeed, some observers were less than enthusiastic about these developments, regardless of who got to live in them. Touring Britain during the early 1930s as part of his research for his book *English Journey* (1934), the Bradford-born writer J. B. Priestley concluded that thousands of near-identical new houses had sacrificed intangible qualities like character in the name of material improvement, and from this forecast the eventual death of working-class culture. There were residents of the new estates who agreed. Little of the infrastructure that had been the bedrock of civic and social life in old working-class communities, including public houses, had been transported to the new towns. Families instead chose to socialize within the walls of their spacious new houses or the gardens behind them. Bored and disappointed, some people found it hard to adapt and decided to return to the cities they thought they had left behind. Although this phenomenon was nowhere near as widespread as late twentieth-century critics of state planning later claimed, the fact it happened at all indicated that change was never going to be easy for everyone.

Long before these problems emerged, however, Lloyd George's coalition government decided to apply the brakes to house building. The underlying reason was a change in the country's economic circumstances. The post-war restocking boom was over by spring 1920, and a sharp and difficult downturn had hit Britain's economic output hard. GDP fell by 6 per cent and official unemployment rose sharply. The typical rate of unemployment had been 4.5 per cent in the years leading up to the war and as low as 2 per cent a year earlier. But the downturn sent it soaring to more than 11 per cent, with areas dominated by heavy industry, like the North East, suffering rates of more than 16 per cent. At almost exactly the same moment, the Bank of England raised its base rate, which set the rate for the rest of the economy, in an effort to tackle inflation. Interest rates were running at 7 per cent, a historically high level without the gold standard's restraining effect. Many politicians and commentators decided the country's £8,000 million debt, which was taking almost 25 per cent of gross government income to service, was a much more pressing concern than building new houses.

WAR ON WASTE

Britain's economic position in the early 1920s was much more complicated than simple sums about income and outgoings. For one thing, the country's struggles stood out in the context of the global economy. While most of its competitors, with the exception of Germany – which had its own problems thanks to the economic punishment handed out under the Versailles Treaty – experienced a recovery of some sort, Britain was discovering that it could not trade its way out of trouble because it had lost overseas markets during the war and stood little chance of getting them back. The costs of manufacturing and industry in Britain, particularly wages, were higher than in the countries that had taken its business. In stark contrast to the USA, where there was a long industrial boom, unemployment ran at close to 10 per cent for most of the decade. The question for the coalition was what they could and should do in response.

Some politicians, used to thinking their responsibility was to Britain's balance sheets and that everything else would take care of itself, thought taxation might be the answer to Britain's debt problems. The snag, however, was that rates were still much higher than people were used to in peacetime. Not only was income tax still at 30 per cent, but Austen Chamberlain, the Conservative Chancellor of the Exchequer, had retained the excess profits tax, much to the annoyance of leading businessmen and industrialists. The Labour Party had an alternative solution. It proposed a 'conscription of wealth', arguing that the rich should be asked to make a monetary contribution that matched the sacrifices the working classes had been asked to make in the trenches. But representatives of finance did not have to try too hard to convince the coalition that the policy would be unwise.

With further borrowing out of the question, there was just one other option: cutting back on expenditure. Although this approach had a particular appeal to those who longed for a return to the Gladstonian ideals of small government and sound finance, calls to rein in government spending took many different forms when many people believed war heroes deserved rewards. The most influential was the 'anti-waste' campaign led by Alfred Harmsworth, founder and owner of the *Daily Mail*, who had been made Baron Northcliffe in 1904. The *Daily Mail* had been created during the late nineteenth century as a pioneer of 'new journalism', which treated news not as a process of instruction but a form of entertainment to be judged almost purely in terms of sales. Northcliffe targeted lower-middle-class readers, including women, whom newspapers had never previously courted, and addressed them as busy, hard-pressed and prudent people whose interests were constantly under threat. Fashioning itself as the challenger to *The Times*, the newspaper of the establishment, the *Daily Mail* broadened the definition of news beyond the traditional diet of parliamentary and foreign affairs to include what would later become known as 'human interest' stories, which, in another departure from *The Times*, were accompanied with scores of photographs and pictures. Thanks to its low cover price, which was subsidized by significant amounts of advertising, the *Daily Mail* was the country's biggest-selling newspaper by the early 1920s, with a circulation in excess of 1.3 million copies.

The *Daily Mail* pushed a strong line on government spending: it was out of control and involved pouring hard-working taxpayers' money down the drain at a moment when the cost of living was on the increase. Evidence that this message was having an impact came in late 1920 and early 1921, when Lloyd George's coalition was defeated at by-elections in Wrekin, Dover, Hertford and Westminster St George's by candidates from the Anti-Waste League, a nominally non-partisan but Tory-leaning organization that had been founded by Lord Rothermere, Northcliffe's younger brother. Lloyd George's response was to form a committee headed by Sir Eric Geddes (1875–1937), a successful railway manager whose administrative and logistical expertise had helped the government get munitions, men and supplies from factories, bases and warehouses to the frontline during the second half of the war. Staffed by businessmen almost as impatient as Geddes himself, the committee was asked to work with the Treasury to identify suitable spending cuts and efficiencies. Their recommendations, delivered in early 1922, were stark: the government should cut approximately £87 million out of a supply services budget of around £528 million.

Having put government spending on the chopping block, Lloyd George was required to wield what became known as the 'Geddes axe'. Some ministers, including Fisher at education, fought their ground. But cuts were the story across the board. While even the army faced up to 40 per cent reductions in spending, the more far-reaching ideas about educational reform, such as institutions for part-time and technical students, dropped off the agenda completely. In a pre-emptive move, Lloyd George had reduced house-building targets by half and moved Addison out of the Ministry of Health long before Geddes's committee had reported back. However, the writing was on the wall when Addison was replaced by Sir Alfred Mond, the founder of ICI and an enthusiast for the swinging axe. Only projects that had reached the point where local authorities were no longer able to break contracts were allowed to continue. Grants for slum clearance were also scaled back dramatically, and abolished completely for private builders.

The dream of homes fit for heroes was not the only thing that seemed to be over in 1922: the coalition that had been elected to build them came to an end too. A meeting of Conservative backbenchers, who later renamed themselves 'The 1922 Committee', decided they would not fight the forthcoming general election on a coalition platform. Party politics was back, twelve years after the last general election to have been fought on such terms. Things were not quite as they had been before, however. In addition to the Tories, voters could choose from two varieties of Liberal: Lloyd George's coalition – or National – Liberals, and Asquith's Independents. As the official party leader, Asquith had kept control of the Liberals' finances, forcing Lloyd George to build an alternative support structure and leaving him with few options other than remaining on good terms with the Conservatives, whose formidable resources dwarfed his own.

However, as became clear when the votes were counted in November 1922, the biggest difference from the last election to be fought on traditional party-political terms, and the one that posed the biggest problem for the Liberals, was the emergence of the Labour Party as a significant presence in Parliament. If the Geddes axe had suggested that an attempt to wind the clock back to a world before the war was under way, then the presence of 142 Labour MPs, more than both factions of the Liberal Party combined, made it clear that, even if it could be done, it might not be straightforward. More than anything else, though, the steady growth of the Labour Party, from just two MPs in 1900, posed serious questions of the Liberals and the part they might play in putting British domestic politics back together after almost ten years of disruption. Having introduced old-age pensions and national insurance and a raft of smaller measures, such as free school meals, but then having helped to swing the Geddes axe at what had looked like the next phase of progressive social reform, were the Liberals now a spent force? In short, was their general election triumph in 1906 actually the end, rather than the beginning, of the Liberals' leading role in British politics?

7

The Man You Can Trust

The general election held in November 1922 was the worst the Liberal Party had experienced since modern party politics began almost three-quarters of a century earlier. While Lloyd George's National Liberals won just sixty-two seats, Asquith, who had returned to Westminster via a by-election in Paisley in 1920, rivalled him with an equally paltry fifty-four MPs. Even a united Liberal Party would have stood in the shadow of a Conservative government and its 345 seats. But trouble was coming at the Liberals from the left too. After losing his seat in 1918, thanks to his pacifism, Ramsay MacDonald, a founding member of the Labour Representation Committee, had returned to Westminster as MP for Aberavon in south Wales and been quickly restored as the leader of the Labour Party. On this occasion, though, he was flanked by 141 other MPs, which made him leader of the official opposition in the House of Commons.

The result was not the end for the Liberals, who continued to hold enough seats to have at least a say in parliamentary affairs for most of the 1920s. But it was not a blip either: their influence was waning and, though they did not know it at the time, their victory in 1906 was the last time the Liberals would form a majority government. For people involved in progressive politics, especially those who had played important roles in shaping new liberalism – the active and interventionist form of liberalism that aimed to reconcile individualist and socialist conceptions of political and economic freedom – at the turn of the century, this situation threw up a number of generation-defining questions. Was the writing on the wall for the Liberal Party? Was Labour now the political party of the future? Was it time for the Liberals to give up on Lloyd George's scheming and throw their lot in with Ramsay MacDonald? The answers mattered to anyone who had thought the 'People's Budget' marked a new dawn in British politics.

But, during the decade after the First World War, when it came to social policy – the aspects of government spending and intervention aimed at alleviating poverty and improving welfare – the arguments that mattered were not solely on the left. The Tories had to face up to the realities of modern Britain, where the Liberals' once controversial tax reforms and pension and national insurance schemes were now a fact of life, there was soon to be universal suffrage, and the Labour Party claimed to speak for the working class in Parliament. Nevertheless, in becoming the biggest party, if not always the sole party of government, for most of the 1920s, the Conservatives had the opportunity to shape social policy according to their ideals. The very poorest Britons had been the targets – and then beneficiaries – of government intervention during the nineteenth and early twentieth centuries. Now it was the middle classes that saw their situations improve during the interwar years, thanks not only to the economic policies pursued by the Tories under their new leader Stanley Baldwin, but also to a Conservativism that aimed for (though it did not always deliver) a democracy in which everyone had a stake.

THE BIG LOAF RISES AGAIN

British politics might have appeared very different when Andrew Bonar Law became Prime Minister and faced up to Ramsay MacDonald at the despatch box in the House of Commons in November 1922, but it looked a lot more familiar a year later. Although Britain had kept some of its wartime taxes, and was interested in shielding some of its most precariously positioned industries from the worst effects of the transition to peace, the world had not descended into a tariff war as some politicians and commentators had feared it might. Bonar Law, whom Asquith had refused to appoint to the Treasury in 1915 because he was a tariff reformer, had been forced to commit his party to free trade, lest the Conservatives looked indifferent to long-term concerns about the impact of protectionism on working-class living standards. Yet when he was struck down by serious illness after six months in Downing Street, Bonar Law was succeeded as Prime Minister by another tariff reformer, Stanley Baldwin (1867–1947), a former manager of his family's steel company. Baldwin displayed less tact on the matter. Addressing the Tory Party conference in October 1923, he declared himself open to protectionism. The resulting outcry from his opponents and disquiet among members of his own party, unnerved by a possible departure from the course set by Bonar Law, forced Baldwin to call another general election.

The reappearance of a serious divide in British politics over the issue of free trade looked like it might be a boon to the Liberals, who had managed to regroup without healing the split between Asquith and Lloyd George. Historically the party of free trade, they had won a huge majority under Henry Campbell-Bannerman seventeen years earlier thanks to a campaign centred on slogans such as 'Big Loaf, Little Loaf' – a reference to the impact they claimed economic protectionism would have on working-class living standards. The problem for both Liberal factions, however, was that they were no longer the only defenders of the big loaf. The Labour Party also supported free trade. As they put it in their election manifesto, Labour believed that tariffs 'foster a spirit of profiteering, materialism and selfishness, poison the life of nations, lead to corruption in politics, promote trusts and monopolies, and impoverish the people'. Free trade was a component of what Labour described as 'practical idealism': social reconstruction that continued what the Liberals had started, and which made more use of tools such as public works to tackle unemployment and a capital levy to pay off the country's war debt.

The Conservative-leaning press, including the *Daily Mail*, the *Daily Express* and *The Times*, made hysterical noises about these proposals, telling their readers that Labour was a coalition of Bolshevists and European socialists hell-bent on destroying the British way of life. In reality, however, Labour was promising a version of the collectivism that had been typical of the trade union and co-operative movements that had helped found the party and which continued to play a key role in its politics. Indeed, Labour did not propose to use anything other than conventional liberal economic policies to achieve their main aim of making life better for the working classes.

Ramsay MacDonald (1866–1937), Labour's leader, played an important part in shaping this platform. An illegitimate child raised by his mother and grandmother in a small fishing port in north-east Scotland, MacDonald might have been present when protesters rioted following the Social Democratic Federation rally in Trafalgar Square in 1886, but he was no violent revolutionary. He was a political progressive, with an evolutionary view of socialism and the Labour Party, who had joined the Fabian Society and was at home with new liberals like Leonard Hobhouse, with whom he shared a belief in the ethical aims and dimensions of politics. MacDonald believed the Labour Party needed dreamers and idealists, but that it also had to be trusted to hold power. He wanted Labour to earn its credentials as a serious party of government. To that end, and following the example of its Fabian Society founders – including the Webbs, who aimed to capture the attention of middle-class intellectuals – the party had attempted to broaden its base beyond the trade unions. Individuals had been allowed to join the party for the first time in 1918, and it had made concerted efforts to disseminate its message in the media – a task the Webbs had started in 1913 when they founded the *New Statesman*.

In the general election of December 1923, MacDonald's approach appeared to be paying off. The Conservatives remained the biggest party, with 258 MPs, 86 fewer than they had returned a year earlier. But the issue of free trade dominated the election, and the two parties that had campaigned for it were numerically superior, albeit only once the Liberals' 159 seats were added to Labour's 191. Baldwin was allowed to try to form a government but Lloyd George – determined to clear a path back to power for the Liberals and secure his position within his own party at the expense of Asquith's Independents – wanted to engineer a situation that served his long-term interests. Much to the displeasure of some in his party, who objected on principle to the idea of propping up a socialist government, Lloyd George decided the Liberals should back Labour and keep the Tories out. His support for Labour, though, was disingenuous. From the start, his aim was to bring MacDonald's administration down the moment it looked like the Liberals might be able to win a new election. Whatever his intentions, history was made: Ramsay MacDonald became Labour's first Prime Minister.

There was a predictable panic in some quarters about the prospect of a Labour government: Lloyd's of London even offered an insurance policy against the effects of their decisions. But, as MacDonald promised, his administration was a deliberately orthodox project. Labour kept its promises about free trade – they even abolished the duties on luxury goods Reginald McKenna had introduced during the war – and were restrained when it came to social policy. John Wheatley, who had risen from Lanarkshire's coalfields to become Minister of Health, passed a Housing Act that went some way to restoring Christopher Addison's ambitions for mass house building that had fallen victim to the Geddes axe. Labour offered local authorities a subsidy of £9 per house per year for forty years and, in an effort to tackle the main problem of housing for the poorest members of society, shifted attention back to the construction of publicly owned property. By 1933, when the subsidy was abolished, approximately 500,000 houses had been built under the scheme.

Yet when it came to the idea that a socialist plot was afoot, Labour's opponents did not let up. MacDonald, who had decided to serve as Foreign Secretary as well as Prime Minister because he did not think he had enough reliable colleagues to fill every Cabinet position, normalized relations with the USSR, which had been internationally isolated since the overthrow of the Romanov monarchy and the rise of the Bolsheviks in 1917. Under MacDonald's auspices, Britain signed a trade agreement with the Soviets, the terms of which included Britain making a £30 million loan to Russia. Unimpressed Tories and tariff reformers were quick to present MacDonald's diplomatic manoeuvres as the kind of act of disloyalty the country should expect from socialists. There were more than 1.4 million people out of work in 1924 and 1925, over 7 per cent of the working-age population. Rather than help them, the Tories argued, Labour was using British money to prop up their comrades abroad.

Always on the lookout for anything he could turn to his advantage, Lloyd George saw an opportunity to hatch the plan he had been sitting on since agreeing to back MacDonald in December 1923. The Liberal leader actually supported Labour's policy towards the Soviets, especially their sensible efforts to resolve financial questions that were outstanding from the fall of the Tsarist regime when the Bolsheviks had seized assets owned by British businesses and individuals, as well as those of Russian opponents who had been forced into exile. But he also thought he could use these suspicions about a socialist conspiracy to turn the public mood against MacDonald's administration. When rumours circulated that the government had put pressure on the Attorney General to drop incitement to mutiny charges against J. R. Campbell, the editor of the communist newspaper *Workers' Weekly*, who had urged soldiers to disobey orders if they were asked to fire on striking workers, MacDonald was caught out misleading the Commons when he told MPs his Cabinet had not been asked for its opinion, when, in fact, it had. Lloyd George instructed his supporters to vote with Asquith's Independent Liberals and the Tories in calling for an official investigation. Seeing this as a vote of no confidence, MacDonald asked King George V to dissolve Parliament in October 1924, just ten months after he had entered Downing Street.

'Red scare' themes dominated the election campaign. The most famous was the *Daily Mail*'s 'Zinoviev letter', supposedly from the head of the Communist International, the body that promoted communism worldwide, to the British Communist Party, asking its members to infiltrate and establish cells in institutions such as the army and put pressure on the Labour government to ratify MacDonald's agreements with the USSR – an effort that would, the letter argued, accelerate the conversion of the British working class to revolutionary communism. The letter is now known to be a forgery. However, many at the time – including officials at the Foreign Office, who drafted and then made public a response without fully checking the letter's provenance – were prepared to believe it was sensational evidence that the Labour government was complicit in foreign plots to undermine British society.

Lloyd George's calculation that Labour's problems would mean decisive gains for the Liberals could not have been more wrong, though. While Labour suffered a setback when the quirks of the first-past-the-post electoral system translated a 3 per cent increase in their share of the vote into a loss of 40 MPs, it was the Conservatives, with 419 seats and 48 per cent of the vote, who benefitted. The Liberals recorded their lowest ever share of the vote, 17.6 per cent, and were reduced to forty seats. It would take another eighty-six years and a merger with another struggling centre party, the Social Democratic Party, for Liberals to return to government, at which point coalition with the Conservatives would subsequently deliver a not dissimilar outcome.

THE CENTRE GROUND

Sidney Webb, who in 1922 had been elected as a Labour MP for Seaham, a mining constituency in the North East, thought the Labour Party's rise and the Liberals' decline were inevitable. Along with his wife and their allies in the Fabian Society, he believed that history was a march towards socialism. To be sure, the Fabians accepted the journey might be slow and not always proceed in a straight line. But for the Fabians, this winding road only underscored the importance of their belief that victory would be achieved through a gradual and attritional war of ideas. The Labour Party was going to become the dominant force in progressive politics, they argued. It was just a matter of keeping up the pressure and waiting for things to slot into place.

When it came to explaining why politics was moving in the Labour Party's direction during the early twentieth century, the Webbs, their opponents in the Tory party, as well as some Liberals, shared a belief that electoral reform, beginning with the Great Reform Act in 1832, had changed everything. The old property qualification had limited voting to particular sections of society, first the upper classes and then, as the threshold had gradually been lowered, the middle and upper-working classes. Supporters of this system argued that it not only ensured the electorate was made up of people with a stake in society but also prevented the mass of the working classes, the numerically biggest group in society, from bending politics to their will. The Webbs also believed the working classes were likely to use their vote to change British politics. After all, why would the working classes support either the Tories, the party of the aristocracy, or the Liberals, whose conception of political reform meant the most they could hope for was an occasional free meal for their children and limited forms of social insurance? It was obvious, the Webbs thought, that the working classes would demand their own representatives in Parliament. The

1918 Representation of the People Act, which extended voting rights to all men aged twenty-one and over and some women over thirty, had handed a huge voting block to the Labour Party, they argued, and the signs for Lloyd George, Asquith and their party were not promising.

The Liberals' fortunes after their landslide victory at the 1906 general election seemed to support this interpretation of events. While they returned a declining number of MPs on a declining share of the vote, Labour's share of the electorate increased dramatically, from around 7 per cent before the war to more than 37 per cent by the end of the 1920s, when there was universal suffrage. The Liberals also suffered much more than they might have done thanks to the first-past-the-post voting system – a situation they might have avoided had they not dropped the second-preference vote allocation system, which transfers ballots from losing candidates to ranked alternatives, from the 1918 act. During the twenty years before the war, Liberals had reached agreements with trade unions and the Labour Representation Committee to field mutually agreeable candidates or not run against one another. After 1918, however, when MPs were finally waged – a concession Labour had squeezed out of Lloyd George in return for their support during the hung parliaments after the 'People's Budget' – Labour was in a financial position to contest more seats than ever. The Liberals became the party of the centre: a party that not only seemed less radical than their challengers to the left but which also contained a faction that had recently done business with the party to their right. They faced finishing second to different opponents in different places and therefore losing out everywhere.

The Liberals' problems were not solely down to electoral sums. For one thing, there were questions about whether they had adapted to the realities of a multi-class electorate. Each of the three main political parties considered their policies to be in the country's best interests. But only the Liberals failed to marry their beliefs with a new approach to securing the support of different parts of the electorate. While Labour invested heavily in local organization, including door-to-door canvassing, the Conservatives, who by the mid-1920s counted more than 700,000 people among their members, cultivated support in business, the media and the suburban middle classes, particularly by stoking fears of what an organized working class might do. The Liberals, however, not only failed to maintain a grassroots electoral machine all year round, they only employed party agents at elections, meaning they were poorly prepared for the practice of politics in an era with so many new voters to reach.

Yet for all their deficiencies when it came to politics on the ground, the Liberals still had the support of writers, intellectuals and social reformers outside Westminster who could be relied on to champion their cause. Seebohm Rowntree, the York chocolate manufacturer and philanthropist whose survey of his home city had made such an impact on the discussion of poverty at the turn of the century, and doyens of new liberalism such as Leonard Hobhouse, who had provided a rationale for welfare policies from pensions to national insurance that were implemented under Asquith, were among those who kept the liberal faith. A younger generation of liberals was also emerging, including the economist John Maynard Keynes, who had become widely known after quitting the Treasury delegation to the Versailles peace conference and writing *The Economic Consequences of the Peace* (1919), a scathing and far-sighted critique of the punishing terms the Allies wanted to impose on Germany, which, he argued, were simply storing up trouble for the future.

These thinkers became the Liberals' intellectual establishment, whose thoughts on the party's future filled the pages of newspapers and periodicals like the *Manchester Guardian*, the *New Statesman* and *The Nation*. They also came together in places such as the Liberal Summer School, which met annually and alternately in Oxford and Cambridge, where participants reflected on the Liberal Party's problems and tried to thrash out new and exciting ideas. Such was the Liberal Summer School's status that Lloyd George gave it £10,000 from his private war chest to investigate Liberal policies on industry. The result, *Britain's Industrial Future* (1928), became widely known as the 'Yellow Book' and showed the influence Keynes and his colleagues at Cambridge were starting to exert on the party. Free trade was important, they suggested, but it should not be the end point of the government's involvement in the country's economic affairs. The aftermath of the war, when British manufacturers had lost overseas markets, inflation had more than doubled prices by 1920, unemployment had risen and stayed at a level that made it look like a systemic problem not a short-term blip, and government debt had reached eye-watering levels, showed that a new and much more active approach to the economy was needed. A Liberal government, they argued, should be prepared to intervene in the economy in ways the Liberals had never considered advisable before, including with heavy spending on public works as a means of tackling unemployment. But, in doing so, Liberals could rest assured that, counterintuitively, they would be making free trade work better, rather than subverting it.

Others, alienated by the direction of travel under Lloyd George and a party riven with factions, abandoned the Liberals. Winston Churchill, who had argued that Lloyd George's coalition with the Conservatives could be the basis for a new centre party that could stop the socialists from ever taking power, was the most prominent Liberal to decide he had had enough. Having lost his seat in 1922 and become estranged from most of the party, Churchill returned to Westminster two years later as an independent anti-socialist MP for Epping, on the outskirts of east London, where he was endorsed by the local Conservative Association. He was convinced that Britain needed a government that was close to liberalism's constitutional and individualist traditions. Churchill was soon back in the official Tory fold.

By contrast, Christopher Addison, the Liberal Minister of Health who had been in charge of creating 'homes fit for heroes' after the war, and J. A. Hobson, the economist who had linked unemployment at home with imperial expansion abroad via the theory of underconsumption, were among those who decided that Labour was the future. Switching allegiances was not always a happy experience. Hobson was uncomfortable with aspects of the Labour Party's approach to politics, especially the power the trade unions wielded in its decision-making processes. But as another Liberal-turned-Labour member, Charles Trevelyan, explained in 1925, he, Hobson and many others had concluded that Labour was 'an enormously better instrument for fighting economic wrongs and profiteering and monopoly than Liberalism ever was or could be'. Indeed, the switch was easy, Trevelyan wrote, because he had not been required 'to shed anything of my Liberalism, except the party name'.

These converts to Labour's cause were joined by a new generation of social reformers and political thinkers who in an earlier generation were likely to have been liberals. R. H. Tawney, based at the London School of Economics, where his brother-in-law William Beveridge was director, explained in books such as *The Acquisitive Society* (1920) and *Equality* (1931) his vision for a British social democracy – a place where equal rights to liberal values like freedom of conscience were accompanied by equal opportunities in the economic sphere. Tawney believed that the state should be prepared to intervene, modify and, when necessary, transform capitalism to make it deliver on the promises that nineteenth-century liberals had made but never delivered for most people. He thought Labour was the party not only most committed to this idea but also most likely to be in a position to realize it.

Of course, this discussion had little impact on the business of government during the second half of the 1920s. After three general elections in two years, the new Conservative administration that succeeded Labour's in November 1924 ran for a full five-year term. Although that period was far from plain sailing, it did see the unfolding of a new vision of Conservativism on the political landscape, inserting into the conversation about welfare and social policy a voice that had not been heard clearly since the Balfour administration at the beginning of the century. In the process, the Tories were able to make their mark on the philosophy and practice of social insurance in Britain.

SAFETY FIRST?

When things were particularly stressful, Stanley Baldwin could not sit still. Rather than let this affliction get the better of him, he developed coping mechanisms such as holding a pipe to conceal his nervous twitch. These props and mannerisms became an important part of his public image as a commonsense politician, drawing on his family's move from farming to the iron business during the nineteenth century to find practical and 'common sense' solutions to the country's problems. Baldwin's political philosophy became known as 'national' Conservativism, which was rooted in traditional Tory strengths, such as respect for private property and the paternalism that once inspired the Tories to campaign for limits to working hours and child labour in factories, but infused with the kinds of values that had led him to back national insurance and pensions before the war. Baldwin tried to forge a moderate and caring Conservativism that looked like something with which disillusioned Liberals could reconcile themselves.

As part of his 'national' approach, Baldwin constructed a Cabinet that was intended to reach out to the different factions of his own party as well as to sympathizers at the fringes of the Liberal factions. He tried to convince Reginald McKenna, whom Asquith had appointed as Chancellor of the Exchequer in preference to Bonar Law during the war, to return to the Treasury. McKenna, however, was concerned about Baldwin's well-known sympathy for tariff reform and the potential for his government to tilt towards economic protectionism. When McKenna turned down the Prime Minister's invitation, Baldwin turned to Churchill, then nominally an independent MP. Baldwin wanted to show he was serious when he said protectionism would only be adopted if circumstances demanded it, and he thought Churchill's return would prove it.

As Chancellor, the big issue confronting Churchill was deciding whether Britain should return to the gold standard. For those who believed in the principles of free trade and the approach to government that had guided the country in the years before the First World War, the gold standard was totemic: pegging sterling to the price of gold guaranteed 'sound finance', they argued, and it put serious constraints on any politician who thought they could spend their way to popularity. Britain's departure had only ever been intended to be a temporary measure because the country needed to borrow to fund its war effort. As even the most casual follower of events knew, however, events since the war meant a return was not straightforward. One important issue was parity – the value of the pound against gold. Most people assumed Britain would go back at $4.86, the dollar value of sterling before the war, as both a point of pride and a means of restoring confidence in the economy. Yet inflation meant the pound was actually worth about $4.40 in 1924. Painful adjustments in prices and wages would be required to make up the 10 per cent difference.

A number of decisions had been taken to try to clear the way for a return. Interest rates had been raised to 7 per cent, 2 per cent higher than their wartime levels, in 1920 as an incentive for investors to hold on to sterling, rather than sell it, which was meant to stop the currency from devaluing any further. Insofar as the exchange rate held – making it possible to reduce interest rates to 3 per cent, which, in theory at least, allowed more businesses to borrow to invest when they were struggling to match international competitors – manipulating interest rates worked. But, even after the slump that followed the restocking boom in 1920, the pound hadn't reached pre-war parity. With official figures showing twice as many people out of work as there had been before 1914, the situation seemed precarious. There were plenty of optimists, though, including in the Labour Party and at the Bank of England, who thought parity was not far off. By the time of his 1925 budget, Churchill concluded the circumstances were as welcoming as they would ever be to go back on the gold standard at $4.86.

Historians and economists have not judged Churchill's decision kindly. Instead, they have tended to side with Keynes, whose blistering critique, *The Economic Consequences of Mr Churchill* (1925), which he had rushed to the printing presses, argued that the Chancellor of the Exchequer had made a serious mistake. The immediate, direct and predictable consequence of Churchill's decision was deflation. This was good news for anyone on a fixed salary, particularly the professional middle classes who saw their situations improve as the cost of living fell. The same could not be said, however, of most people working in industry and manufacturing, where adjustment meant either wages had to come down or unemployment had to go up.

This trade-off provided the setting, in mid-1926, for Britain's first general strike. Coal mining was one of the country's struggling industries, and had been particularly troubled since pits were returned to private ownership after temporary government control during the war. Mine owners had demanded miners accept longer hours and lower wages, sparking unrest among workers and forcing the government to keep the peace by subsidizing miners' pay until a Royal Commission could deliver what it hoped would be seen as an impartial verdict on the dispute. When the commission endorsed the mine owners' position, the Trades Union Congress brought out a large number of their members in support of the miners, who rallied under the slogan 'Not a Penny off the Pay, Not a Minute on the Day'. The general strike lasted for nine days in May 1926, when essential services like transport were kept running by middle-class volunteers. The miners stayed out for another six months but were eventually forced back to work that November, with worse terms and lower pay.

From Baldwin's perspective, trouble of this kind was hugely regrettable. But the Tories had been put back into power with a majority of more than two hundred MPs thanks to support from the moneyed and middle classes, particularly those working in commerce and finance. Unemployment and declining wages in manufacturing and industry were a price the government was willing to pay to prevent inflation and ensure the stability of financial institutions, especially as Baldwin's preferred alternative – tariff reform – looked like electoral suicide. Indeed, the Conservatives could point to British industry's lack of competitiveness, which was related to its relatively high wages, and argue that the gold standard was far from the only problem – even if it was disingenuous to suggest, as the Conservatives did, that it was irrelevant.

As Baldwin and his allies tried to fashion a new politics in this context, Conservative intellectuals developed a number of ideas. One was of a 'property-owning democracy', a phrase coined by the Scottish Unionist Noel Skelton (1880–1935) in the Tory periodical the *Spectator* in 1923. Skelton, Baldwin and others wanted to square their party's historical identity as the party of property owners with the new reality of an electorate who possessed all the political rights, but not the economic status, property owners once enjoyed. As Skelton explained, these new Conservatives believed that 'character and a sense of responsibility are rooted in a man's possession of "something of his own"', and that a better Britain would therefore require more property owners. The wager, of course, was that more property owners would mean Tory values being held more widely throughout society, in the process immunizing the electorate against socialist ideas about common ownership. The challenge was to find an acceptable way to turn more people into property owners. Some, including Skelton, thought profit-sharing business models might be the answer – an idea that would enjoy a fleeting renaissance under David Cameron some ninety years later – but there was little sense of how business might be persuaded to adopt such models voluntarily.

The housing market provided hints of a solution (and an indicator of where enthusiasm for a property-owning democracy would lead later in the century). Although the Geddes axe had done for Christopher Addison's 'homes fit for heroes' scheme, subsidies, albeit much reduced, had still been available to local authorities that wanted to build new properties. Under the Conservatives, though, attention shifted towards private builders. The Tories believed that council owned and managed homes were only really necessary for a small segment of the population, and that the 250,000 properties approved before 1922 – half the number the country had been estimated as needing – had more or less eliminated the pragmatic reasons for state involvement in the issue. On this score, the Conservatives were joined by some members of the Labour Party, who thought that the needs of large numbers of people should be met not by government but by voluntary and co-operative organizations, including trade unions. The Tories, however, had quite different concerns. They thought large numbers of people who rented houses were capable of buying new ones – an idea that was not without foundation, given that more than a million properties had been sold by private landlords to owner-occupiers during the interwar years. If new homes could be built for these potential owners it would have a rippling effect, Tories suggested, freeing up homes for the less affluent.

During the 1920s, around 400,000 homes were constructed under the Conservatives' housing policies, followed by almost 3 million during the 1930s when interest rates dropped to 2 per cent, making house building a much more attractive investment than it had been immediately after the First World War. Yet as Nye Bevan, the firebrand Labour MP who served as Minister of Health in the post-1945 Labour government, observed, these new properties were of little use to the people Lloyd George had been speaking to in 1918. For the most part, they were not homes built for the poorest members of society or those facing the most acute need. Rather, the houses were constructed in suburbs near areas of economic growth, often in the south of England where white-collar, salaried workers were doing well off the back of policies that were causing manual workers in the north of the country so much misery, especially during the Great Depression of the 1930s.

These new suburbs were filled with rows and rows of semi-detached properties set back from the pavement, with driveways and garages, paths leading through small front gardens to the door, and large gardens to their rear. Found in areas like Gants Hill on the Essex outskirts of east London, New Malden in Surrey and Kenton in Middlesex, these were houses geared to a growing market of middle-class workers. However, even people employed in better-paid working-class occupations, such as in the print industry and on the railways, could afford to save a deposit as small as £25 on a final £500 asking price. Architects also designed homes for people who aspired to something more than the identikit houses that had appeared in places like Becontree during the 1920s, varying their plans regularly, even on the same street. Some chose properties with bay windows, others houses with porches or small stained-glass feature windows. All, however, were able to settle into a life of suburban comfort, thanks to government decisions that catered to their needs, those of homebuyers, rather than others'.

OLD AGE AND CONTRIBUTIONS

Baldwin's national Conservativism made its mark in other areas too, thanks in large part to Neville Chamberlain (1869–1940). Baldwin and Chamberlain had much in common. Like Baldwin, Chamberlain came from a family that had done well out of the industrial revolution thanks to an investment in a screw manufacturing company, and had followed in family footsteps to Parliament. The Chamberlains, however, had the appearance of an emerging and great political dynasty. While Neville's father, Joseph, had been the pioneering Mayor of Birmingham who had experimented with municipal socialism, buying up utilities such as gas and water during the 1880s, and the most prominent figure among the breakaway Unionist faction of the Liberal Party that eventually merged with the Tories in 1912, his uncle, Richard, had also been a Liberal Unionist MP, and his brother, Austen, Chancellor of the Exchequer under the Conservative Arthur Balfour. Thanks to a steely focus and determination, Neville Chamberlain emerged from his father's shadow to become one of the most important figures in interwar Conservativism, and an essential component in Baldwin's administrative machinery.

Now best known almost entirely for his short stint as Prime Minister during the late 1930s, during which he stepped off a plane from Munich waiving a piece of paper signed by Adolf Hitler and fatefully declared 'peace for our time', Chamberlain is frequently considered a man who was not up to the job when the country needed him most. Yet a popular fixation with that moment has overshadowed a long, distinguished and – in the case of social policy – important career. Like his father, Neville Chamberlain had cut his political teeth in local government, also serving as Mayor of Birmingham, where he had pursued a similar localist agenda. Although Lloyd George dismissed him as 'a good mayor of Birmingham in an off year', Chamberlain did an important job there during the First World War. He successfully managed the day-to-day affairs of a vital cog in Britain's industrial war machine, and created institutions including the Birmingham Symphony Orchestra and the Birmingham Corporation Savings Bank, later renamed the Birmingham Municipal Bank, which invested in the government's war-loan scheme. Elected to Parliament in 1918 as a Conservative and Liberal Unionist member for the Birmingham constituency of Ladywood, Chamberlain was a highly regarded backbencher during the coalition years. He rose quickly, first to the Ministry of Health under Bonar Law, and then to the Treasury in Baldwin's first, brief administration. Chamberlain, though, was never comfortable with high-profile statesmanship. He was a technician – one who enjoyed combing through the small print – and chose to return to Health, rather than the Treasury, when Baldwin appointed a new Cabinet in 1924.

Chamberlain bought into Baldwin's argument that the Tories had to show they could be trusted with social reform, much as MacDonald wanted Labour to demonstrate it could be trusted with the economy. He arrived back at the Ministry of Health in 1924 with a clear plan of action: twenty-five bills he wanted to make law during the life of the Parliament. His starting point was what became the 1925 Widows, Orphans, and Old Age Pensions Act. Since its introduction by the Liberals in 1908, Britain's pension scheme had been debated constantly. Labour and the left had consistently argued that the state pension – initially five shillings a week, a quarter of the average labourer's wage – was too small, should be available much earlier than at seventy years of age, and subjected claimants to an unnecessarily intrusive administrative assessment – the means test. Conservatives, on the other hand, had always been much more concerned with the costs to the public purse. The Liberals' projections of how much money would be needed to pay for their pension scheme had been blown out of the water when the first bill came in at twice what they had predicted. While longer life expectancy had been to blame, the coalition government's decision in 1919 to double payments to ten shillings a week and lift the annual earnings cap to £49 8s a year in response to inflation had put further strain on the scheme, and led to Tory calls to get a grip on government spending.

More importantly, many Conservatives hated the values written into the pension scheme, in that pensions were not contributory: they were funded out of general taxation, meaning wealth was transferred from rich to poor. Eager to address this issue, in 1923 Baldwin asked a committee headed by Sir John Anderson, Permanent Under-Secretary at the Home Office, to investigate how the scheme might be reformed. When Baldwin lost the surprise general election later that year, and Ramsay MacDonald entered Downing Street with the intention of making pensions more generous, it looked like Baldwin's plans might amount to nothing. Chamberlain, however, had been put in charge of a secret Tory committee to shadow Anderson's work, and when he returned to the Ministry of Health after Lloyd George pulled the rug out from under the first Labour government's feet, he did not need to start from scratch.

Significantly, Chamberlain also had a Chancellor of the Exchequer who was willing to work with him. Churchill – a veteran of the great Liberal reforming governments from 1906 to the war – was desperate to prove his credentials to Conservatives who were sceptical about his return to the party. While he had served up the tax cuts the party faithful expected in his first budget in 1925, he also wanted to show that his instincts on social reform were aligned with Baldwin's vision for the Tories and the country as a whole.

When, in April 1925, Churchill announced the general aims of the Widows, Orphans, and Old Age Pensions Act, he therefore took not only the Labour benches but also many members of his own party by surprise. Chamberlain's proposals were based on an important trade-off. On the one hand, he put forward a series of reforms that the left could endorse. The age at which people qualified for a pension was to be lowered from seventy to sixty-five, theoretically freeing up jobs for younger, unemployed workers; payments were to be kept at exactly the same rate; and the despised means test was to be abolished. On the other hand, Chamberlain proposed a significant change to the basic principles of the pension scheme. He wanted to make it contributory, with benefits linked to a person's history of paying into the system, which he believed he could make self-funding. Sixty-five-year-olds would be able to claim a pension under Chamberlain's rules, but only if they had five years of contributions behind them. Everyone, though, would be entitled to a pension at the age of seventy.

Chamberlain planned to graft these rules on to existing administrative arrangements by adding them to the workload of the organizations that ran the country's health insurance scheme, which was also contributory. Unlike health insurance, however, only employees and employers would be required to pay into Chamberlain's pension scheme – 4½d per week from both employer and employee, in the case of men, and 2½d per week from the employer and 2d from the employee in the case of women – meaning the state would no longer help people's planning for old age. As with health insurance, though, women got a poor deal from Chamberlain's suggested reforms. Whereas the Liberals' original scheme had granted women a pension regardless of their husband's circumstances, Chamberlain's new contributory rules only applied to insurable employment, from which 90 per cent of women were excluded. Women were treated as dependants and entitled to pensions based on their husbands' contributions – a decision that, like the Liberals' health insurance reforms fourteen years earlier, put a particular and narrow view of economic and family life at the heart of an important piece of social policy.

Bridge funding would be required from the government for some time to make up the shortfall in income and payments for those who could claim a pension after as few as five years' contributions. Chamberlain's own estimates were that 2010 would be the first year when people would draw truly self-funded pensions, having paid in since the age of sixteen. In the meantime, however, the general gist of these changes resonated perfectly with Baldwin's idea of a new Conservativism. The redistributive features of the old scheme that Tories objected to had been removed. At the same time, the contributory principles – albeit limited ones that did not adjust benefit payments according to contribution history, as many private schemes did – not only sounded like rewards for thrift, independence and industriousness, they also eliminated a number of Labour's biggest complaints about the old system.

Chamberlain also used his experience in Birmingham to reform local government, the institution responsible for delivering most social policies, and in particular its relationship with Westminster. There was a long history, dating back to the Poor Law reforms of the 1830s, of local authorities frustrating and outraging Parliament in equal measure by departing from the strict instructions they had been told to follow, most frequently by ignoring the rule that people enter the workhouse in order to receive help. By the 1920s the issue that riled Conservatives went by the name of 'Poplarism' – a practice named after the staunchly Labour east London borough where Poor Law Guardians were famous for treating paupers and the unemployed much more generously than the rules allowed. Aside from their objections to the shameless flouting of the principle of 'less eligibility' – which the more conspiratorially minded thought was a strategy to buy votes in poor communities – Conservatives were angered by the financial implications. While some Poor Law Unions had been declared bankrupt, Poplar had kept itself afloat by simply refusing to pay its share of the joint costs of a number of metropolitan authorities, including the London County Council and Metropolitan Police.

Although Chamberlain was happy enough to take on uncooperative authorities he thought were guilty of financial mismanagement, especially if he thought they used the funds to push a left-wing agenda (in 1926, he sent commissioners into West Ham and Durham to take over the Poor Law Guardians' responsibilities), he had enough experience of local government to know that many authorities only broke the rules for good reasons. In Poplar, where thirty councillors were gaoled in 1921 for defying instructions to meet their obligations to other institutions, the local authorities' complaint was a not un-common one in urban areas: they, like other poor areas, did badly out of the local rates system. Rich local authorities were not only able to collect more money from their residents than less affluent ones – they also had fewer liabilities.

Chamberlain's attempt at a long-term answer to these difficulties was the Local Government Act of 1929, in which he tried to do what Beatrice Webb's minority report had suggested twenty years earlier: to make a rationalized local authority system the official and main mode of delivery for welfare services. The basic principle behind the act was to complete the trend that had been started during the late nineteenth century, when Poor Law infirmaries started to be moved out of workhouses, separating – both physically and as a point of principle – able-bodied claimants from those who required more specialist care. Chamberlain wanted to abolish Poor Law Guardians, the elected boards created during the reforms of the 1830s, and trans-fer their assets and responsibilities to local government. While Public Assistance Committees took over the Guardians' duties with respect to the able-bodied poor, responsibilities for people who needed help for reasons other than unemployment were handed to local auth-orities, who were allowed to create new committees if they thought they were necessary.

The proposed arrangements had a number of consequences, some of which were logical and practical, others potentially more pro-found. On the one hand, the responsibility for educating children whose care fell under the old Poor Law was transferred to Local Edu-cation Authorities. On the other, however, councils could set up bodies such as health committees to run all the workhouse infirm-aries in their area – something Chamberlain wanted to encourage as part of a shift towards local authorities delivering better and more integrated health services for those they were supposed to help. Yet while some authorities used these new responsibilities – for instance, in the creation of old people's homes for those who could claim a small pension but not support themselves – there was no great rush to buy up institutions such as hospitals, especially when the economic situation worsened the following year.

All of this needed to be paid for, of course. Chamberlain wanted a simple system of central government block grants to local authorities, which would be calculated by determining the numbers of people with different needs, from the unemployed to orphaned children, an authority was responsible for, thereby tackling the complaints that came from places like Poplar. Churchill, however, was keen to integrate local government reform with broader economic policy, which was taking a hit from the country's return to the gold standard. The slump had turned into one of the most severe Britain had ever experienced. With unemployment still above 10 per cent and a return to sound finance not delivering the recovery that many people had either hoped for or expected, Churchill was on the look-out for ways to stimulate trade, industry and agriculture. After tortuous behind-the-scenes negotiations, he agreed to introduce Chamberlain's block grants – but only if industry was exempted from local taxation and subject to a new national business rate instead. Churchill sugared this pill by promising that nobody – by which he meant no Tory local authorities – would end up in a worse position than the one they were already in.

Chamberlain would not remain in post long enough to see the Local Government Act reforms implemented. Baldwin's Conservatives lost power at the general election held in late May 1929, the first to be held with an equal franchise for men and women. Like the election of 1923, no single party held an overall majority and Lloyd George's Liberals held the balance of power. Unlike 1923 Labour, rather than the Conservatives, were the biggest party. Unemployment was the central issue of the day and, insofar as the election was a judgement in any clear sense, it was not a good one for Baldwin, who had pitched himself as 'the man you can trust'. In 1930, as unemployment shot up to over 2 million, more than 12 per cent of the working population, Keynes's argument that Britain needed to put the prevention of unemployment before everything else was looking increasingly wise.

8

Will the Machine Work?

On 11 March 1908, twenty years before unemployment became the central issue in British politics, the Fabian socialists Beatrice and Sidney Webb had held a dinner party at their home on Grosvenor Road, on the north bank of the Thames and a short walk from the Houses of Parliament. The Webbs held these events several times a week as part of their relentless efforts to influence the country's political and intellectual elites. On this occasion they had a very clear goal in mind. Among their guests were the then Liberal MP Winston Churchill, then the Under-Secretary for the Colonies but weeks away from taking over at the Board of Trade as part of Asquith's shake up of the Liberal administration. Also dining with the Webbs that evening was a less well-known figure: William Beveridge, a 29-year-old economist. The Webbs had known Beveridge since the turn of the century, when he had been a resident at Toynbee Hall, the university settlement in the East End of London where, since the mid-1880s, countless Oxford graduates had spent time learning about poverty and deprivation, and they wanted Churchill to hear about Beveridge's work.

Beveridge had spent the best part of a decade studying unemployment, and was known to people like the Webbs as one of the country's most knowledgeable and innovative thinkers on the subject. Indeed, when unemployment came up for discussion at the Royal Commission on the Poor Laws and Relief of Distress, which had commenced work in 1905, Beatrice wasted no time in calling Beveridge to give evidence. Now, as the courses that emerged from the Webbs' kitchen were eaten, drinks were drunk, and cigarettes and cigars smoked, Beveridge let Churchill know all about what he thought the government needed to do if it was serious about tackling a problem that had emerged as a seemingly permanent feature of modern industrial society. The young economist decided not to hold back from criticizing either the Liberal government or his famous and equally forthright dining companion's efforts to defend its policies. But, as Beveridge later reported, he 'came away with a feeling that I had made an impression'. He was right. Less than six months later, Beveridge was working as an adviser at the Board of Trade.

The crux of what Beveridge told Churchill was that, while it might not be possible to eliminate unemployment completely, the state was perfectly capable of making it much less common than it had become during the late nineteenth century. Unemployment was often a consequence of poor organization, Beveridge argued, most notably the unplanned and uncoordinated way many businesses liked to hire workers. Improving on this situation had the potential to be a win–win outcome: industry could become much more efficient and, in the process, the state could reduce the amount of money it spent on the relief of people who found themselves out of work. But there would be a price: the state would have to take a much more active role in the economy by measuring, tracking and understanding unemployment, rather than just picking up the tab when it happened. Building the infrastructure that would enable governments to keep on top of unemployment in such a way was an immense task. Some people, however, wondered if it might be the beginning of an entirely new approach to the economy and society – one in which the state could measure and monitor specific phenomena and make targeted interventions when necessary.

THE PROBLEM OF INDUSTRY

'Unemployment' was used as a noun for the first time in 1888, in an article in an American journal called *Science*. The word's general meaning seemed clear enough: a situation in which someone was willing to work but could not find a job. Thinkers dating back to the classical era of political economy during the late eighteenth and early nineteenth centuries, including Adam Smith and David Ricardo, had accepted that workers might not be able to find a job in any place and at any time. But they struggled to accept the idea that unemployment could be a systemic or structural problem. As those who were heavily influenced by these classical political economists, including the Poor Law reformers of the 1830s, liked to argue, the only sufficient explanation for long-term worklessness was a person's character. By the early twentieth century, though, after events such as the Lancashire cotton famine of the 1860s and the depression that followed the end of the 'Great Victorian Boom' in the 1870s, unemployment looked like a phenomenon that was here to stay. As institutions from Poor Law Guardians to charities to churches dealt with the human consequences of unemployment, economists tried to make sense of the forces that were causing unemployment in the first place. Beveridge's was a name that became more closely associated with that effort than any other.

Born in Rangpur, in the north of modern-day Bangladesh, William Beveridge (1879–1963) had spent the first five years of his life in India with his English mother and Scottish father, who served the Raj as a judge. His childhood was not a particularly happy time; he had been seriously ill in Bengal with a fever that was never diagnosed properly, and then was incredibly lonely after his parents sent him back to England at the age of five for a boarding-school education. Adding to his sense of dislocation was a dissatisfaction with what he was taught. Beveridge loved natural science, particularly the writings of the great biologists such as Thomas Huxley and Charles Darwin. But, as he would often complain twenty years later, he was fed a constant and unremitting diet of the classics – the kind of curriculum that advocates of 'national efficiency' said was the root of Britain's struggles in economics and international affairs at the beginning of the new century – first at school and then at Balliol College, Oxford, where he studied mathematics and classics for three years from 1897. Apparently destined for a quintessentially middle-class career as a lawyer, Beveridge earned his parents' displeasure by changing his mind at the last minute. Following in the footsteps of Oxford-educated intellectuals such as Leonard Hobhouse, Beveridge had been captivated by the 'social question'. He decided he would prefer to spend some time at Toynbee Hall with his friend and soon-to-be brother-in-law, R. H. Tawney.

While many of those who took up residence at Toynbee Hall were fully committed to either the Liberal Party or the labour movement, Beveridge's political views were difficult to pin down. He knew all about the latest ideas coming out of places like the Rainbow Circle – the discussion group frequented by new liberals such as the economist J. A. Hobson and socialists like the future Labour leader Ramsay MacDonald – and had flirted with Fabian socialism, getting to know the Webbs during his time in London. Yet Beveridge was also a regular contributor to the *Morning Post*, a Tory newspaper that would later merge with the *Telegraph*. Indeed, he had not travelled to the East End because he thought spending time in the company of the poor was a good thing in and of itself. Rather, he believed the major challenge for social reform was essentially technical, and that what social investigators needed was high quality observational data, from which the new laws governing society would spring. For Beveridge, there was little difference between society, the economy and nature. Life in the East End, in his view, was an opportunity to start the process that would lead to discovering the economy's version of evolution by means of natural selection.

At Toynbee Hall, Beveridge was introduced to all kinds of approaches to tackling poverty. He watched members of the Charity Organisation Society conduct casework and apply their ideas about self-help and moral character to people struggling with problems such as alcoholism. He observed trade unions recruit members around the Port of London's docks and tried to make sense of how their presence changed workers' employment prospects and employers' behaviour. Beveridge was by no means won over to every cause. While he decided that means testing was a problem rather than a solution when it came to administering benefits, and backed campaigns for old-age pensions and free school meals, he was not convinced by other, sometimes more radical, ideas. He was sceptical of a minimum wage across society – a cause the Webbs had thrown themselves behind – because he believed it put some jobs at risk and, more importantly, he thought the lesson of the work done by Seebohm Rowntree, among others, was that poverty had many more causes than low pay.

As Beveridge would explain in his landmark book of 1909, *Unemployment: A Problem of Industry*, his work in the East End had led him to see unemployment as the issue 'at the root of most other social problems'. The reason was that society 'lays upon its members responsibilities which in the vast majority of cases can be met only from the reward of labour'. If the 'ideal unit is the household of man, wife and children maintained by the earnings of the first alone' then, Beveridge argued, 'reasonable security of employment for the bread-winner is the basis of all private duties and all sound social action'.

For these reasons, Beveridge wanted to do something different to the poverty surveys that had appeared during the previous two decades. Where Booth, Rowntree and others had explored the day-to-day experience of poverty, he was interested in the more abstract phenomenon of unemployment, which he saw as providing the framework within which those people's suffering was played out. Beveridge pored over census returns, records on industrial production collected by the Board of Trade, and local authority records on pauperism with the aim of building a picture of the economy's ebbs and flows. Unemployment's deep social consequences would only be fixed, he argued, if people spent more time reasoning from empirical data than they did moralizing about an individual's perceived character failings.

As his book's subtitle indicated, Beveridge concluded that a significant amount of unemployment was structural and caused by the way industries were organized. There were, certainly, men who were without work because they lacked the motivation to find it. But, he argued, anyone who thought those people were the major problem were deeply misguided, because there were all kinds of obstacles in the way of even the most energetic and driven workers. There was cyclical unemployment: periods when industries experienced downturns, such as seasonal lows in the seaside towns where increasing numbers of people were able to have holidays during the summer, meaning that there was much less, and sometimes no, work available at some points in the year. Unskilled workers also had trouble acquiring accurate information about where jobs could be found. Yet their problems were in many ways negligible compared to the challenges faced by skilled workers whose trade was in decline, perhaps because technology had made their skills redundant or too costly compared to workers in another part of the world. How were these workers supposed to know which industries had skills shortages that would last long enough to justify the time and effort it would take to retrain?

Beveridge found that the most consistent problems were experienced by casual labourers: men who had to go to companies every day to find out if there was work. Unionized industries were far from perfect, not least when it came to the friction between trade unions and employers. However, there were benefits for both sides when trade unions controlled access to work, helped set wage rates, and could supply employers with a reliable stream of good-quality workers. Employers in casual labour markets, on the other hand, maintained a surplus of workers, not simply to keep wages down but to ensure they were never short-handed. The somewhat paradoxical result, as Beveridge observed for himself, was industries where large numbers of people found it difficult to secure regular work but companies frequently needed more workers.

Beveridge explained how this happened by asking readers of *Unemployment* to imagine a scene he had encountered many times during his time at Toynbee Hall: ten wharves that each employed between fifty and a hundred men per day, half of whom were regular staff and half of whom were reserves. Each of those ten wharves was likely to experience similar high and low points throughout the year thanks to general fluctuations in trade. But they were also likely to have their own individual fluctuations within those peaks and troughs. An economist looking at the ten wharves as a whole would not be able to see these smaller deviations from the general trends throughout the year. However, for the reserve labourers, who were being turned away, these fluctuations were all that mattered. 'The greatest barrier to free movement in any area', Beveridge explained, 'is ignorance among the men as to the demand for labour in different directions.' The goal had to be, therefore, to spread information about where work could be found as widely as possible. To be sure, 'even if every man knows exactly how many men will be wanted next day at each wharf', this would not mean everyone would find a job. It would, though, be a start.

Beveridge called this possible world in which information about vacancies circulated freely the 'organised fluidity of labour'. All kinds of institutions, including trade unions and large employers, would need to contribute to its realization, but all would reap its rewards. Yet the institution that would gain the most, Beveridge thought, would be the state. If he was right, improved labour mobility would mean more people in jobs, and more people in jobs would mean less pressure on poor relief services. This result would be hugely significant for the public finances, not to mention the myriad social problems closely connected to unemployment, from the psychological despair experienced by men without work to the disorder and rioting that happened when times were tough for a large and geographically concentrated group of people. The scale of these rewards was important, Beveridge believed, because the state was the only agency with the power and resources, including money and information, to create the employment environment he had described.

'ORGANIZED FLUIDITY OF LABOUR'

A particular institution was at the heart of Beveridge's vision of the 'organised fluidity of labour'. He had learned about labour exchanges – places where employers could locate workers and vice versa – from Percy Alden (1865–1944), a popular Liberal MP, former student of the Idealist philosopher T. H. Green and member of the Fabian Society, who could often be found conversing with the likes of J. A. Hobson and Ramsay MacDonald at the dinner parties that were an integral part of progressive politics in the capital. Alden had set up his own university settlement, Mansfield House, in Canning Town, about five miles east of Toynbee Hall, where local men, many of whom worked on the docks and at the nearby Tate & Lyle sugar refinery, were offered the opportunity to participate in sporting activities as well as political and religious education. But Alden was just as interested in national solutions to problems like unemployment, to which end he had travelled throughout mainland Europe to study such things as labour colonies – camps where the unemployed were sent for rehabilitation. His account of what he had seen, *The Unemployed: A National Question* (1905), was a hugely influential book that introduced men like Beveridge to possibilities beyond the Poor Law.

The recently unified Germany was the pioneer when it came to using labour exchanges as part of a publicly funded effort to tackle unemployment. Although he had read reports on the German system by Alden and others, Beveridge's commitment to the idea of transferring it to Britain began to crystallize after the Webbs urged him to travel to Germany and see it at first hand. What Beveridge found in Berlin, Cologne and other cities in September 1906 was a system of more than 4,000 exchanges – some government run, others state-supported but operated by organizations like trade unions and charities – filling more than 1.25 million job vacancies every year. As he told readers of the *Morning Post*, which helped fund the trip, and the *Economic Journal*, one the country's oldest specialist economics publications, for which he wrote a more detailed scholarly study, he was deeply impressed. The exchanges not only generated statistics for government, which used them to understand more about the movement of and demand for labour; they were also integral to Germany's compulsory national insurance scheme, which covered more than 12 million workers and provided old-age pensions.

Labour exchanges were not an alien concept in Britain. During the first decade of the twentieth century there were twenty-four 'labour bureaux' operating in the country. Beveridge had access to the exchanges in London thanks to his Toynbee Hall connections, and he hoped he might be able to use them to run a trial of his ideas about how they could be used more effectively. He ran into trouble, however, when local trade unions learned about his project. The unions were suspicious about the idea of a young economist trying to circumvent existing arrangements in labour markets. Aside from concerns about how their role as gatekeepers to employment in certain sectors might be affected, the unions thought employers were likely to use labour exchanges as a means of recruiting workers to break strikes.

Despite these challenges, Beveridge was encouraged to persevere, particularly when Beatrice Webb decided to champion his work: first by inviting him to give evidence to the Royal Commission on the Poor Laws and Relief of Distress, and then by introducing him to Winston Churchill at the March 1908 dinner party. It was an encounter that convinced Churchill that labour exchanges could help make the Liberals' plans for unemployment insurance work better. Shortly after, he had offered Beveridge an advisory role at the Board of Trade to help put the idea into practice.

When he arrived in Whitehall, Beveridge found himself working alongside the Board of Trade's Permanent Secretary, Hubert Llewellyn Smith (1864–1945), who had joined the civil service through its open-competition exams in 1893. The two men had much in common. Llewellyn Smith had been a contemporary of the new liberal theorist Hobhouse at Oxford and, like Beveridge, a Toynbee Hall resident – a fact that did not go unnoticed by the Labour MP George Lansbury, who later remarked in his autobiography that the university settlement had become a launchpad for ambitious and sometimes cynical social reformers who had their eye on careers in government and administration. Llewellyn Smith also put a premium on empirical social research. Having contributed work on migration to Charles Booth's survey of London during the late 1880s, he moved to the Board of Trade, where he was employed as a labour commissioner in the mid-1890s. Under his direction the Board of Trade started to collect and analyse unemployment statistics more systematically, and established itself as a conciliation service for industrial disputes. Working alongside Llewellyn Smith helped Beveridge understand how his vision of labour exchanges as instruments of economic calibration might become an administrative reality.

The first fruits of the two men's collaboration was the Labour Exchanges Bill, which began its passage through Parliament in June 1909. Although the bill endorsed the general principle of setting up a national network of labour exchanges, the details of such a scheme still needed to be worked out. To that end, Churchill established a Labour Exchanges Branch within a new Labour Department at the Board of Trade and, in September 1909, gave Beveridge the job of running it. Beveridge's vision for the new system was ambitious. As a starting point, he wanted specialist exchanges for small towns where there was a single or just a few major employers, a general labour exchange in every town with more than 100,000 residents, and multiple exchanges in larger cities. He also wanted regional networks, with a major town or city as the focus for Divisional Clearing Houses, through which exchanges could communicate with each other via direct telephone lines and a dedicated postal service. Making all these institutions communicate with one another in a way that sent information about jobs circulating so that vacancies were filled quickly seemed like a big ask. Beveridge, though, was filled with enthusiasm; it was a difficult challenge, he thought, but one that could be met.

After assembling a team of assistants, Beveridge met people and institutions, such as employers and Local Education Authorities, whose co-operation in directing new labour market entrants towards the exchanges would be necessary if the system was going to work. While he fretted over small details – like where the labour exchanges should be in each town in order to maximize the flow of information and access to vacancies – he spent a huge amount of time explaining how the system was supposed to work, trying to win over the still-sceptical trade unions. At the same time, Llewellyn Smith's national insurance proposals, with which Beveridge had been intimately involved, were on a slow journey through Westminster – a process that would not be complete until 1911.

The delay caused by the House of Lords' decision to refuse to pass Lloyd George's 'People's Budget' led to subtle but important changes in the government's understanding of the purposes that labour exchanges could serve. In theory, labour exchanges could be set up and operated for no other reason than to improve the efficiency with which job vacancies were filled. The Board of Trade, however, was responsible for unemployment insurance too. In addition to matching people with jobs, labour exchanges were meant to act as the gateway to unemployment benefit, with failure to find work at an exchange considered proof that the requisite effort had been made. Yet for a scheme of that kind to be successful there had to be a high level of participation from both employers and potential employees. To that end, the Liberal government offered employers an incentive: labour exchanges would take care of all their administrative responsibilities, including keeping employees' contribution records, under Part II of the National Insurance Act – so long as they recruited all their workers through the exchanges.

The new era began in July 1912 when, after months of preparation, more than 100 new exchanges employing more than 15,000 workers, who helped run the exchanges and administer national insurance, were up and running. As Llewellyn Smith and Beveridge had suggested would be the case, most of the first claimants six months later were from the building trade, which experienced a lull every winter when rain and freezing temperatures frequently brought construction work to a halt. By the First World War there were more than 450 labour exchanges across the country, helping some workers find work further afield than they had been able to look in the past. But there were a number of problems that stopped the system functioning in anything like the way Beveridge wanted it to. Administrating national insurance turned out to be overwhelming at times. Moreover, some of the organizations that were expected to use the exchanges grew frustrated with them. Predictably, trade unions resented the state wading into territory they were used to calling their own. Most trade unions took pride in the quality of workers they put forward for jobs, especially where the closed shop – the requirement for men to belong to a specific union in order to be employed in particular workplaces – operated. Labour exchanges, however, could be less discerning and often supplied men who had fewer skills, not to mention less interest in the jobs in question, than unions and employers themselves thought necessary. Labour exchanges promised much but, for the time being at least, many people opted for the human touch that was characteristic of old and occasionally fraught relationships.

WEALTH AND WELFARE

Beveridge was far from being the only economist of his era who was drawn to questions about patterns in the economy and their underlying causes. There was growing interest across Europe and America in the mysteries of the trade cycle – the expansion and contraction in economic activity that led to booms and recessions. Theorists including Knut Wicksell in Sweden and Ludwig von Mises in Austria, not to mention economists and statisticians working in American organizations like the Washington, DC-based Brookings Institution, were interested in whether the ups and downs that all industrial economies seemed to go through exhibited a common pattern, and if they could be linked to definite underlying causes. While answers seemed a long way off, the benefits of making progress towards them were obvious.

Governments, businesses and individual workers themselves could make suitable plans for spending, investment and saving if they knew exactly when downturns were on their way.

Although they had provided the foundation for arguments about the importance of letting markets operate unhindered, the great and cele-brated minds of earlier years, including Adam Smith and David Ricardo, had written little that provided much insight into the questions econ-omists were asking by the early twentieth century. Classical economists had talked about a world made up of three homogeneous classes – workers, capitalists and landowners – and economies dominated by agriculture. But by 1900 the world had changed. Industrialization meant new modes of production, new trading patterns and different ways of living, especially for those who had migrated to Britain's grow-ing towns and cities where new jobs were to be found. Economists had tracked these changes and developed new theories to explain what was going on. Sometimes, they modified old ideas to suit the new context; on other occasions they made significant departures, as when John Stu-art Mill distinguished between laws of production and distribution, suggesting society had much more choice about where wealth ended up than many classical economists liked to admit.

One phenomenon that signalled an important shift in modern economies was the increasingly prevalent practice of buying things for pleasure and status value rather than simply need, a habit that had grown along with the middle class during the nineteenth century. Department stores like Le Bon Marché in Paris, Macy's in New York and Harrods in London had been created to serve a growing and affluent group of customers who were looking for ways to express their identity. Stocked with luxury goods and mass-produced items churned out by mechanized factories at home and abroad, these stores turned shopping into an experience, spreading ideas about fashion in clothes and home furnishings.

Economists such as the Liverpudlian W. S. Jevons (1835–82) looked for new tools to explain these phenomena. Drawing heavily on math-ematics and the rapidly developing science of psychology, Jevons reconnected with the utilitarian philosopher and political theorist Jeremy Bentham's pleasure/pain formula, according to which humans decide their course of action by calculating the sum total of happiness that is likely to accrue. Jevons argued that the value of things was decided mostly by the people who consumed them, not – as economists from Smith to Marx had believed – by the labour that went into making them. Moreover, he thought consumption was not a static phenomenon but a dynamic one, governed by rules like 'marginal utility', whereby people attach the most value to their first experience of something. In turn, Jevons argued, demand was not limitless, nor was it constrained simply by the money available to buy an item, but subject instead to constant and sometimes tiny shifts thanks to psychological and sometimes non-rational factors. Jevons thought this insight was the basis for a new kind of economics, more like physics than politics, and that it would revolutionize people's understanding of how markets operated. His work was a starting point for what came to be called 'neoclassical' economics, so called because it revised traditional assumptions about how producers and consumers behave in market settings.

These developments helped produce a new strand of research called the 'English school of welfare economics' – a name coined in 1919 by the American Walton Hamilton. Welfare economics was associated with a loosely connected but influential group of thinkers, including Beveridge, who were interested in the question of how market economies might be made to function better and, in the process, meet a range of needs that were not always considered strictly economic. Looking around, they thought they could see good reasons to be confident about this project. Even taking into account the downturns after the 1870s, capitalism was producing more goods and wealth than any economic system had in history. Surely there was a way of organizing things that kept free-market enthusiasts happy but that also gave most people a fair chance of enjoying the fruits of that growth?

Posing this question within the framework of political liberalism was not new. Back in 1848 John Stuart Mill had written about his hopes for an 'advanced Liberalism' in his *Principles of Political Economy*, and suggested that individuals acting out of self-interest might not always produce widely beneficial results for the whole of society. Social surveyors such as Booth and Rowntree had also shown that poverty was much more complex than had once been understood, with people being pulled down into poverty and pushed back up again by forces beyond their control. Moreover, the likes of Leonard Hobhouse and J. A. Hobson had tried to develop a programme that paid as much attention to economic opportunity as it did political freedom. Conceptually speaking, though, welfare economics owed most to utilitarianism, in particular Bentham's dream of evaluating and reforming government institutions according to their efficiency and contribution to the overall happiness of individuals and society. Welfare economists wanted to create a system that kept market structures and the incentives provided by competition, but that was not blind to the way wealth, happiness and the goods that were necessary to satisfy basic needs were distributed across society.

The name most closely associated with welfare economics was Arthur Cecil Pigou (1877–1959). A pacifist who volunteered for the Friends' Ambulance Unit during the First World War, Pigou was a serious and deeply moral thinker, not to mention a favourite of his former teacher, Alfred Marshall, often called the first professional economist, whom Pigou succeeded in 1908 as Professor of Political Economy at Cambridge. Pigou's main interests were connected with the topic of market failure. According to economic theory, markets should allocate things efficiently, as long as they are not interfered with. In Pigou's view, however, there were lots of cases in which markets seemed to be neither behaving as economists thought they should do, nor achieving broader goals – namely, greater wealth and prosperity for everyone.

As he explained in books like *Wealth and Welfare* (1912) and *The Economics of Welfare* (1920), Pigou thought markets could fail for lots of reasons. Modern industrial society required investment in all kinds of areas, from infrastructure such as roads to new equipment for factories to scientific research that produced ideas and technologies on which future innovation might be based. But the people who could afford to pay for those things could not be relied on to do so, often because returns on their investments would not come for years, even decades. For their part, consumers could also frequently disregard the long-term costs of their actions. Some were short-sighted, paying most attention to satisfying their immediate wants and desires; others had no option but to make choices with bad long-term prospects, frequently because they had limited means and could only buy the cheapest of the options that were available to them. The problem, Pigou argued, was that society, rather than the individuals in question, ended up shouldering the costs, especially when it came to something like health. A lifetime of over-indulgence or poor nutrition, for instance, could result in needs that people were incapable of meeting on their own, leaving others – compassionate and caring as they should be – to step in to help.

Pigou believed that market failures of these kinds were much more common than economists and politicians liked to assume. He examined different tools that governments might use to correct them and, in so doing, ensure markets produced social welfare as well as wealth. The basis for his deliberations was the 'national dividend', a concept he borrowed from Alfred Marshall, his old mentor at Cambridge. Pigou defined the national dividend as the product of everything a country had inherited throughout history, combined with the efforts of its current citizens – the 'fruit of the activities of the people working in conjunction with the accumulated results of past activities and with the materials and forces provided by nature'. His main claim was that economic welfare would increase for everyone if the national dividend was as large as it could be, allowed to grow constantly rather than subject to frequent contractions, and distributed fairly, with the poorer members of society getting as big a share of it as possible.

Social reformers envisaged all kinds of ways to achieve these goals, some of which were more realistic than others. The Fabians, of course, proposed a 'national minimum': redistributing wealth so that nobody was allowed to fall below a certain threshold, whether it was in wages, education or health. Pigou, however, believed taxation was the best means of making progress. He thought there should be levies on activities that could be shown to have an adverse impact on social welfare, such as alcohol consumption, which was bad for people's health and, according to some, their morals too. Conversely, he believed governments should offer incentives, including tax breaks, for investments that might deliver wider benefits, such as paying for medical research or a new stretch of railway track.

As critics pointed out, there were problems with Pigou's approach.

Most obviously, it was difficult to measure or even define welfare. Lionel Robbins (1898–1984), an economist based at the London School of Economics who would later become widely known for the 1963 report on higher education that led to the expansion of the British university system, argued it was impossible to calculate the sum of different people's judgements, and that Pigou's work was a well-meaning but flawed enterprise. Other welfare economists believed these difficulties could be overcome if different methods were used. The Italian economist and sociologist Vilfredo Pareto suggested that governments should intervene in markets if they could make one or more people better off without making anyone else worse off. Yet Pareto's proposals were just as slippery as Pigou's. After all, his critics argued, is there an intervention that does not cost someone something?

SAMPLING WELFARE

During the interwar years, the idea that it was possible to use quantitative methods to identify where governments might intervene and then evaluate their impact on social welfare spread across the social sciences. In 1936 Seebohm Rowntree repeated his survey of York, thirty-nine years after he started the work that led to *Poverty: A Study of Town Life*, eventually publishing the results in 1941. His aim was to 'help those interested in social well-being to measure the degree in which a typical provincial city has benefitted from the efforts put forth during this century to improve social conditions', such as pensions and social insurance, not to mention the scattered services and helping hands some people had access to via schools and health centres. As they had in 1897, Rowntree and his vast team of assistants knocked on doors throughout York, this time visiting more than 16,000 families to ask them about their incomes, expenditures and lifestyles.

In his new survey, which formed the basis of a book he was writing about incomes and family health, his 1937 revision of *The Human Needs of Labour* (originally published in 1918), Rowntree had to confront some of the problems with the methods he had used first time round. Specifically, he reflected on how, back then, he had categorized around 18 per cent of York as living in 'secondary poverty', a condition caused by spending on unnecessary items; now, he concluded that the categorization fell far short of the scientific exactness to which he aspired. Back in 1897–8 he had, for instance, instructed his interviewers to ask neighbours if people were heavy drinkers, which meant all kinds of value judgements and unverifiable pieces of information being included in the classification process. He also realized that if he was to try to do the same again, he and his investigators might fall into a trap. What counted as 'obvious want and squalor' changed over time, not least because rising standards of living meant goods once available to the relatively well off became cheaper and more widely available. It would be easy to judge some people as not showing signs of poverty because they had things that were not commonplace in the late 1890s, when, by 1936 standards, they were not well off at all.

Focusing on what he had called 'primary poverty', people and families with an income inadequate for the most basic needs, including a meagre diet and fuel, Rowntree updated his original estimate of the amount of money needed to get by to 43s 6d a week for a man, woman and three children. Insisting that, once again, he had taken a hard line in order to identify the number of people who genuinely found it difficult to get by, he reported that primary poverty was down from 15.46 per cent in 1899 to 6.8 per cent. While things had undoubtedly got better for many, Rowntree did not think there was all that much to celebrate. It was genuinely difficult to compare information from his two surveys, beyond estimates of those who had enough money to buy a meagre list of essential items. In fact, he believed that a broader definition of poverty, one that included people who lived precariously above the poverty line and incorporated the poverty cycle he had identified back in 1899 (which described how events like the birth of a child or illness of a relative suddenly made an income inadequate), meant there was actually a much bigger problem in 1936 than there had been before. Indeed, he suggested that if the category of secondary poverty was used, anything up to 42 per cent of people could be counted as living in poverty in 1930s' York.

There was also an effort to bring Charles Booth's work up to date. A new survey of London, which started in 1928 and took four years to complete, was directed by Beveridge's former boss at the Board of Trade, Hubert Llewellyn Smith, who had worked on Booth's original project during the late 1880s. In addition to collecting and collating publicly available data about the capital, this new project included a household survey led by the statistician Arthur Bowley (1869–1957), whom Sidney Webb had plucked from his schoolteacher's job when the London School of Economics opened its doors in 1895. Bowley devised a new poverty line, tied to what Rowntree had called 'primary poverty', which he set at forty shillings per week for a family. He then sent more than 180 investigators to 38 of London's boroughs to conduct face-to-face interviews with people who were asked all kinds of questions about their daily lives, from the amount of money they earned and the number of hours they worked every week to how much of their income they spent on rent.

Unlike the famous surveyors of half a century earlier, however, Bowley did not believe it was necessary to examine and count everybody in order to reach reliable conclusions. He thought that social researchers simply needed to look at a large enough sample of the people or things they were interested in, as he had done in a series of four small surveys in places that included Reading, Warrington and Bolton. A randomly selected sample of a suitable size – 10 per cent in the case of Bolton – delivered almost exactly the same results, statistically speaking, as a comprehensive survey but was much faster and, crucially, cost rather less money. The result, published in nine volumes between 1930 and 1935 as the *New Survey of London Life and Labour*, was information about more than 30,000 households' incomes and outgoings, which was used to create new versions of Booth's famous colour-coded maps.

Yet this survey was just the tip of the iceberg when it came to developments in social research during the interwar years at the London School of Economics, where Beveridge had been installed as director by Sidney Webb. Using the administrative skills he had picked up at the Board of Trade and then at the ministries of food and munitions during the war, Beveridge proved adept at securing grants from the Rockefeller Foundation, the American philanthropic organization created during the first decade of the twentieth century as a means for the oil baron John D. Rockefeller to dispense with some of his vast fortune in a tax-efficient way. The $500,000 Beveridge secured for the School between 1923 and 1937 helped it to hire all kinds of social scientists, from the liberal economist Friedrich Hayek, who joined the School from Vienna in 1931, to Beveridge's brother-in-law R. H. Tawney, who became the leading economic historian of his generation and a hugely influential critic of what he called the 'acquisitive society'. Lionel Robbins, who had been an undergraduate at the School and then Beveridge's research assistant during the late 1920s, when he was putting together a second edition of *Unemployment: A Problem of Industry*, also rose through the ranks, becoming Professor of Economics when aged just thirty-one.

Following up on his youthful passion for the natural sciences, Beveridge also used some of the Rockefeller funds to establish a department of social biology, which was headed by Lancelot Hogben, a leading geneticist and renowned socialist who was building a reputation as one of his generation's most prolific and accessible science communicators, later writing very popular books, including *Mathematics for the Million* (1936) and *Science for the Citizen* (1938). Hogben and his colleagues aimed to build a new and modernizing science that brought statistics to bear on questions that had worried social reformers since the turn of the century, especially those connected with concerns about population trends and degeneration. Some of their most important work was built on a programme of mass intelligence testing in private and state-funded schools across the Greater London area. The researchers' aim was to ascertain whether privately educated schoolchildren, who monopolized university places and prestigious jobs, were actually more intelligent than their state-school counterparts. Based on test results from more than 10,000 children aged between nine and twelve, they concluded that 80 per cent of the children who met the criteria for high intelligence were among the group whose parents did not pay for their education. A huge amount of talent was being allowed to fall by the wayside, these researchers argued, because the state stopped spending money on educating children at the age of fourteen.

The appetite for social science and its capacity for shining a light on social problems was not confined to universities during the middle decades of the twentieth century. This enthusiasm was particularly prevalent among the liberal and left-leaning members of the upper-working and lower-middle classes, who, following in the footsteps of the national efficiency movement, saw subjects like economics and sociology as an alternative to traditional literary culture, which was dominated by a social and cultural elite who perpetuated their values through the public schools and Oxbridge universities. Social science was closely connected to social reform and looked like a vehicle for rationality, modernization and progress, rather than misty-eyed nostalgia about the past. Not only did it offer the opportunity to think about changing society for the better, it also provided a chance for self-discovery and improvement for those who participated in it, largely because it took seriously the effort to understand social and cultural experiences that were otherwise marginalized or hidden from view.

The most famous of these social science projects was Mass-Observation – an independent social research organization that was created in 1937 by the poet and journalist Charles Madge and the anthropologist Tom Harrisson, with help from the filmmaker Humphrey Jennings. Madge, Harrisson and Jennings called on volunteers up and down the country to help them construct an 'anthropology of everyday life'. At its early height, in 1938, Mass-Observation could claim to have almost a thousand volunteers, most of whom had been recruited through adverts in the *New Statesman*, the magazine founded by the Fabian Society. In reality – and still impressively – the organization had around a hundred active contributors spread throughout England and Wales, while it had offices in Bolton and London, where its early studies were focused. Volunteers were asked to keep diaries in which they recorded their thoughts and feelings on specific issues and topical questions, noting down what went on around them in their local communities – from the films their friends and relatives liked to watch to the frequency with which they liked to gamble. The aim was to build up a repository of information on working-class life, which was studied as a culture in its own right, rather than as an inferior version of middle-class existence, and as a largely ignored engine of social improvement. Supplemented with surveys and questionnaires, Mass-Observation used their volunteers' correspondence as the basis for reports on state-of-the-nation issues, from people's savings habits to the place of the public house in community life to (later on) the impact of rationing during the Second World War.

Opinion polling also commenced as a serious practice during the mid-1930s. Although it became commonplace during the late twentieth century, the idea that public opinion was important and could be measured using scientific techniques, rather than inferred by great minds that had a unique connection to the British public, was revolutionary prior to the Second World War. Indeed, for people like Henry Durant (1902–82), who founded the British Institute of Public Opinion, the UK branch of the American firm Gallup, in the same year that Mass-Observation was created, opinion polling was a kind of direct democracy. Durant believed it was possible to establish what the British people really thought about key issues in between general elections if the sample surveying techniques used by Bowley in his household survey of London were applied more regularly. Pollsters could keep citizens and governments in touch at all times, Durant argued, and make sure politicians were held to account in the theatre of public opinion, rather than simply during infrequent general election campaigns. People could be turned into active and engaged citizens throughout the year, and government made better, by feeding their opinions into the decision-making process at all times.

In the years after the Second World War, these seeds would grow into a new academic discipline: social policy, which flourished in the United Kingdom, almost uniquely among European nations, and North America. The London School of Economics was at the forefront of this movement thanks to the intellectual and institutional infrastructure that was developed by Beveridge during the interwar years. While T. H. Marshall, one of Britain's most important sociologists of citizenship and social class, joined the School in 1925, his post-war successor as head of the School's Social Science Department, Richard Titmuss, an actuary from Luton who held no formal educational qualifications (but who became known as the 'high priest of the welfare state' after discovering his ability to calculate fire risks could be applied to questions about social class and life chances), published his first book, *Poverty and Population: A Factual Study of Contemporary Social Waste*, in 1938. But social policy – a field that sat at the intersection of economics, sociology, social work and politics – was not confined to the capital. The 'red brick' universities – a reference to the construction materials that made educational establishments in places such as Liverpool and Birmingham stand out from Oxbridge colleges' ancient spires – also embraced the field after the Second World War, when there was a surge in enthusiasm for thinking about how experts could help the country respond to its social needs.

During the 1930s, however, the British state was less interested in the notion of social science as a means of democratic engagement than it was in the idea that expert knowledge could fix a more immediate set of problems. Governments had consulted social scientists in the past. But they had always done so when they needed help with specific issues and at key junctures, like when Churchill had invited Beveridge to work at the Board of Trade or Royal Commissions had been appointed to investigate a particular question. Social scientists had always been just one of many groups involved in those processes and few had more than a fleeting association with the state. With economic turmoil having turned into depression, things were changing. Politicians were convinced social scientists, and economists in particular, should be brought into government on a more permanent footing.

9

In the Long Run We're All Dead

In August 1925 the economist John Maynard Keynes was back in Cambridge, a city he knew well. The son of a famous philosopher and economist, he had spent his early years there and, after boarding at Eton, had returned to study and teach at the university. Keynes, though, had always wanted something more than the just the cut and thrust of scholarly debate. Recently married to the enigmatic Russian ballet dancer Lydia Lopokova, the 42-year-old Keynes was a public intellectual and a deeply political animal, as happy discussing the gold standard with David Lloyd George at Westminster as he was avant-garde literature with Virginia Woolf at his house on Gordon Square in Bloomsbury. As *The Economic Consequences of the Peace* (1919), his best-selling critique of the economic punishment meted out to Germany at the Versailles peace conference, which Keynes had witnessed first-hand as a Treasury delegate, showed, there was a significant audience who wanted to hear what he had to say about current affairs.

That summer, Keynes was in Cambridge to talk to the Liberal Summer School, the organization that had been established as a forum for liberals to discuss how to rejuvenate their flagging party, both intellectually and institutionally. Keynes himself was a well-known liberal and understood the party's predicament: stuck between the Tories, who had secured power under Stanley Baldwin and his 'national' Conservativism, and Ramsay MacDonald's Labour Party, whom many people thought was the future for progressive politics. In pondering this situation, Keynes told his audience, he had come to some clear conclusions. He knew he was not a Tory, because the Conservative Party 'promotes neither my self-interest nor the public good'. Yet he knew he was not a Labour Party man either.

Labour certainly had some good ideas, but ultimately it was a 'class party', Keynes argued, 'and the class is not my class'. For all their faults, the Liberals were the party for him. 'I can be influenced by what seems to me to be justice and good sense,' he explained, 'but the *class* war will find me on the side of the educated *bourgeoisie*.'

Keynes was also clear, however, that his support for the Liberals was dependent on their building on the work they had started after their landslide election victory in 1906. The Liberals had to work hard to maintain their reputation as the party of free trade, he argued, but, at the same time, they had to continue to innovate when it came to protecting everyone from those policies' downsides. Britain and the world had changed since the birth of liberalism during the early nineteenth century, he explained, and it was necessary for the Liberal Party to continue to change and adapt too, making use of what supporters such as himself had to offer. 'I believe that in the future, more than ever,' Keynes told his audience in Cambridge, 'questions about the economic framework of society will be far and away the most important of political issues. I believe that the right solution will involve intellectual and scientific elements.'

William Beveridge's efforts to help the government modernize the processes through which people found work had been emblematic of earlier hopes that specific aspects of the economy might be brought under control. By the late 1920s, however, a growing number of economists, politicians and social scientists believed the state could go much further; they thought it was now possible to create an economy that delivered both prosperity and fairness, not only through the redistribution of wealth, as many nineteenth-century social reformers had imagined, but also by consciously and deliberately preventing some of the worst problems from happening in the first place. Rather than create something like national insurance and then spend time debating whether it was viable in the face of a significant economic downturn, they asked, why not try to prevent millions of people from losing their jobs in the first place? As Keynes, who did more than anyone else to explain how that could be done, put it in 1925, why not make the 'transition from economic anarchy to a regime which deliberately aims at controlling and directing economic forces in the interests of social justice and social stability'?

A NECESSARY INGREDIENT FOR THOSE
ENTRUSTED WITH POWER

Britain had all kinds of problems during the interwar years but none seemed bigger than the economy. The country had one of the world's biggest trading economies, but there was little in the way of optimism about its performance. As Britain had stumbled and dragged itself through the 1920s, with high unemployment a persistent feature of economic life and political debate, it became increasingly apparent that the economic clock was not going to turn back to the world before the war. Industries such as iron and steel and coal were in decline for a range of reasons: from employers' reluctance to modernize by investing in new technology and their workers' skills to an unwillingness or inability to make what were likely to be painful adjustments in the face of fierce competition from abroad. Government after government struggled to understand what was going on and to formulate a response.

For those who had been arguing since the turn of the century that the country needed more experts to deal with the highly complex demands of the modern world, an important part of the failure to accurately diagnose and treat these economic problems was that the state employed few economists in formal, long-term roles. In 1919 the Board of Trade in Britain had created the job of Chief Economic Adviser to the Government, to which it had appointed Hubert Llewellyn Smith, who had worked on labour exchanges with Beveridge. Yet few ministers took Llewellyn Smith's post seriously, leaving him and his successors to focus, somewhat impotently, on overseas trade rather than the domestic economy. Indeed, at this time even the Bank of England had just one full-time professional economist: Henry Clay, previously Professor of Political Economy at the University of Manchester.

This state of affairs might have been frustrating for some, but it was unsurprising given the nature of the advice most economists had issued up to this point. The state hardly needed massed ranks of experts in Whitehall to tell them to let markets do their job. Moreover, economists themselves had grown wary of becoming involved too heavily in politics. Alfred Marshall, the first British political economist to regularly call himself the more scientific-sounding 'economist', was particularly worried about the problems that might result from doing so. Despite significant experience of Royal Commissions and discreet lines of communication with the Tory Prime Minister Arthur Balfour, Marshall was generally reticent about making public interventions. He believed they eroded trust in the scientific credentials of the profession he was trying to build, largely because they had the potential to reveal that economists could not always agree among themselves beyond fundamental principles.

Marshall believed John Stuart Mill's distinction between economic science – the part of political economy that involved understanding the principles underpinning economic phenomena – and the art of government – which required moral judgements about how to respond to a particular set of circumstances – could resolve the tension between expert knowledge about the economy and open questions about what to do with it. The self-styled progressive sections of the political and intellectual classes, in particular new liberals such as J. A. Hobson and Fabians such as the Webbs, thought it was obvious that professional economists, schooled in this technocratic way of thinking, should be brought into government. As Beveridge explained in 1924 in an article for *The Nation and Athenaeum*, a liberal newspaper owned by a consortium headed by Keynes, he, like Hobson and the Webbs, believed that modern governments were faced with 'problems in the field of economic science as technical as those raised by war in the field of military or naval science'. The time had come, Beveridge argued, 'when the Government of this country should have a general intelligence division for economic problems – a staff of experts not engaged in administration and not attached to any one Department'. Britain needed what he called an 'Economic General Staff'.

These ideas seemed close to penetrating Whitehall during the general election of 1929, when the country's stubbornly high unemployment was the unavoidable battleground. The Conservative Prime Minister Stanley Baldwin, 'the man you can trust', who had been in power since late 1924, suggested a strategy of 'Safety First' – a slogan borrowed from a First World War campaign to reduce the number of road traffic accidents in London. He promised further help for industries like coal and steel, which continued to struggle against foreign competition, and funds for improving the railways and roads, on which those industries (among many others) depended. Nevertheless, the Tories argued, the best way to improve the economy would be to persist with the tax policies they had laid out during the last Parliament. These included the relief from local rates Churchill had offered to industry as part of Neville Chamberlain's local government reforms, and 'imperial preference', the practice of offering low duties on goods traded between members of the British Empire, as a way of increasing the volume of trade.

Lloyd George's Liberals approached unemployment from a different angle. Under the influence of thinkers like Keynes they argued that 'there can be no national health, no widespread prosperity, there can be no national happiness and contentment so long as more than a million of our fellow-countrymen are unable to find work and earn wages by their work'. The Liberal Party offered a massive programme of loan-financed public works, detailed in their pamphlet *We Can Conquer Unemployment*, which Seebohm Rowntree helped write and was published in 1929. It gave breakdowns of the number of jobs that would be created by different projects, such as road and bridge building – 350,000 workers – and further investment in national infrastructure, including the telephone network. Unemployment stood at what felt like an unbearable number, the Liberals argued, but their plans would see it decline to manageable levels and bring the economy under control within a year.

For their part, Ramsay MacDonald's Labour Party, turfed out of office by Lloyd George four and half years earlier, attacked the Tories in their manifesto for sitting 'supinely with folded arms . . . waiting for Providence or charity to do its work' when it came to unemployment. While restating their rejection of revolutionary socialism – which the press had accused them of wanting to force on Britain when MacDonald had been in Downing Street in 1924 – Labour's manifesto offered a heartfelt criticism of the wrongs of a system that was causing so many people so much suffering. They promised more generous benefits for the unemployed, and to stop people who had paid into the national insurance fund from being denied payments when their entitlements ran out. Like the Liberals, they also promised to invest in electrification, house building and transport infrastructure, as ways of creating jobs and modernizing the country.

When the ballots were counted on 30 May 1929, the day of the first general election at which women in Britain were able to vote on the same terms as men, the Conservatives had the most votes but Labour the most seats, with 287. MacDonald had, however, fallen short of a parliamentary majority, meaning that once again he would need support from the Liberals, who had returned just fifty-nine MPs, to form a government. On account of being the biggest party in the Commons, though, the second Labour government had a stronger mandate than the first, encouraging MacDonald to make a number of bold early moves, including the appointment of the country's first woman Cabinet member: Margaret Bondfield, a former shop assistant who had left school at fourteen and had risen through the trade union ranks, who took over as Minister of Labour. Everything seemed set for MacDonald to pick up where Lloyd George had forced him to leave off in the Parliament before last.

Yet in late October 1929, five months into this second spell in government, came the Wall Street Crash. Financial assets that had ballooned during the 1920s, with the US undergoing massive growth driven by an industrial boom, were wiped out, leading to a worldwide collapse in investment and production, and unemployment rates of 25 per cent and upwards. Thanks in part to the rough decade it had just experienced, Britain did not feel the impact as hard straight away; experts, including Keynes, suggested that the country would be able to avoid the worst of the storm. But the effects of the crash eventually bled into the economy. The Great Depression that followed saw the number of unemployed workers more than double in 18 months: 2.5 million by early 1931; 3.5 million a year later. Many of these workers – especially in areas like the North East, where heavy industry, already under pressure, took a massive hit from the collapse in global demand – had no hope of finding another job any time soon.

MacDonald's strategy for Labour had always been evolutionary. He made no promises about overthrowing capitalism, much to the eternal disappointment of those on the left of his party who criticized him for insufficient radicalism and ambition. MacDonald had aimed to improve working-class living standards through reforms to the existing system, and thought that in doing so he would show that Labour were a serious party of government that could be trusted to run things, albeit in a fairer way than the Liberals and Conservatives had managed. The question was whether MacDonald could stick to that path when some were wondering if what they were now witnessing was the end of capitalism itself.

THE EYE OF THE STORM

In the face of economic disaster, Ramsay MacDonald did not know what to do. His staunchest critics inside his party suggested his gradualist strategy had suddenly been found wanting. Britain was in the midst of what looked like a fundamental crisis of capitalism – the perfect moment for far-reaching change – and he had nothing to offer. To many outside the Labour Party, MacDonald simply looked confused, rather than the authoritative figure he had always wanted to appear. In MacDonald's defence, nobody else really knew what to do either. The whole developed world had been sucked into an economic catastrophe, meaning Britain's own problems would now be exacerbated by collapsing global trade.

Many suggested Labour should follow conventional advice and cut spending. Others proposed MacDonald should abandon the commitment to free trade that had been so important to his economic platform. The country could stimulate its industries by imposing tariffs on imports and pursuing imperial preference, as the Tories proposed. It could even come off the gold standard, just four years after Churchill had put it back on, so the Treasury was freed from its constraints, including severe restrictions on state spending, should more be thought desirable.

Although MacDonald was struggling to find a way out of what he called an 'economic blizzard', he thought he knew who might be able to help. In January 1930 he appointed a group of experts to what he called the Economic Advisory Council. Unlike the experts already employed by the state, the council would not be attached to any single government department. Instead, it was asked to consider the economic aspects of policies across government, appointing sub-committees through which it could draft in further expertise if required. The council's weekly discussions were appropriately wide-ranging. Were there enough biologists to ensure the UK could pursue advanced agricultural policies? Should Britain build a tunnel under the English Channel (an idea that had been dreamt up during the early nineteenth century but received serious attention as a potential public-works scheme during the mid-1920s)? Could the country's national insurance schemes be restructured so that money currently spent on benefits for workers who had exhausted their entitlements was spent on public works instead?

Members of the Economic Advisory Council included Sir Arthur Balfour, the head of a hugely successful Sheffield steel company, G. D. H. Cole, the leading political theorist of guild socialism, and the economic historian R. H. Tawney. Most prominent among them, however, was Keynes, who had succeeded Alfred Marshall as the leading economist at Cambridge. Keynes was an exceptional self-publicist, skilled in what he called the 'art of persuasion', who knew exactly how to make an impact on debates beyond university seminar rooms and the House of Commons. He had ridiculed the decision to put Britain back on the gold standard, writing *The Economic Consequences of Mr Churchill* (1925), the title of which deliberately echoed that of his earlier book on the Versailles peace conference and which offered a critique that was no less withering in its attack on what Keynes thought were political choices presented as economic necessities.

As a liberal who had been the inspiration for Lloyd George's proposals to tackle unemployment by borrowing to pay for public works, Keynes believed economists were selling themselves short when they insisted that economic matters would resolve themselves in the full-ness of time. As he famously put it in 1923, in *A Tract on Monetary Reform*, economics was easy and fundamentally pointless if that timeframe was used, because 'in the long run we are all dead'. He and his professional colleagues could use what they knew about the econ-omy to help their fellow citizens in the short term, rather than simply telling them 'when the storm is long past, the ocean is flat again'.

Keynes saw the Economic Advisory Council as an opportunity to funnel these ideas into government and especially into the Treasury, which was particularly resistant to the suggestion it do anything other than balance the national books. To do so, however, Keynes had to get the rest of the council to agree with his interpretation of what was happening to the world economy. As he told MacDonald, he thought there was a better chance of doing so if the discussion only involved economists, rather than a mixture of people with different interests and concerns who might be daunted by his often intimidatingly powerful command of economic theory. 'It may be that economics is not enough of a science to be able to produce useful fruits,' Keynes wrote. 'But I think it might be given a trial, and that we might assume for a moment, if only as a hypothesis, that it can be treated like any other science, and ask qualified scientists in the subject to say their say.'

Keynes was typically compelling and MacDonald allowed him to form a Committee of Economists, whose job was to provide a theoretical framework for the council's discussions. He recruited a mixture of economists at different stages of their careers, from the eminent – the welfare economist A. C. Pigou – to the more recently established, such as the London School of Economics' Lionel Robbins, and rising stars like Richard Kahn, who had started work on what he called the 'multiplier effect', the idea that money produces a rippling effect in the economy if the first recipient goes on to spend it elsewhere. Keynes circulated to his fellow council members a questionnaire about policies such as tariffs and problems in areas including employment, prices and wages, so he could gauge what everyone thought and devise a suitable strategy to persuade them of his views. He believed he stood a reasonable chance of bringing most of the committee round to his way of thinking. In particular, he thought he could get broad agreement on a strategy to stimulate the economy through 'cheap money' – low interest rates intended to encourage private investment – and public works to reduce unemployment.

Two of Keynes's chief obstacles were Pigou and Robbins. Pigou had supported going back on the gold standard at pre-war parity in 1925, and was sceptical about public works as a general rather than special measure. But he also thought the country's persistently high unemployment was linked to high wages, which he believed were sustained by economic and institutional inflexibility, including workers who stayed in depressed areas rather than move to places where more jobs were available, and employers who failed to make their businesses and industries more efficient. Although Pigou was not prepared to back proposals for tariffs, he had come to see the country's situation as serious enough to warrant temporary experiments with policies such as wage subsidies, which he thought might encourage businesses to take on extra workers. In this respect, while he did not agree with everything Keynes wanted to put in the committee's report, he did feel that he could sign off on some of it.

Robbins, however, felt much more strongly that Keynes was taking the committee in a wrong-headed and dangerous direction. Robbins believed that allegedly short-term measures, in particular tariffs to protect vulnerable but important industries, would encourage excessive borrowing and prop up bad investments, which he argued were among the most significant causes of the crash. To be sure, he agreed with Pigou that high wages were a significant barrier to recovery and future progress. But Robbins was unable to reconcile himself with any of Keynes's proposals, believing they would cause markets to seize up and stop them from sweating out the fevers that had infected them. Quite remarkably, Robbins insisted on producing a minority report, to which he was the only signatory.

Yet by early 1931, when the council came to consider both Keynes's proposals and Robbins's dissenting document, the economy had taken another turn for the worse. Unemployment was continuing to rise and the country's deficit was increasing thanks to a combination of declining tax receipts and rising spending liabilities, including benefits for those who were now without work. Conventional wisdom was that the government should do something to show it was tackling the deficit. If the government did not, the argument went, it might struggle to secure loans on reasonable terms, which it might need to do to stay on the gold standard. MacDonald wanted to support the Chancellor of the Exchequer, Philip Snowden, and his commitments to free trade and the gold standard, in part because of Labour's long-term commitment to free trade as the means of achieving higher living standards for the working class, but also because he wanted to prove the party was not out to transform the country radically and rapidly. However, free trade was now being loudly questioned, especially in influential and popular right-wing newspapers like the *Daily Mail* and *Daily Express*, in ways it had not since of the turn of the century when Joseph Chamberlain had led the campaign for 'tariff reform'.

While they deliberated over these huge questions of political and economic philosophy, MacDonald and Snowden decided to tackle one issue – government spending – in the way Lloyd George had done when he had called on the former railway manager Eric Geddes a decade earlier: by appointing a committee to investigate the government's outgoings, with the aim of restoring confidence in sterling by demonstrating that Britain had things under control. The result, delivered in a report that landed on Labour ministers' desks in June 1931, was the opposite of what the Prime Minister and Chancellor had hoped for. The seven-member committee's head, the wealthy insurance official George May, applied the kind of unforgiving reasoning to the situation that the most enthusiastic advocates of balanced budgets and sound finances might have expected. By assuming that Britain should pay its debts off at the same rate it would if it was in the midst of a boom, and pay for everything else, including unemployment insurance, out of the revenue it could raise at that moment in time, May's report put the government's deficit at £120 million. According to these figures, the country was going bankrupt fast. May prescribed savings of £96 million and specified that two-thirds of that should come from spending on unemployment benefits, with much of the rest made up by cutting the salaries of state employees, including school teachers. As Keynes told MacDonald, the proposal was blinkered: it might slash government spending right away but it would also reduce its income, not least because it would take away from those affected money they would otherwise spend, eventually depriving the Treasury of taxes.

For Labour MPs and ministers, however, there was a more specific and urgent concern. Insurance offered an unemployed man 17s a week, plus an additional 9s for dependent adults and 2s for each child – significantly less than the 43s 6d that Seebohm Rowntree estimated a family of five needed to live on the poverty line five years later. Why, Labour MPs asked, should they tell people trying to get by on such meagre sums to make do with even less? MacDonald believed he could find a way through these conflicting interests but his package of less extreme cuts satisfied neither those who thought May had issued a warning that had to be heeded nor the Labour Party and its supporters, including the trade unions, which refused to countenance any reduction in unemployment benefit. MacDonald, however, refused to back down, especially after Snowden used an even more pessimistic set of assumptions to revise May's estimate of the deficit upwards by £50 million. He could find few people in government or at institutions like the Bank of England who thought he shouldn't follow May's recommendations, or that he should adopt the kinds of alternative proposals offered by Keynes. Labour could not be held hostage by the trade unions, MacDonald argued; country had to come before party.

To everyone's surprise, MacDonald managed to secure a Cabinet majority for his revised programme of cuts. But he won by just two votes and his opponents, led by Arthur Henderson, one of Labour's first Cabinet ministers in Asquith's wartime government fifteen years earlier, refused to go along with the result. The second Labour government collapsed as a result. Believing that a general election so soon after the last one would do more harm than good to international perceptions of Britain's stability, MacDonald held a meeting at Buckingham Palace on 24 August 1931 with King George V, the Conservative leader Stanley Baldwin and the Liberal MP Herbert Samuel, who stood in for Lloyd George, who was recovering from a prostate operation. The outcome was an agreement that MacDonald should form a national government to see the country through its immediate difficulties. With a Cabinet composed of four Labour MPs, four Tories and two Liberals, this cobbled-together administration raised taxes and made the cuts May had demanded, including a 10 per cent reduction in unemployment benefits. MacDonald was expelled from the Labour Party as a traitor, along with the other Labour MPs who stuck with the national government, in late September 1931.

The national government's programme did not get off to an overwhelmingly positive start. In mid-September 1931, more than a thousand sailors at the Invergordon naval base in northern Scotland went on strike for two days when they heard that the lowest-paid among them were going to have their wages cut by 25 per cent. The Royal Navy looked like it was on the verge of mutiny, causing a run on the pound – the exact opposite of what MacDonald believed he would achieve by sticking to May's recommendations. With no tools left in its financial toolbox, the government had no choice but to come off the gold standard. All the pain and suffering MacDonald had insisted was necessary for the national interest looked like it might be for nothing.

'THE GRADUAL ENCROACHMENT OF IDEAS'

After long and often acrimonious discussions, MacDonald decided to call a general election in October 1931. He asked the electorate to give his national government a 'doctor's mandate': permission to do whatever it would take to drag the country out of the hole down which it seemed to be disappearing. Arthur Henderson and a tiny group of Independent Liberals under the sixty-eight-year-old Lloyd George, who objected to an election being called at all, were no match for MacDonald's calls for the country to unite in the national interest. The opposition returned to Westminster with fewer than a hundred MPs between them, and Labour were reduced to fewer than sixty seats. As MacDonald's critics never ceased reminding him during the three years he struggled on, his national government was not dominated by the party he had once led, but by the Tories, who won more than 470 of its 554 seats.

The 10 per cent cut to unemployment benefits that had been implemented at the height of the crisis, introduced on top of other restrictions such as exclusions for married women and seasonal workers, expired in 1934. Rather than simply extend those measures, the government tried to reform the legislation that framed them. Following in the footsteps of Neville Chamberlain's pensions legislation of the 1920s, and the Baldwinite path of marrying welfare to sound finance, the Unemployment Act of 1934 aimed to make unemployment benefits self-funding, but in a way that made the scheme look more generous and more spendthrift. The number of people who were covered actually increased, exceeding 15 million people once agricultural workers were allowed to join the scheme in 1936. Moreover, while benefit rates were restored to their former levels, entitlements were set at twenty-six weeks – a marked improvement on the fifteen weeks that workers had under the old legislation.

Predictably, there was a catch. Any apparent generosity to the short-term unemployed looked like it was offset by the government's attitude to those out of work and receiving benefits for longer than twenty-six weeks. The national government wanted to use means testing – a long-term object of hate on the left and among claimants themselves, who resented the humiliation of officials asking intrusive questions about their home lives – to assess people who had exhausted their standard entitlement. Such claimants were also to be transferred from the care of the National Insurance Statutory Committee, which covered what were considered ordinary and short-term cases, to new Unemployment Assistance Boards. The boards were asked to apply rigid and standardized benefit scales and, later in the decade, to help claimants find work, sometimes by retraining, other times by moving away from depressed areas. There was significant public dissent against what looked like a measure to stigmatize the long-term unemployed, especially when it was discovered the new benefit scales were much less generous than the ones used by the Public Assistance Committees that had handled such cases in the past. The government, concerned that it was being seen to treat vulnerable people badly, postponed the new scales' implementation by a year and made them more generous in practice than they had looked on paper.

The national government also tried to breathe life into trade and tackle the country's long-standing balance of payments problems. Their efforts were confirmation that the doubts about free trade – a policy that, almost uniquely, had managed to unite politicians, intellectuals, the media and the public for the best part of a century – that had been growing since the early 1920s had finally overwhelmed its supporters. Chamberlain, now the new Chancellor of the Exchequer, pushed for further protectionist measures. A 10 per cent tariff on unfinished and semi-manufactured imports was introduced, and before long 'Empire Free Trade', another name for imperial preference – which many politicians assumed was a guarantee of beneficial trading terms – was being pursued as a strategy for reviving the country's ailing industries. Despatched to the Imperial Economic Conference in Ottawa in 1932 to negotiate preferential tariff agreements, Chamberlain found few countries in the mood to accommodate him. He got deals that kept the cost of Britain's food imports down but he made little headway in convincing countries such as Canada, India and South Africa to offer terms that would help Britain's manufacturers and heavy industry at the expense of their own.

For critics of protectionism, Chamberlain's failure to build harmonious and mutually beneficial trading relationships out of protectionist principles was unsurprising. But while the likes of Lionel Robbins had a well-rehearsed and often resonant set of responses to tariff proposals, other ideas about interfering with the economy that were growing in popularity posed greater difficulties. With the word 'reconstruction' having fallen by the wayside by the mid-1920s, when all the momentum, not to mention money, had disappeared from the projects that had been touted after the First World War, the word 'planning' had started to appear more frequently in British political debates. Generally used to refer to a vaguely defined modernizing project to transform society and eliminate the downsides of capitalism, planning captured the imaginations of large numbers of politicians and social scientists during the 1930s.

Interest in planning was piqued by alternative economic and social models being tried elsewhere in the world. The 1917 revolution in Russia had enabled communists to experiment with a range of different tools, from central state planning to scientific management techniques, in an attempt to increase productivity and redistribute economic goods. Despite its totalitarianism, the USSR fascinated many on the British political left, who believed the Soviets had shown that it was possible to avoid the miseries of the Great Depression and create an economic system that was not only fairer but much more efficient than capitalism. Intrigued by what the Soviets claimed to have achieved, in the 1930s many went to look for themselves. The Webbs even wrote a book about what they had seen, *Soviet Communism: A New Civilisation?* (1935). They dropped the question mark two years later.

One of the earliest enthusiasts for planning on the Labour benches was the charismatic heir to a baronetcy, Oswald Mosley. A former Unionist who had stood in the 'coupon' election of 1918, when Lloyd George had fronted a Conservative-dominated coalition, Mosley had joined the Labour Party in 1924, after MacDonald had formed his first administration. A passionate believer in the idea that the organization, money and effort that had gone into the First World War could also be applied to peacetime problems, Mosley was impatient with the country's response to poverty and economic decline long before the Wall Street Crash had made the situation even more serious. Recognizing his energy and enthusiasm, MacDonald appointed him to a post outside the Cabinet – Chancellor of the Duchy of Lancaster – and asked him to prepare proposals for bringing unemployment down. Stitching together a patchwork of ideas drawn from the likes of J. A. Hobson, the new liberal economist, Mosley demanded that MacDonald and Snowden drop their commitments to free trade and sound finance and instead pursue a programme of mass public works and investment, including road building. Mosley wanted an economist like Keynes to head something like the economic general staff Beveridge had described.

Frustrated that nobody appeared willing to act on his proposals, Mosley resigned his government position and formed the New Party in March 1931, believing that the existing political parties were in thrall to vested interests that stood in the way of progress. He almost immediately began his rapid and notorious descent from impatient maverick, keen to experiment with ideas from the radical fringes of progressive politics, to poisonous pariah, forming the British Union of Fascists after visiting Benito Mussolini's Italy in 1932. Flanked by his vicious army of 'black shirts', Mosley travelled the country giving fevered and paranoid speeches about the need to fight the enemies within. By 1936, he had added anti-Semitism to his anti-communism. Famously ejected from London's East End during the battle of Cable Street, he ended up a social and political outcast, interned for most of the Second World War.

Although few others who shared Mosley's interest in planning embraced populism or fascism, most shared his belief that the British establishment was insufficiently equipped to tackle the country's problems. Political and Economic Planning – a new type of organization that would come to be called a think-tank – was founded in 1931 in response to a special supplement of the *Week-End Review*, a new periodical set up by journalists who had resigned en masse from the liberal *Saturday Review* when its board of directors instructed them to support Empire Free Trade. The journalists had numerous objections to the policy, including moral concerns about trying to solve Britain's problems by exploiting overseas territories. Overall, however, they considered Empire Free Trade to be protectionism by another name and therefore unlikely to bring back prosperity.

The supplement's lead writer was Edward Max Nicholson, a twenty-seven-year-old ornithologist who would serve as Herbert Morrison's most senior civil servant in the post-1945 Labour government, and would go on to help found the World Wildlife Fund in 1961. Nicholson believed British government was organized for a nineteenth-century world and, as such, had inevitably been found wanting during the 1930s. He desired a new national plan: one that not only met the immediate challenges facing Britain but that also seized the opportunity for the country's wholesale modernization, transforming everything from its political institutions to its business practices to its infrastructure.

PEP, as Political and Economic Planning was known for short, was supposed to be the research organization that converted Britain's elites to planning and then furnished them with all the information they needed to do their jobs. Its founding members were drawn from all walks of life. In addition to Nicholson, they included the biologist Julian Huxley, the civil servant and director of the Bank of England Sir Basil Blackett, the vice-chairman and joint managing director of Marks & Spencer Israel Sieff, and the head of the department of political economy at University College London, Noel Hall. Their work was wide ranging, touching on agriculture, industry, regional development, healthcare and schools. As the organization developed during the 1930s, special research groups and subcommittees were established and experts recruited, including the architect and town planner John Dower and the population expert Alexander Carr-Saunders, who succeeded Beveridge as director of the London School of Economics in 1937.

Like the Fabian Society, PEP was determined not to leave things to chance when it came to the making their ideas count. Rather than hope their work might be picked up by those in positions of power, PEP delivered it directly to them. Situated in headquarters in Queen Anne's Gate, a stone's throw from the Houses of Parliament, PEP produced pamphlets summarizing the outcomes of their research, known as 'broadsheets', and sent them to a 2,000-strong mailing list of politicians, businessmen, trade union leaders, academics and public intellectuals. At the start, when it was under Nicholson's influence most heavily, PEP's work was rooted in a strong central planning agenda. By the end of the 1930s, however, and in reaction to the direction people like Mosley had taken the idea, PEP had evolved into a more moderate body, taking 'planning' to be something more like forecasting and managing, with a focus on the interventions government might make in a bid to improve its use of the resources – economic, human and natural – at its disposal.

WHERE TO DRAW THE LINE?

Keynes was not a planner, but he benefitted from the growing interest in it. His main problem throughout the 1920s and early 1930s had been formulating a coherent theory that satisfied both his colleagues in economics and the politicians he was trying to influence. There was a good prima facie case for the efficacy of things like public works when it came to changing the course of economic events. Thanks in large part to the housing boom driven by the construction of semi-detached suburban houses for the middle classes – not to mention government spending on rearmament in light of the growing threat from mainland Europe – unemployment was cut from 23 per cent in 1933 to 10 per cent four years later. Yet Keynes found it hard to explain exactly what was going on in a way that satisfied other economists. He had laboured for almost seven years over *A Treatise on Money* (1930), his first book on economic theory, and was pleased with what he thought were important breakthroughs, including his argument that savings and investment were not always equal, which he thought demonstrated that an increase in the latter could drag an economy out of depression. But Keynes had struggled to make the different parts of *A Treatise on Money* hold together. Though to the uninitiated his worries about his use of contradictory assumptions about output – at some points stationary and forcing prices up and down; at others variable in response to those changes – were opaque, they mattered to both his critics and those who wanted to believe it was possible to manage the problems out of the British economy.

The General Theory of Employment, Interest and Money, published in 1936, was Keynes's resolution of these problems. A complex book, *The General Theory* was the product of five years of hard work at Cambridge with some of the rising stars of economics. At its heart, the book was about the unstable ebbs and flows of modern economies and the question of why, contrary to traditional accounts, markets had yet to resolve their deep-lying problems. Keynes offered theories about each aspect of economic activity, including spending and employment, but he also had explanations of how they related to each other which painted a picture of how economies were products of subtle psychological states. Richard Kahn's multiplier effect, first discussed by the Committee of Economists, linked investment and demand. An employed worker would spend his earnings on goods and services that would need to be supplied by other workers, who in turn would require goods and services themselves. Keynes's theory of 'liquidity preference' – the idea people will hold on to their money rather than spend or invest it when times are uncertain – explained why demand was linked to interest rates. 'Effective demand', the aggregate of demand throughout the whole economy, was at the intersection of all these things. A thriving economy required people to want and be able to purchase goods and services. Governments simply had to throw out the rulebook about balanced budgets and sound finance; they even had to run short-term (and occasionally huge) deficits if it meant growth further down the line.

Although Keynes did not think he had overturned the ideas of every previous school of economic thought, he knew, after almost twenty years in the public eye, that capturing people's attention would be much easier if he made bold claims about his work. It was no use saying other economists were sometimes right but only in a specific set of circumstances. Keynes told his readers that his book had smashed a tradition that had dominated 'the economic thought, both practical and theoretical, of the governing and academic classes of this generation' and for the previous century. He knew a book like this would demand to be read, and insisted his publisher sell it at the bestseller price of five shillings – around a third of what people would have expected to pay for a heavy-going academic treatise.

Economists were fascinated by *The General Theory*. The book contained no simple formula or policy prescription, and there were aspects of economic activity, including the international dimension to trade, that received much less attention than they expected. As such, it presented economists with a challenge: Keynes seemed to be saying something important but they needed to understand what it was before they could make up their minds about whether he was right or wrong. The root of their difficulties with *The General Theory* was the level of analysis Keynes offered. Economists usually discussed transactions between individuals and businesses, assuming that the sum total of those interactions took care of themselves, most obviously when markets adjusted to changes in circumstances by raising or lowering the prices of goods or forcing unprofitable companies to close. Keynes, however, took individuals and businesses for granted. Instead, he focused on their aggregates, giving an account of how each category of economic actors or phenomena, from governments and consumers to demand and interest rates, behaved in general. As such, he painted a picture of a field that would soon become known as 'macroeconomics'.

An early product of economists' efforts to understand *The General Theory* was one of its most important: the 'IS-LM model' of the relationship between investment, savings, liquidity preference and money. It was developed in 1937 by the Cambridge-based economist John Hicks, who wanted a simple way to represent the aggregate relationships Keynes wrote about. The IS-LM model was a diagram with GDP, the sum total of a country's goods and services, on one axis, interest rates on the other, and two curves, the intersection of which represented equilibrium. The sloping curves, which Hicks moved around to explore how changes in one part of the economy impacted on others, were an early example of a new mindset Keynes helped encourage. Economists, particularly younger members of the profession, wondered whether the IS-LM model could ever be more than a representation. Maybe the economy could be manipulated in the same way Hicks did when he moved curves up and down on his diagrams? Few progressive economists in Britain thought that central planning, with production targets for industries set by the state, could work. But this more moderate sense of the economy as something that could be managed seemed well within the grasp of modern governments.

Keynes's name and ideas became fixtures in public culture both at home and abroad, especially in the USA, where the *New York Times* published his open letters to President Roosevelt, urging him to be even bolder in his plans for public works and investment as part of his 'New Deal' for the American people. Yet not everyone was so enamoured with Keynes's ideas, or believed there was a benign version of planning that could be derived from them. After a four lecture audition-cum-interview, in which he had explained his belief that efforts to stimulate economies artificially were doomed to failure, the Austrian economist Friedrich Hayek had been awarded a permanent chair at the London School of Economics as a professor of economics in 1932. A tall, serious-looking man with thin-rimmed circular glasses, Hayek was deeply worried about the state of Britain. In his view, nineteenth-century Britain had shown the world how to liberate people from political tyranny, throwing off the laws that protected the aristocracy at everyone else's expense, as Parliament had done when it repealed the protectionist Corn Laws in 1846. But he was worried the country was now losing its nerve. Having witnessed hyperinflation in post-war Austria, he thought Keynes was mad to think cheap money would bring anything but pain, as people stopped saving and borrowed and spent instead.

Hayek's bigger concern about Keynes, however, was a belief that the enthusiasm for intervening in the economy that his work helped encourage would infect people's minds with ideas more dangerous than the consequences of hyperinflation. Thanks to his mentor, the Austrian economist Ludwig von Mises, Hayek had a deep aversion to anything that sounded like planning. Governments could not do without markets, Mises and Hayek argued, because they were the most accurate and efficient way of telling what people wanted. Little would have to go wrong in a state-run economy for things people needed to be in short supply while things they did not need piled up.

More importantly, though, Hayek believed that attempts to influence economic outcomes constituted infringements of basic freedoms and, as such, were anathema in Britain, the pioneer of the liberal tradition. Economic planning required governments to interfere with anything and everything that went into the production of goods – from workers' wages to the price consumers paid to companies' profit levels. Once an authority started making decisions of that kind, it was imposing all manner of restrictions on individuals. While the jobs people could do would be dictated by the goods the state deemed necessary, the things they could spend their pre-determined earnings on would be limited for the same reasons. Many enthusiasts for planning, of course, suggested any erosion of freedom was a trade-off people were willing to make because they obtained higher goods like social welfare, which they could not generate on their own. But, like other critics of welfare economics, and as he would later explain more fully in *The Road to Serfdom* (1944), Hayek thought this argument was misleading. After all, who actually had a definition of social welfare that everyone could agree on?

Despite their disagreements over these issues, Hayek and Keynes were friends who debated their differences on economic and political matters both in print and behind closed doors. In fact, while Hayek wrote approvingly of Keynes's pamphlet *How to Pay for the War* (1940), which featured a compulsory savings scheme that was meant to help keep inflation under control, and accepted there were special circumstances in which the state would have to interfere with markets, Keynes declared himself to be in 'deeply moved agreement' with *The Road to Serfdom* and accepted that there were legitimate worries about governments infringing the rights of individuals via economic policy. Keynes, however, concluded that the real issue dividing them was not whether a line should be drawn between citizen and state, but the question of when and where to draw it. He was far from the only person to reach this judgement. Indeed, when war began in September 1939, another of Hayek's old adversaries, William Beveridge, started a journey that would show how much beliefs about the best way to secure freedom and prosperity for the British people had changed since the world of nineteenth-century liberalism Hayek revered.

10

Half-way to Moscow

'It's extraordinary the interest people are taking in it,' remarked one thirty-five-year-old Londoner on 2 December 1942. 'When I went down to the Stationery Office to get it, there were queues of people buying it; and I was looking at it on the 'bus, and the conductor said "I suppose you haven't got a spare copy of that?" ' The book everyone was after was Beveridge's *Social Insurance and Allied Services*. Interest around the 172-page report, backed with almost 130 further pages of graphs and tables detailing average life expectancy and administrative costs, among many other things, had been building for months. Beveridge had not told anyone exactly what was in it. But the economist and social reformer was by now a well-known public figure, thanks in part to his appearances on the BBC's hugely popular Sunday afternoon radio show, *The Brains Trust*, which featured a panel of experts answering audience questions. He had been dropping hints about his forthcoming publication for months, raising the public's expectations about what he was going to recommend. The government had played its part in piquing interest in Beveridge's work too: without saying why, it had kept the report back for almost a month.

Why did Beveridge have Churchill's wartime coalition government so worried? As readers who laid eyes on *Social Insurance and Allied Services* found out, the answer was complicated. Beveridge had dug deep into more than thirty years of state-backed social insurance history, from the ground-breaking old-age pension and national insurance schemes established by the Liberals before the First World War to Neville Chamberlain's pension reforms of the 1920s to the national government's efforts to change unemployment benefits during the previous decade. In so doing, he had made a series of strong recommendations aimed at simplifying the patchwork of schemes covering sickness, unemployment and old age and, above all, making them fairer. Yet, mindful of the moment into which his report was being published, Beveridge had spiced his discussion of arcane details of government administration with some stirring rhetoric. War with Germany and Japan had raised the stakes. It was time, he argued, for the country to pay people back for their sacrifices, and in a way that made up for the 'homes fit for heroes' that had failed to materialize after the First World War, twenty years earlier. Beveridge, indeed, had a vision: of a new Britain that would conquer 'five giant evils on the road to reconstruction' – squalor, ignorance, want, idleness and disease.

As *The Times* – a newspaper hardly renowned for its endorsement of far-reaching social change – put it, Beveridge's plan was 'a plainly realizable project of national endeavour ... comprehensive in its sweep without losing grip on the economic and administrative realities'. More importantly, it involved 'no new departure in principle from the policies and methods which have characterized the development of the British social services during the last half century'. Such familiarity and continuity did not mean Beveridge had nothing new to say, though. The government had wanted administrative patches, and sober extensions of the state's responsibilities. Beveridge, however, had delivered much more. His proposed social security system would only work, he explained, if society and the economy did too. His report told the country that the state could and should be more than a fire-fighter taking responsibility for putting out the worst blazes when they had already started; it should prevent them from being lit in the first place.

'I DIDN'T FEEL WELFARE WAS UP MY STREET'

When, in 1937, Beveridge left the London School of Economics after eighteen years as its director, he was exhausted. A well-connected man, he had a number of job offers, including one from a new think-tank, the National Institute of Economic and Social Research, which needed a director. After some deliberation, however, he decided to head back to Oxford, where he had been an undergraduate four decades earlier, to take over as Master of University College.

Returning to his alma mater involved sacrifices. He had to take a significant pay cut and move away from the busy capital, where he felt close to the political action. Oxford had its perks, though, such as a free college house with fifteen living rooms, and far fewer responsibilities than his old job. Moreover, Oxford had branched out in directions of which he approved. The university now had an honours degree in Philosophy, Politics and Economics and a new Institute of Statistics; it had also accepted a benefaction from Viscount Nuffield, who had made his fortune from the Morris Motor Company, which was being used to create a specialist social science college. Beveridge was able to immerse himself in research once again, including into one of his long-standing obsessions: a study of the history of prices and wages since the twelfth century. He also returned to the problem of unemployment. He wanted to reconnect with his days of gathering statistics from labour exchanges and government departments, and finally discover what caused the trade cycle's peaks and troughs. At almost sixty, however, he delegated the task of slogging up and down the country to a research assistant, a recent graduate in the new Politics, Philosophy and Economics degree named Harold Wilson.

Beveridge and Wilson had written several chapters of a book on their research by the time Britain went to war with Germany in September 1939. Even though he was now in his early sixties, Beveridge expected the government to invite him to join what everyone expected to be a massive administrative and planning operation in London; he even wrote to ministers offering his services. Yet he was ignored as Britain failed to make a rapid transition into a full-blown war economy. Following the failure of his policy of appeasement towards Hitler during the late 1930s, Prime Minister Neville Chamberlain endured a difficult opening to the conflict, despite not having to commit British forces to any meaningful battles for seven months, the period known as the 'phoney war'. Continuing to believe, forlornly, that military might and organization would not be the main factor in defeating Germany, Chamberlain struggled to convince Parliament and the public that he had a strategy to win the war. Contrary to custom and expectations, the leaders of the opposition Labour and Liberal parties declined to form a wartime coalition with the national government.

Beveridge was therefore not alone among academics, experts and administrators in finding himself deemed unnecessary in Whitehall during the early stages of the war. He joined a group including the former editor of *The Economist*, Walter Layton, and Arthur Salter, who had sat on Ramsay MacDonald's Economic Advisory Council during the early 1930s, who met regularly at Keynes's house in Bloomsbury to chew over the government's decisions. Beveridge did not hold back from making the thoughts he aired in those meetings more widely known. As he outlined in *The Times*, a month after the outbreak of war, he had a vision of a 'war without waste', run by an 'economic general staff' and a small War Cabinet of the kind David Lloyd George had used twenty years earlier, and thought it essential that Chamberlain embrace the idea immediately.

However, when Britain's first significant military foray – an effort to push the Nazis back in Norway – went wrong in April 1940, starting a chain of events that saw the resignation of Chamberlain and his replacement by Churchill in May, it became clear there were other reasons Beveridge found himself out in the cold. Other members of the group who met in Bloomsbury were invited to take up government jobs, most notably Keynes, who landed the most prestigious position as consultant to the Chancellor of the Exchequer. Beveridge thought his relationship with Churchill, who back in 1908 had plucked him from relative obscurity to help build the Liberal Party's unemployment insurance programme, meant he would be called up too. Two months later, however, he was still waiting.

Beveridge's record in the Ministries of munitions and food during the First World War, when he had been one of the most prominent figures calling for the government to do anything it thought necessary to beat Germany, was one reason he was deemed surplus to requirements. Back then, he had earned a particularly bad reputation among trade unionists by helping to turn temporary and voluntary agreements about working conditions into law – law that the unions had believed was a land grab, using the excuse of war to permanently undermine collective-bargaining arrangements and wage rates.

Churchill decided something other than Beveridge's continuing calls to suspend any and all terms and conditions was required. Ernest Bevin, the General Secretary of the Transport and General Workers' Union, stood unopposed in a by-election for the south London seat of Wandsworth Central shortly after accepting an invitation to sit in the cabinet as the new Minister of Labour. The aim was to keep workers, who were already annoyed that war had meant a premature end to a Royal Commission on workmen's compensation, happy by having their interests represented at the heart of government as Churchill accelerated the pace of economic and organizational change.

In June 1940 Bevin asked Beveridge to accept a commission that involved developing a new department of welfare, which Bevin thought should be related to the existing process of factory inspections. Beveridge, however, was unenthusiastic. He 'didn't feel that welfare was up my street' and turned Bevin down. Instantly regretting the decision to be so picky about what he would and would not do, Beveridge did not make the same mistake when Bevin approached him again the following month, with a request to carry out a small manpower investigation. Beveridge knew that the study was relatively unimportant in the context of both the government's manpower operation and the war economy as a whole. But, having spent ten months on the outside looking in, he was grateful to be involved in government work at all.

Beveridge returned to London, living in and working out of the basement of the palatial Pall Mall headquarters of the Reform Club, before relocating to a house on Richmond Terrace, not far from Downing Street and next door to the Labour leader, Clement Attlee. Before long, however, Beveridge was antagonizing people again, not least because he continued to make it known in public where he thought the government was going wrong. Ministers decided they had had enough of him and that they wanted him out of sight. They believed a highly technical and potentially dreary new committee that they thought was unlikely to trouble newspaper headline writers, the Inter-Departmental Committee on Social Insurance and Allied Services, would be the perfect place for him. Bevin broke the news in early June 1941. Beveridge was, he recalled, 'frankly a little sad at what I was asked to do'; others reported they saw tears in his eyes.

Welfare issues were on the government's agenda for a number of reasons. From the moment war had started, the Labour Party had been calling for the government to put resources into thinking about post-war reconstruction, arguing that the British people could not be let down by poor planning as they had been after 1918. There had been some additional spending on pensions, offset by increased contributions, in 1940, when five shillings a week was added to the benefit (albeit after a means test), and the age at which women married to insured men could claim a pension was lowered to sixty. But war had required much more significant interventions elsewhere. Accepting that civilians could not be left to take care of their own healthcare in the face of probable aerial bombing, the government created the Emergency Medical Service by linking together around two-thirds of the country's hospitals, including local authority and voluntary institutions. These facilities shared resources, including staff, and transferred patients according to their needs, as part of a plan to provide civilian and military patients with treatment in the case of severe and sustained attacks.

The Emergency Medical Service was not without its problems. Some hospitals, paid by the government to keep beds available for emergencies, struggled to maintain enough space for people who needed long-term care. Yet the service had a number of transformative effects. Since running the service involved stocktaking, this gave the government an unparalleled comprehensive picture of country-wide provision. Hospitals suddenly found themselves with freshly kitted out operating theatres, the opportunity to call on specialists who had previously been found only in private practice or at elite teaching hospitals, such as plastic surgeons, and access to the UK's first national blood transfusion service. As a state of total war and aerial bombing made the line between civilian and war wounded blurry, the list of groups eligible to use the service expanded from a narrow group of service personnel to most people engaged in war work, vulnerable civilians such as children and pensioners, and anyone who had a fracture, dislocation or sprain. Indeed, by 1945, more than 30,000 people a day were making use of rehabilitation schemes for those left disabled in some way by their injuries. Although these numbers were a relatively small fraction of the population, the public knew there was an unprecedentedly wide range of circumstances under which they could access free hospital care.

Beveridge, however, had not been asked to do anything as seemingly exciting or ground-breaking as co-ordinate the Emergency Medical Service. His uninspiring mission statement, handed to him by Arthur Greenwood, the deputy Labour leader, who had been put in charge of reconstruction policy, was 'to undertake, with special reference to the inter-relation of the schemes, a survey of the existing national schemes of social insurance and allied services, including workmen's compensation, and to make recommendations'. Moreover, his fellow committee members hardly suggested the government expected anything radical to come back to them. Greenwood had assigned civil servants from the seven government departments involved in administering Britain's social insurance schemes. Beveridge's fellow members included Mary Agnes Hamilton, a former Labour MP and, like Beveridge, a contributor to *The Brains Trust*; Sir George Epps, the government actuary, who was invited to test assumptions about insurance risks and their costs; and Daniel Chester, an expert on public utilities from Manchester University who had been drafted into the economic section of the War Office in 1940.

Suitably uninspired, Beveridge gave the committee little attention for most of the rest of 1941, choosing to carry on work on other projects, including on manpower and, later, a fuel-rationing scheme – a points-based system that would have involved issuing coupons to households throughout the country – that the government thought was ingenious but ultimately unworkable. By November, however, Beveridge decided he had no choice but to get more involved with the committee. He did so at the moment when it was entering the stage of hearings and interviews with expert witnesses. Contributors included veterans of the previous half-century of debates about social reform, such as the social surveyor and businessman Seebohm Rowntree, and the MP and family allowances campaigner Eleanor Rathbone, as well representatives from bodies such as Political and Economic Planning, the British Medical Association, the Fabian Society, the Trades Union Congress, and the Association of Approved Societies. Discussions ranged over issues large and small, including what counted as an insurable risk; the problems faced by men injured at work; the definition of a healthy diet; and the question of whether social insurance was a field that needed to be managed by a single government agency.

That November, with scant regard for the work his colleagues had done up until that point, Beveridge imposed himself on proceedings. His favourite ideas and policies got plenty of exposure; those he did not like were often dismissed quickly or passed over entirely. He started issuing memoranda outlining his thoughts on existing government services and what he believed should be the committee's next steps. In so doing, he made it clear he was interpreting Greenwood's instructions in the broadest possible terms. Technical and administrative solutions were important – but only once fundamental assumptions and first principles had been considered. Nothing, Beveridge argued, should be off-limits. The committee was going to have to think big: to propose drastic changes to the way government ran social insurance.

As far as the rest of the committee was concerned, Beveridge's about-turn was a major headache. The civil servants were in a particularly difficult position. Aside from the danger of intruding into political territory that would put their administrative neutrality at risk, a report of the kind Beveridge was interested in producing had the potential to commit departments and ministers to far-reaching changes – should the civil servants sign them off. No department was more concerned than the Treasury, whose representative, Edward Hale, told his colleagues that massive increases in public spending were on the horizon should the most radical ideas on the table make it into the final report.

The Cabinet was worried that the committee was getting out of hand. Shutting it down was impossible; it would only antagonize the trade unions, among others. But that left a limited number of possible solutions. The Treasury suggested adding extra members to the committee as a way of diluting Beveridge's influence. Greenwood, though, decided on a different course of action. Writing to Beveridge in January 1942, he told him that 'the departmental representatives should henceforth be regarded as your advisors and assessors on various technical and administrative matters with which they are severally concerned'. The final report would be Beveridge's: 'it will be signed by you alone,' Greenwood told him, 'and the departmental representatives will not be associated in any way with the views and recommendations on questions of policy which it contains'. Everyone but Beveridge had been absolved from responsibility for the report's contents.

Despite – though perhaps as much because of – being given this freedom over the committee, Beveridge continued to rage at the government. In March, he told readers of *The Times* and *News Chronicle* that the government was insufficiently serious about post-war reconstruction, failing to recognize that looking to the future was part and parcel of the war effort. Journalists, desperate for the inside story of his report, bombarded him with interview requests. Although he turned most down, the few he accepted did little to ease the Cabinet's collective mind. Shortly after he had delivered his report, in November 1942, the *Daily Telegraph* quoted him – inaccurately, he would later protest – as saying he was on the verge of taking the country 'half-way to Moscow'. As the Cabinet continued to sit on the report, the publishing house Penguin, noted for its iconic, mass-market paperback publishing, sensed the public interest and offered to publish it, if the government had no intention of doing so. There seemed little chance Beveridge was going to go away quietly.

A TIME FOR REVOLUTIONS, NOT PATCHING

Beveridge's sole-authored report was presented to Parliament in late November 1942 and finally published by His Majesty's Stationery Office on 1 December. As the government and then the public discovered, his proposals were a complex package. Beveridge had surveyed the country's existing social insurance provision and explained in fine-grained detail how half a century of legislation meant Britain had a wide array of schemes covering all kinds of eventualities, from old age to industrial injury. As he pointed out, these schemes were quite extensive compared to many other countries' arrangements. But they were also patchy and inconsistent, largely because there was no overarching vision or philosophy, which in turn made it difficult for politicians, civil servants and the public to understand what social insurance was meant to achieve, beyond bailing some people out of some situations some of the time. Instead, Beveridge's report recommended the government create a single ministry to run social insurance and embed a single set of values in all legislation. This would be a significant undertaking, but the government was actually much more worried about a number of Beveridge's other substantial recommendations. Although he had declined to describe them in any great detail, Beveridge had argued that anyone who accepted the case for his rationalized system of social insurance would concede the case for a series of more transformative commitments to state involvement in society and the economy too.

Understandably for a document written by an individual who wanted to impose his vision on a problem, Beveridge's report displayed an overwhelming concern with simplicity and consistency. As things stood, he explained, social insurance consisted of layers and layers of legislation covering health, unemployment and old age, and a myriad of external agents who were responsible for applying them. Moreover, there were huge differences in the benefits to which different people were entitled. If people were able to join a large and rich friendly society, for instance, they could be entitled to a service such as dental treatment, for which the society could pay out of its annual surplus. Those joining a small, less prosperous society, however, could expect little beyond treatment from an approved doctor. The rules the state had set out were often no better. An insured adult with a wife and two children was entitled to a weekly unemployment benefit of 38s – but if he became sick his income would drop to 18s. A seventeen-year-old boy, on the other hand, would receive 9s a week in unemployment benefit, yet in the case of finding himself out of work because of illness, the benefit would actually rise to 12s. Bringing order to this near chaos was essential. It would, Beveridge stated, make the state's provisions 'more beneficial and more intelligible to those whom they serve and more economical in their administration'.

When it came to the content of this rationalized scheme, Beveridge's proposals were actually fairly tame. He did not suggest that benefits be paid out of general taxation, as those on the left believed they should be as a matter of social justice. Instead, he advised sticking with principles with which politicians and the public were familiar. 'Benefit in return for contributions,' he wrote, 'rather than free allowances from the State, is what the people of Britain desire.' Social insurance, he proposed, should merge two templates: the universal and compulsory scheme Neville Chamberlain had used to reform pensions during the 1920s; and the tripartite system of contributions from individuals, employers and the state which the Liberal Party had used for unemployment insurance forty years earlier. Lists of approved trades and occupations that excluded most people, including the self-employed and almost every woman in gainful employment, would be a thing of the past. So too would be the opportunity to opt out, as a small number of industries, such as finance, had been able to do since the 1920s, arguing that their low unemployment rates meant government schemes need not apply. Everyone, Beveridge insisted, should pay into the scheme, not only because they might need it at some unforeseen point in the future, but also because they did not go about their work in isolation from the rest of the economy. Finance might have a low unemployment rate but, as the world had seen less than fifteen years earlier, financial crashes put blameless people in manufacturing and heavy industry out of work.

Beveridge's proposed scheme was universal in other senses too. It would be funded by flat-rate contributions, deducted automatically by employers, who would fix stamps to insurance documents as confirmation. Contributions would be high: 4s 3d a week, three times the 1s 10d a week a man paid out for health insurance, unemployment insurance and the state pension scheme. But in reality, Beveridge argued, 4s 3d was not that much. Figures collected by the Ministry of Labour shortly before the war showed that, over the course of a year, the average industrial family was spending a little over 6s a week on things Beveridge's plan would cover, including private insurance that added hospital cover to the panel doctor they could access via the government's health insurance scheme, medicines and dental treatment. Indeed, he thought that when people could see the benefits to which they would be entitled in return, they would think his scheme was a bargain. He had divided the population into six different groups – four of working age, bookended by children and pensioners – and explained how everyone, including those who were wilfully excluded from existing contributory schemes (such as housewives) would be entitled to something depending on their needs and ability to pay.

Wage earners would be insured against unemployment, temporary incapacity, permanent disability and the effects of old age which meant they could no longer support themselves. Furthermore, they would have access to a thirteen-week maternity allowance, a grant for funeral expenses, and assistance in the case of marriage breakdown. Even the self-employed would be entitled to many of these benefits, albeit with stricter conditions, such as a thirteen-week qualification period for unemployment benefit, which reflected the absence of an employer's contribution.

These benefits would not involve the hated means test, which Beveridge believed was not only intrusive but also inefficient. Why was it necessary to spend time assessing anything more than the legitimacy of a claim, he argued? A far simpler approach – one that everyone could understand and would be easy to administer – was to link benefits to subsistence: what individuals and families required to survive in modern society. Beveridge had two points of reference when it came to explaining what this concept of subsistence meant in practice. The first was the idea of a national minimum – a basic standard of income and living that everyone in a civilized society should be entitled to – promoted by Fabians, including Beatrice and Sidney Webb, as well as other enthusiasts for 'national efficiency', during the early twentieth century. The second was the quantitative methods that had been developed in social science and medicine during the previous century. By using the most up-to-date information on prices and a realistic view of what people needed to survive – including Rowntree's pioneering calculations of the number of calories required for a healthy diet – the new benefits would be a significant improvement on the existing system and a world away from the old Poor Law's principle of less eligibility. Under the pre-war system, an insured family of four where the father was unemployed and the mother did not work could expect to receive thirty-eight shillings a week; Beveridge proposed they be entitled to at least fifty-six shillings and possibly more, depending on post-war inflation.

There were, of course, problems with these proposals, which Beveridge and his advisers had discussed at length. Some concerns were to do with the way a universal system would be perceived. Beveridge knew that critics, particularly those on the right and centre right, would struggle to reconcile themselves with anything that looked like a 'Santa Claus' state: one that gave out gifts to everyone regardless of need or contribution to society. However, as he outlined in his proposals, a universal system did not mean the wholesale redistribution of wealth, as most critics on the right of the political spectrum feared it would. On the contrary, as Rowntree had demonstrated in his second survey of York during the 1930s, it would be possible to keep everyone on or above the poverty line by redistributing wealth between members of the working classes, rather than from the middle and upper classes to those below them. Indeed, Beveridge stressed that his aim was a system of social security that did 'not stifle incentive, opportunity, [or] responsibility'. He wanted 'a national minimum' but also 'room and encouragement for voluntary action by each individual to provide more than that minimum for himself and his family'.

Other problems were linked to the capacity of Beveridge's system to cope with demand. Would his proposed social insurance system be able to withstand the pressure of paying the same flat-rate pension to everyone as soon as they turned sixty-five? After all, when the Liberals had introduced an old-age pension in 1909 they had quickly discovered the costs were more than double the amount they had estimated. Beveridge argued that the country's demographic profile was a predictable challenge. The state collected vast swathes of information, not least via its existing social insurance provision, which enabled statisticians to give plenty of advance notice about the number of people likely to qualify for a pension and the length of time over which they might draw it. It was hardly beyond the state's abilities to devise a plan that matched financial capacity with demand. Beveridge's own suggestion was a transition period, in which the government would build up its pension funds and have time to assess the proper rate at which to pay people. He proposed that for the first twenty years of the scheme payments should be made at a rate below subsistence, with means tests used to identify those who needed further financial support. He also thought that it would be possible to build up cash reserves and keep pressure off the scheme by offering people incentives, such as higher basic pension payments, to work past sixty-five.

There was also the question of what to do about people who did not pay into his proposed system. Surely universal benefits would be ripe for exploitation by some of these people? For centuries, critics of any attempt to understand poverty in terms of anything but individual character had painted apocalyptic scenes of huge numbers of feckless people milking the system. Such fevered imaginings had little to do with reality, as the experience of running social insurance since 1911 – not to mention the Poor Law before that – had shown, and as the Royal Commission on the Poor Laws and Relief of Distress had documented almost forty years earlier. While there were certainly people who were happy to take handouts rather than work, they were, Beveridge argued, in a small minority. There was no need to build a system around them and punish the rest of the population in the process. For those unable to meet his contribution requirements, Beveridge suggested a slimmed-down version of national assistance, the system introduced by the national government during the mid-1930s for those who had run down their entitlements. These national assistance payments would be less generous than social security benefits and subject to means testing, which would leave scope for administrators to use their judgement. Indeed, Beveridge went so far as to argue there was a case for criminal prosecutions and punishment of anyone who persistently avoided the responsibilities to both themselves and their family that he had outlined.

Then there were issues that threatened to undermine the possibility of a genuinely universal, country-wide system. One of the biggest challenges was rent. Beveridge's benefits included an estimated proportion of recipients' housing costs. There were massive and well-documented differences in the rents charged for roughly equivalent homes in different parts of Britain, though. How could there be flat-rate benefits when the cost of subsistence varied so widely, and for reasons that had little to do with individual choice? Beveridge was acutely aware of this difficulty. He understood that, in addition to presenting him with a complex technical difficulty, housing was an issue with deep emotional pull, given successive governments' failure to fulfil Lloyd George's promises of 'homes fit for heroes' a quarter of a century earlier. But there seemed something wrong about looking for blame in the benefits that were paid out rather than the needs they were meant to meet. In housing, 'as in other respects', Beveridge wrote, 'the framing of a completely satisfactory plan of social security depends on a solution of other social problems'. Each of his proposals was tailored for a particular purpose, yet none would succeed on their own. Beveridge believed the government could not cherry-pick: it had to accept the whole of his report or none of it.

As readers who made it through to Part VI of his report discovered, it was this kind of argument that was the source of the government's concerns. More specifically, the government was deeply worried about what Beveridge called his 'three assumptions': allowances of eight shillings a week, to be paid to families for the upkeep of each child after their first, up until they left full-time compulsory education; a free and universal health service; and economic policies that prevented mass unemployment. The government could not have his plan for social insurance without also committing to these things, Beveridge explained, because his scheme would only work in a particular social and economic context. The problem for the government was that those extra commitments could not be paid for or run by the social insurance scheme he had described – child allowances and a health service would require funds from general taxation. 'Assumption' was understatement at its finest.

Beveridge's reasoning was relatively simple. Child allowances were necessary as part of the attack on want. Rowntree's account of the poverty cycle had shown how the birth of a child and the years of expense that followed were one of the major reasons people fell below his poverty line. More than thirty years on, Rowntree and others had emphasized during the committee's hearings that family size was, after unemployment, the leading cause of poverty. Payments that contributed towards the cost of raising children would not only alleviate poverty, they would require less government intrusion than other possible solutions such as setting wage rates so that workers could support a family on one income. Indeed, Beveridge believed that payments for every child after a family's first would not only preserve individual responsibility, they would also address concerns statisticians and social investigators had raised over the previous decades about the country's low birthrate. 'In the next thirty years housewives as mothers have vital work to do', Beveridge explained, 'in ensuring the adequate continuance of the British race and of British ideals in the world', not least because the working-age population would need to be big enough to support people who did not work, whether because they were old or young, in poor health, or unable to find a job. Child allowances would not provide anyone with a reason to start a family – but they would offset the cost of having a bigger one when they did.

A national health service was also necessary, for reasons of both social justice and hard-headed economic reasoning. Following the same chain of thought as Edwin Chadwick a century earlier, Beveridge argued it was in the state's interest to provide a free health service, including hospital treatment, because it would keep the numbers of people claiming sickness-related benefits to a minimum. The service would not only help prevent illness in the first place but also rehabilitate those who were injured, ill or disabled yet capable of again becoming economically productive citizens.

Similarly, Beveridge argued, it was essential for governments to keep employment levels as high as they could for preventative reasons. A social insurance system with indefinite flat-rate benefits would collapse if there were regular sustained periods of high unemployment. Beveridge suggested that his system could tolerate an unemployment rate of 8.5 per cent among the main class of able-bodied workers, which was not that far off the lower rates experienced during the 1930s. It was, nevertheless, a target that would require the government to intervene in the economy one way or another. A healthy labour market went hand in hand with a healthy population. If jobs and healthcare were available freely, then the Ministry of Social Security would find it easy to test an individual's willingness and ability to work.

Beveridge's report made no attempt to flesh out what his assumptions would look like in practice. Nevertheless, he made no bones about what he thought they and the administrative system of social insurance he had described would create: a new and better society that the British people deserved. 'Freedom from want cannot be forced on a democracy or given to a democracy,' he wrote in closing.

> Winning it needs courage and faith and a sense of national unity: courage to face facts and difficulties and overcome them; faith in our future and in the ideals of fair-play and freedom for which century after century our forefathers were prepared to die; a sense of national unity overriding the interests of any class or section.

Beveridge wanted his readers to know he believed in these ideas and that 'in this supreme crisis', the war that threatened their way of life, the British people would 'not be found wanting, of courage and faith and national unity, of material and spiritual power'. Beveridge was sure they would win the war, but he was equally convinced that, given the chance by the government, they could secure the peace they deserved too.

THE BOOM AND THE BOYCOTT

The month following the publication of *Social Insurance and Allied Services* was a period Beveridge described as a 'boom' for himself. More than 100,000 copies of his report were sold in four weeks – figures unheard of for a government document, not to mention one about insurance. Beveridge and his report became a staple topic for newspapers and the newsreels that were shown before the main feature at cinemas. But he himself 'remained a private citizen going about in omnibuses and third-class compartments', rather than the 'functionary with an escort' he would have been if he was a full-time government employee. Nevertheless, people recognized him: some would sit and stare; others wanted to talk. He was deluged with letters offering congratulations and sharing often heart-breaking stories, such as the elderly woman who wrote to tell him about how she had raised eight children, lost a son during the First World War and had three grandchildren serving in the current conflict, yet was reduced to 'sponging on my unmarried daughter' because she was not covered under existing pensions legislation. These people believed Beveridge had a plan for a better future – one that would eliminate the indignities that they or people they knew had been forced to suffer.

Yet, as compelling as these encounters often were, they were not necessarily an accurate indicator of how popular Beveridge's proposals were with the general public. After all, plenty of people, including members of the skilled working classes, thought they received a decent service from their local hospital or trade union insurance schemes. Did they want the kind of wholesale change Beveridge had outlined, and to be compelled to pay into a government scheme?

Indeed, would the middle classes who paid to see private doctors take kindly to the idea that, as they might see it, they should have to see a panel doctor like the currently insured working classes?

The pollster Henry Durant believed it was possible to find out. The founder of the British Institute of Public Opinion had astounded newspaper editors by correctly predicting the result of a by-election in West Fulham before the war. Two weeks after the publication of Beveridge's report, Durant commissioned a survey in 150 parliamentary constituencies, the details of which were published soon after as *The Beveridge Report and the Public.* The British Institute of Public Opinion found that a remarkable 95 per cent of people knew about Beveridge's proposals. While there were criticisms – particularly of old-age pensions, which many respondents deemed not nearly generous enough – most measures were approved of wholeheartedly, including the idea of a national health service, which was endorsed by 88 per cent of those surveyed. The rival surveying organization, Mass-Observation – specialists in qualitative, rather than quantitative, data (and which Durant dismissed as 'high-level journalism') – found similar levels of enthusiasm, even if most respondents were hazy on the specifics. 'It seems all right to me,' one twenty-eight-year-old man reported. 'It would be all right to be able to stop worrying about tomorrow, or your old age, or what was going to happen to the kids.'

Contrary to some expectations, support was also high across social classes. Working-class respondents were certainly the most enthusiastic about Beveridge's proposals but the middle classes were also quickly persuaded of his report's merits. Indeed, even though only 57 per cent of total respondents said they thought they would be better off thanks to Beveridge, 76 per cent of the upper-income group, and 90 per cent of those who worked in a profession – a group that included lawyers, accountants, engineers and civil servants – supported his plan. 'People's views on whether the Report should be implemented do not seem to have been directly influenced by their calculation of whether they personally are likely to gain or lose,' Durant wrote. 'They seem to have approached the question from the angle of the public good.'

Beveridge's scheme was received so positively for a number of reasons. While some of these were related to specific proposals he had made, attitudes were also shaped by the broader context in which they were published. The principle of contribution meant it could not be dismissed as something-for-nothing. The upheaval of war, too, had been important in softening and reshaping attitudes. The actuary-turned-social scientist Richard Titmuss – who advised the government on health statistics during the war and was asked to write the official history of social services afterwards – believed that organizations like the Emergency Medical Service had opened people's eyes to the possibility of extending welfare services beyond what many politicians had considered desirable or possible in peacetime. He also thought wartime evacuation, designed to protect the most vulnerable people in densely populated and mainly urban areas from aerial warfare, had played an important role. Town and country, working class and middle class, had been brought face to face as 3 million people from cities like London and Liverpool were moved to either specially constructed camps or private homes in places such as Devon, Cornwall and other rural areas during late 1939 and early 1940.

Evacuation was an eye-opening experience for all involved. As documented in the pages of medical journals, including *The Lancet*, and reports written by government officials sent to observe the process, hosts were shocked by children arriving poorly clothed, undernourished and filthy dirty. They complained frequently about their young guests wetting the bed, seeing it as a sign of a neglected upbringing rather than as an involuntary psychological response to a traumatic situation. There were stories about children struggling to adjust to life in homes that were very different to the slums they had left behind. One often-repeated story involved a family's horror at the moment a six-year-old child from Glasgow defecated on their living-room carpet, only for the child's mother to tell them they should have done the polite thing and gone in the corner.

Such experiences, in Titmuss's view, raised middle- and upper-class awareness of the human dimensions of problems that many had only ever read about before the war and, in the process, made them more open to calls for more government help. As even *The Times*, the newspaper of the Establishment, put it shortly after the Dunkirk retreat in July 1940, it was no longer good enough to define British values in 'purely nineteenth-century terms'. After the war, it asserted, democracy could not be a kind that 'maintains the right to vote but forgets the right to work and the right to live'. Freedom could not 'mean a rugged individualism which excludes social organisation and economic planning'. Equality could not mean 'a political equality nullified by social and economic privilege'. 'Economic reconstruction' was going to have to involve 'maximum production' but it would be useless without 'equitable distribution'.

Talk of this kind had taken on a new meaning just a month before *Social Insurance and Allied Services* appeared, when Lieutenant-General Montgomery led Allied forces to victory at El Alamein in Egypt, the Allies' first major breakthrough on land, and repelled the Germans from key strategic targets in the Middle East and North Africa, including oil fields and the Suez Canal. The Ministry of Information, latching on to the idea that *Social Insurance and Allied Services* could be a useful piece of propaganda, started referring to it as the 'Beveridge Plan'. The Army Bureau of Current Affairs produced a pocket version of the report, approved by Beveridge himself, and a translated summary was dropped behind enemy lines in mainland Europe as part of an effort to stir up support among the civilian population for the Allies' efforts.

Such enthusiasm was not matched elsewhere in government. Some MPs and government officials complained that it was inappropriate for troops to discuss what they considered a politically contentious and controversial topic. The cheap army edition of *Social Insurance and Allied Services* was withdrawn after just two days. By the end of January 1943, two months after the report had been published, MPs had still not debated Beveridge's report in the House of Commons. Rumours circulated that he might try to force the issue by standing as an independent candidate at a by-election in Watford, hoping that a comprehensive victory would show the weight of public opinion was behind him. But, following some friendly advice from the canny old political operator Lloyd George, who, recalling Tory efforts to block his own social insurance proposals, suggested keeping relations with the government as cordial as possible, Beveridge decided against the move.

On Tuesday, 16 February 1943 the House of Commons finally began discussing Beveridge's proposals in a three-day debate. Introducing the report to a tense chamber, Arthur Greenwood, the deputy Labour leader – who, in putting Beveridge in charge of the Inter-Departmental Committee on Social Insurance and Allied Services, had given him the opportunity that he had seized with both hands – acknowledged that there was widespread and cross-party interest in Beveridge's suggested scheme. 'No document within living memory has made such a powerful impression, or stirred such hopes,' Greenwood told MPs. 'The people of the country have made up their minds to see the plan in its broad outline carried into effect, and nothing will shift them. The plan for social security has struck their imagination.'

The debate that followed was lively, with Labour MPs jeering and heckling anyone who tried to argue against the report. The government tried to fudge the issue. Rather than promising to implement Beveridge's report, it opted for a much weaker resolution: approving it in principle but merely welcoming it as a helpful guide as to what might be included in plans for post-war reconstruction. The biggest parliamentary revolt of the war followed: 119 MPs, including almost every Labour backbencher and Lloyd George (casting his final vote in the Commons) filed through the opposition lobby, against 335 MPs who chose to support the resolution.

In the months that followed, the political landscape was gradually reshaped. Some Labour members had their doubts about *Social Insurance and Allied Services*, in particular Beveridge's emphasis on subsistence and contribution, which they considered insufficiently radical and likely to prop up a version of the insurance system that existed before the war. Yet many influential Labour intellectuals, including R. H. Tawney and Harold Laski, Beveridge's old colleagues from the London School of Economics, were happy to talk up the report's progressive values. While Labour committed itself to implementing the plan, and called on the government to do so immediately, Churchill waited until March before giving a public statement on it. Even then, he talked about Beveridge's plan in heavily circumscribed terms, dwelling at length in one of his radio addresses to the nation on the problems of binding future governments, operating in unknown conditions, to specific schemes. Churchill explained that he was in favour of a unified compulsory insurance scheme, underpinned by contributory principles, covering health and unemployment, not to mention a raft of other things Beveridge had not discussed, including better educational opportunities for the young; a society where everyone was covered 'from the cradle to the grave'. But, he argued, there could be no promises until the war was won.

Some Labour MPs, such as the firebrand Welsh backbencher Aneurin Bevan, were distinctly unimpressed, seeing the government's refusal to commit to Beveridge's report as the latest proof of its insufficient engagement with post-war reconstruction. Bevan and his colleagues demanded that Labour consider ending the electoral truce that had held since the beginning of the war, and to use the threat of disruption in Parliament to extract commitments from the government to Beveridge's plan. However Attlee, the Deputy Prime Minister – who had angered the likes of Bevan by steadfastly supporting Churchill throughout the early stages of his premiership, even when many observers thought he was pursuing a flawed war strategy – discouraged his party from stirring up trouble. There was little to be gained from such an approach, he argued, when the response to *Social Insurance and Allied Services* had put clear daylight between Labour and the Tories and there was still a war to be won. Attlee had realized what Churchill, apparently, had not: that in distancing himself from the Beveridge Plan, Churchill had conceded ownership of the future to Labour.

Parliament's weak resolution of support and Churchill's temporizing also marked the beginning of what Beveridge described as a government boycott of both him and his work. He refused to go quietly. Along with his Oxford colleague G. D. H. Cole, Beveridge established the Social Security League, which held packed community meetings across the country throughout the rest of 1943 in an effort to keep the call for his report to be implemented in full and immediately going. Beveridge also found there was interest in his work from abroad, particularly in the USA, where social activists and social scientists invited him to speak, hoping to inject momentum back into President Roosevelt's 'New Deal', which had become stalled after a promising start in 1932. Government officials worried that Beveridge might give his American hosts (who included universities, labour organizations and the Rockefeller Foundation) who were paying for his trip the impression he represented the government's views. Yet ministers decided their concerns were outweighed by the strength of their desire to get him out of the public eye. They gave him permission to travel to America with his wife in early May 1943, where he stayed for three months. Beveridge knew that all was not lost. But with a war still to win and a government intent on putting the Atlantic Ocean between them, the day when his plans for social insurance might become a reality looked some way off.

II

Constructive Progress

On 4 June 1945, at the Prime Minister's Buckinghamshire retreat of Chequers, Winston Churchill prepared to make a radio address to the nation. Less than a month earlier, Germany had surrendered unconditionally to the Allied forces in Europe and, shortly after, Churchill had called a general election. Now, he was campaigning to lead Britain through what was likely to be a difficult period of reconstruction.

Having been less than enthusiastic about endorsing Beveridge's social insurance plan, Churchill now assured the British people that the Tories were fully committed to what had been outlined in *Social Insurance and Allied Services* two and half years previously. Labour, led by Clement Attlee, was promising similar things, but in his radio address to the British public Churchill wanted his listeners to understand there was a very real choice on offer. Labour's policies would require a 'political police', he claimed, because they 'would have to fall back on some form of Gestapo', albeit one that would be 'no doubt very humanely directed in the first instance'. This turned out to be more than a throwaway line. 'GESTAPO IN BRITAIN IF SOCIALISTS WIN', screamed the front page of the following day's *Daily Express*: 'they would dictate what to say and do, even where to queue'.

In comparing Labour to the Nazis, Churchill wanted to present the Tories as the inheritors of the liberal tradition; to reassure the country that, in the likely confusion and struggles of post-war reconstruction, the Conservative Party would provide the kind of solid reforms that people could intuitively understand. Depicting Labour – which had never yet secured a parliamentary majority – as unfamiliar, foreign, even dangerous, was a simple and, Churchill believed, effective rhetorical tool, given it had been used so effectively against them during the 1920s, when they were often portrayed as a vehicle for international communism.

Yet, as Attlee pointed out in an elegant and effective response the following day, anyone who was worried about foreign ideas infiltrating British politics might like to think about the connection between Churchill's words and those of the Austrian economist Friedrich Hayek, the London School of Economics professor who had clashed with John Maynard Keynes over the causes of the Great Depression during the 1930s. Churchill's invoking of the Gestapo was obviously indebted to Hayek's argument, set out in his international bestseller *The Road to Serfdom* (1944), that well-intentioned efforts to interfere in economic matters were a slippery slope that inevitably led to infringements on basic freedoms and, eventually, to totalitarianism. It seemed uncharacteristically naïve of Churchill to think he could convince Britain that Labour – a party that had opposed the appeasement of Hitler before the war and with whom Churchill himself had been in government only a few weeks earlier – was somehow a threat to the British way of life.

Despite the pollsters' prediction that Labour would win, newspapers and commentators seemed shocked to find out the British people agreed with Attlee when the votes were counted across almost three weeks in July 1945 – a delay necessitated by the large number of postal votes sent by soldiers stationed overseas. Labour had won 393 seats and a thumping majority of 146, securing their status as an independent party of government for the first time. The Liberals, on the other hand, were reduced to just twelve MPs – confirmation, if confirmation were needed, that they were a spent force. The British public had been brutal. Thirteen Conservative ministers, including Harold Macmillan, who had been Secretary of State for Air for little more than a month, and Brendan Bracken, the former Minister of Information who had seen the propaganda potential of Beveridge's report, lost their seats.

The result was an endorsement of not only Labour's proposals for social security but also a range of further economic controls that people (including Beveridge) had argued were necessary, both for the transition from war to peace and to ensure that the proposals worked.

Labour had no intention of turning this into what Hayek later called 'hot socialism': strict central planning and a government that forcibly organized markets by setting wages and controlling individuals' fundamental rights to produce, buy and sell what they wished. Rather, the new government embarked on a course of economic management with a view to building the institutions that would provide a basic standard of living for all. For the likes of Hayek it still looked very much like sacrificing economic freedom in the name of a higher goal. But for those who cast their votes for Attlee's party it was what Beveridge had described as a 'very British revolution': a moment of modernization that made sense not because it was completely different or new, but because it involved extending to everyone rights and obligations that only a few had possessed in the past.

'ESSENTIAL SPRINGS OF MATERIAL PROGRESS'

Back at the start of 1943, Beveridge had been so sure he was going to be involved in taking his plan forward that he had told University College, the Oxford college where he was Master, that they would need to find a temporary replacement for him while he was away on government business. Given that his reputation had been built on his research on unemployment during the first decade of the century, and that he had been working on the subject again at Oxford, fleshing out what he had called 'Assumption C' – high and stable levels of employment – might mean in practice seemed like a task he was ideally suited to. He approached Attlee, as Churchill's coalition deputy, and Brendan Bracken at the Ministry of Information to ask if they might be able to commission him to work on the topic. But, with many in the government unhappy with the way Beveridge had conducted himself during the early stages of the war and in the build up to his report's publication, those talks ended up going nowhere. As a consequence, Beveridge made an important decision in April 1943: he would 'go ahead on my own'.

Beveridge had enjoyed both the freedom he had been granted on the Inter-Departmental Committee on Social Insurance and Allied

Services and the assistance from the committee members Arthur Greenwood had eventually decided to put him in charge of. As a consequence, he decided he wanted to study employment in the same way. Hiring premises on Bruton Street in central London, Beveridge recruited a group of consultants whom he believed would provide the ideas he needed to assemble a set of policy proposals for high and stable levels of employment. These consultants included the Hungarian Nicholas Kaldor, an economics lecturer at the London School of Economics; Barbara Wootton, another LSE lecturer and a former member of the Labour Party's Research Department; Joan Robinson, one of the most gifted economic theorists of her generation, who had produced pioneering work on imperfect competition; and E. F. Schumacher, a political refugee from Nazi Germany.

Beveridge was able to do this thanks to support from three sources. The first was Kenneth Lee. A Manchester-based businessman who had served on a Royal Commission into the coal industry during the mid-1920s, Lee was the Director General of Raw Materials at the Ministry of Supply. David Astor was the son of the fantastically wealthy proprietor of the *Observer* newspaper and a graduate of Oxford's Politics, Philosophy and Economics degree, who helped recruit writers such as the radical Hungarian intellectual Arthur Koestler to his father's newspaper during the early stages of the war. The group's dominant figure, however, was Edward Hulton, the owner of the country's leading photo-journalism publication, the *Picture Post*, who had inherited a fortune from his father, a newspaper proprietor who counted the London *Evening Standard* among his many titles. Hulton had stood unsuccessfully for Parliament as a Conservative Unionist on two occasions during the interwar years and put profits from the *Picture Post* into the Home Guard Training School. But, as he explained in his book *The New Age* (1943), reading *Social Insurance and Allied Services* had been a transformative moment for him. Beveridge had persuaded Hulton that the future was a mixed economy, involving intelligent use of government controls and more extensive social services.

Beveridge's choice of consultants was a testament to a new consensus that was taking shape among economists, particularly young economists. A decade earlier, there had been fierce disagreement, most famously between Keynes and Hayek, about the causes of the Great Depression. According to Hayek the depression was a monetary matter, with roots in financial markets that had seen rapid credit expansion. When those booms came to an end and the credit started to dry up some people discovered they had made poor investments; others simply decided to pull out of deals that offered what they considered inadequate short-term returns. The results were painful: businesses went under and unemployment shot up. But, Hayek argued, governments had to let this process work itself through, allowing the economy to right itself. Keynes disagreed. He believed the problem was that the financial collapse had caused a contraction of demand throughout the economy, which brought everything to a grinding halt as producers suddenly had nobody to sell their goods to. The good news, according to Keynes, was that governments could do something about this situation: they could jump-start the economy by creating jobs through infrastructure projects, which, thanks to the multiplier effect, would cause demand to ripple outwards through the economy. The state could then safely withdraw when everything was moving again.

Nicholas Kaldor had been one of the economists who had worked closely with Hayek at the London School of Economics throughout that debate. When Hayek first arrived in Britain during the early 1930s, Kaldor had translated his work from its original German and helped him with his English during his correspondence with Keynes. Yet by 1943, and to Hayek's dismay, Kaldor had been converted to Keynesianism. Joan Robinson, meanwhile, was a member of the 'Cambridge Circus' – the group of young economists who met with Keynes to scrutinize his work in the years leading up to the publication of *The General Theory of Employment, Interest and Money* in 1936, and who scathingly described Hayek's ideas as a 'pitiful state of confusion'. For these economists, Hayek's liberalism was hopelessly out of date; Keynes's technocratic macroeconomics was the future.

Along with the likes of G. D. H. Cole, a guild socialist who believed in sharing power between the state, industry and consumers and Beveridge's co-founder of the Social Security League, these consultants had important impacts on Beveridge's thinking. They dragged him away from the idea that 'Assumption C', high and stable levels of employment, could be achieved only through conventional state planning with governments controlling production and supply, and towards Keynes's belief that it could be done through demand management. The distinction sounded highly technical (and Hayek believed it was largely meaningless), but it was hugely significant. Beveridge was convinced that by continuously identifying long-term infrastructure projects, and being prepared to run up big deficits to pay for them, governments could keep unemployment below 3 per cent – significantly lower than the 8.5 per cent unemployment threshold that he had estimated was necessary for his social insurance plan to be sustainable.

In this respect, Beveridge's 1944 report on his and his consultants' work, *Full Employment in a Free Society*, was quite different to *Social Insurance and Allied Services*. Rather than detailed proposals for post-war legislation or instructions on demobilization, *Full Employment in a Free Society* contained general suggestions for peacetime economic structures and policies. Beveridge, though, was wary of critics like Hayek. He went out of his way to emphasize that his recommendations did not entail a shift towards totalitarianism via state planning. His general goal of full employment left plenty of scope for discussion about and differences on individual issues, including nationalizing the means of production – which, some socialists believed, was the answer to many of Britain's social and economic problems. Political values, including freedom of expression and assembly, the peaceful change of government and free choice of occupation would all be safe, Beveridge argued. Indeed, his policies had been designed, he asserted, 'to preserve all the essential springs of material progress in the community, to leave to special efforts its rewards, to leave scope for change, invention, competition and initiative'.

When he finished his report on 18 May 1944 Beveridge had a major problem: thanks to rationing there was no paper to print it on. Much to his annoyance, it took a further six months for *Full Employment in a Free Society* to see the light of day, giving the government the opportunity to jump into action by starting what he called a 'White Paper chase' – a rapid succession of documents indicating the likely content of post-war legislation – which had all been written without his input.

THROWING MONEY DOWN THE SINK?

The school system had been a thorny topic of discussion among social reformers and governments since the late nineteenth century. Support for the extension of free education for children existed for a variety of reasons. One was the concern, in the light of the widening electoral franchise, that more people would need to be better equipped to make decisions that had previously been the privilege of property owners only. Another was the worry that a failure to educate and train young people, particularly in matters connected to science and technology, meant Britain was falling behind its international rivals, and especially Germany, which had excelled in fields such as chemical engineering. By the early twentieth century, thanks to the national efficiency movement, these issues had been fused with ideas about social justice. Not only was Britain failing to offer opportunities to bright and capable children, it was wasting their talents and therefore squandering one of its most valuable resources. For the left as much as the right, educational reform was an easy sell because it could be used to support arguments about the importance of hard work and self-improvement, not to mention opportunity, on the pathway to individual success.

In 1936, after taking over from Ramsay MacDonald as Prime Minister for the second time, Stanley Baldwin had agreed to raise the school leaving age from fourteen to fifteen, but the outbreak of war had meant the change was never implemented. During the Blitz, work on school reform had rumbled on quietly in the background. The 1941 document *Education After the War*, more widely known as the 'Green Book', summarized the Board of Education's ideas about further reforming the school system, and a committee led by Sir Cyril Norwood, the president of St John's College, Oxford, had subsequently been appointed to formulate plans for the secondary school curriculum that it would require. The consensus among education experts was that there were different types of children with different aptitudes and that they should be divided into different kinds of schools, in which they would be taught subjects appropriate to their particular capabilities, at an appropriate stage of their development.

Grammar schools that offered places to children who could demonstrate high ability via an intelligence test, usually taken at the age of eleven, and institutions that offered what had long been known as a technical education, preparing children and young people for a life in industrial employment or some kind of trade, were examples of what these experts had in mind.

However, as the history of educational reform over the previous century had shown, there were major challenges for anyone who wanted to organize schools in Britain into a single system. One of the biggest was religion. Churches had been a major provider of education for centuries, instructing millions of children in the three Rs. Given that schools were an opportunity to build strong relationships with young minds, instilling religious teachings and creating a new generation of parishioners who would put their hands in their pockets when collection plates went round at Sunday services, churches guarded their independence fiercely. But while some church schools were excellent, others were not, often because low and fluctuating levels of funding left them with too few teachers and inadequate facilities. They were also a subject that had stirred strong political emotions at numerous points during the previous five decades. After the 1902 Education Act, when Arthur Balfour's Tory administration had made it legal for public money to be used for secondary schooling, religious schools could claim state support on certain conditions – namely a say, though not a decisive one, in how they were run. The decision angered many. While the fact that the state funded schools at all was a matter of great discontent for liberals, who objected on grounds of freedom of conscience, religious dissenters were often irate if they had no choice but to send their child to a Church of England or Catholic school, leading to complaints about Rome or Canterbury 'on the rates'.

Another problem was public schools, where the country's elites sent their children and which held a stranglehold over access to the ancient universities. These establishments had been the subject of criticism by the likes of the Fabian Society and their associates among the national efficiency movement, who suggested public schools' focus on classics and literature, rather than sciences and technology, was impacting on the quality of people available to lead the country. Boarding-school life had also received an increasingly negative press during the early twentieth century, with exposés of the cruelty that permeated the hierarchies among the student population: the practice of 'fagging', through which older pupils would enlist younger ones as servants, was notorious enough to have an entry in the *Encyclopaedia Britannica*. As demand for public-school places dropped among the middle classes, famous schools like Harrow shrank in size and less well-known ones, which charged reasonably modest fees, were in the kind of perilous financial state that suggested some might start closing soon.

The man charged with tackling all these issues was the President of the Board of Education and Chairman of the Conservative Committee on Post-war Problems, R. A. Butler (1902–82). Like Beveridge, Butler had been born in India to British parents, and sent to Britain for a boarding-school education. After graduating from Cambridge, he had married the daughter of a wealthy textile manufacturer, whose decision to gift Butler an income of £5,000 a year enabled him to choose politics over more financially lucrative careers. Affable and supremely clever, Butler seemed to have everything required for a career at the very top of politics, except the calculated ruthlessness that helped people get there. He held a number of government positions, including India Under-Secretary in the national government and junior posts at the Foreign Office and Ministry of Labour under Neville Chamberlain. But, after supporting appeasement – not as a cover for rearmament but as a principled position – Butler was marginalized by Churchill, who had sent him to the Board of Education in July 1941.

Like Beveridge, while Butler did not consider his wartime assignment a compliment he made the best of his situation, throwing himself into the task of solving seemingly intractable problems. Assisted by his parliamentary secretary, the Labour MP James Chuter Ede (1882–1965), who had been a teacher during the first decade of the twentieth century, Butler met leaders from Anglican, Roman Catholic and dissenting churches. He listened patiently to their long list of concerns and grievances and encouraged them to consider the conditions under which they might join a national education system. Yet while Ede helped Butler make headway with religious schools, Butler, an alumnus of Marlborough College whose relatives included headmasters of

Harrow and Haileybury, made markedly less progress with public schools. Butler had an intimate knowledge of how such schools worked and appreciated the problems they posed – particularly if they existed outside a national education system and therefore continued to allow the wealthy to segregate themselves from everyone else. He nevertheless skirted around solutions that involved asking these schools to make significant compromises, and was unwilling to see them go to the wall.

Churchill had not given Butler's work much thought until November 1942, when the publication of *Social Insurance and Allied Services* saw him casting around for something to compensate for his refusal to commit to the Beveridge Plan. Butler saw his chance and found a willing accomplice in Kingsley Wood, the Tory Chancellor of the Exchequer, who told him he would 'rather give money for education than throw it down the sink with Sir William Beveridge'. Butler quickly prepared a White Paper, *Educational Reconstruction*, which was published in July 1943. Flagging the instrumental importance of education to the country's future, and showing signs of his own public-school background, Butler stressed its less tangible benefits and role in the development of individual identity and character. Education, he argued, was the glue that kept communities together; it would play an essential part in helping people withstand the social, economic and cultural challenges that would come their way in the years after the war.

Much like *Social Insurance and Allied Services*, Butler's vision involved proposals with which the public were familiar. He had looked into long-standing complaints about the deficiencies of technical and vocational education, as well as ideas about providing nursery places for all children and continuing part-time education for adults – suggestions mooted after the First World War, but which had never got off the ground. Butler had concluded that the days of cash-strapped schools with classes of fifty or more pupils, sometimes filled with children of different ages who were simply counting down the days until they could leave, should come to an end. But he had also embraced the principle that equality of opportunity did not mean equality of outcome, let alone giving children the same things on the way. Children should have a progressive schooling experience, one in which they moved through distinct stages alongside others of the same age. But, after receiving the same basic instruction for six years, at the age of eleven children should be divided into groups according to their perceived ability, aptitude and aspiration. There would then follow four more years of education in either a grammar, modern or technical school that would prepare them for their adult lives.

Butler's discussions with church leaders had delivered a very British compromise. Although the ultimate responsibility for schooling would lie, legally and financially, with a new Ministry of Education, the job of administering schools would fall to local authorities, which in turn would be responsible to local communities. Church schools would have a choice about how they fitted in to this system: they could become either 'controlled' or 'aided'. If they opted for the former then the local authority would take over the school's management. The quid pro quo, however, was that the school could claim all its costs from the local authority and, in a deal Butler had struck with church leaders, insist on the teaching of an approved non-denominational religious instruction syllabus. If the school opted to be aided, though, the local authority would only provide day-to-day running costs, leaving the church to pay for everything else, including buildings. The advantage for the church was that they would retain control over day-to-day decision-making. Either way, the schools got a stable income and their aim of compulsory religious instruction, while the state was able to integrate them into a new national school system.

These ideas were translated into legislation during 1944, culminating in the Education Act that was passed in August that year. The Butler Act, as it became known, contained a number of radical measures, such as an end to fees for all but a small number of grammar schools, meaning middle-class parents could not use their wealth to bypass the eleven-plus entrance examination as many had done in the past when their children had failed it. The act also made legal provision for a massive expansion in college places and nursery schools, and established the goal of eventually raising the school-leaving age to sixteen. Ultimately, though, the act was quite conservative, especially after the government had scrambled to remove an amendment guaranteeing equal pay for female teachers, which had been introduced by the Tory backbencher Thelma Cazalet-Keir, and which threatened to push estimated costs up by anything up to a quarter (not to mention increasing the perceived risk of similar demands from women employed in other government services). The provision of college places and nursery schools remained optional for the local authorities who would ultimately have to plan and run the new system. Despite much fevered speculation, the public-school system was left alone. In fact, thanks to the decision to abolish grammar-school fees, they would receive a much-needed boost from middle-class exiles from the new state system after 1945.

Beveridge welcomed this extension of education but he was also frustrated by the government's decision to suddenly accelerate its plans for post-war reconstruction without his input. From February to September 1944, as he waited for paper to become available for him to print *Full Employment* and the Allies successfully executed their plan to push the Nazis back by landing on the beaches of Normandy early in June, more White Papers appeared, setting out commitments to comprehensive social insurance based on flat-rate contributions and benefits, a National Health Service, and economic policies that aimed to produce high and stable levels of employment. These documents did not go into every detail; all kinds of questions still needed to be answered, from how the country would actually staff a universal health service to what a full employment policy meant in practice, before these ideas could become reality. In principle, however, Churchill's government had accepted everything Beveridge had been arguing for, assumptions and all. He was happy that progress was finally being made, but also (not unreasonably) convinced that the government was excluding him out of spite. He decided it was time to enter the world of electoral politics. Having spent his career just about keeping his party political sympathies to himself, preferring to appear as a rational and aloof technocrat who was interested in a number of progressive political causes, he declared for the Liberal Party and entered Parliament as the MP for Berwick-upon-Tweed in October 1944. Beveridge hoped it was a move that would put him in the right place to influence further developments. But not even he would escape the electorate's unforgiving judgement at the general election that was held less than ten months later.

LET US FACE THE FUTURE

In July 1945 Britain had a new Prime Minister. The Labour leader Clement Attlee was cut from rather different cloth from Churchill, the man he had defeated. A Haileybury-educated former solicitor with a thick moustache, thinning hair and quiet demeanour, Attlee looked entirely unremarkable – or, as some contemporaries put it less flatteringly, boring. If Attlee 'had got up in the Commons and announced The Revolution', one Tory MP was reported to have said, 'it would have sounded like a change in the regional railway timetable'. Attlee, though, was unyielding. A former soldier – he had served in the horrendous Gallipoli campaign of 1915, directed by Churchill – he had weathered a barrage of criticism from his own party for his perceived lack of radicalism. He was convinced that the state had to fix the problems with capitalism and make society work for everyone – and now, he was determined to put his convictions into practice.

Labour's manifesto, *Let Us Face the Future*, reminded the nation of the other parties' broken promises at the end of the First World War. Labour promised wide-ranging changes to the social insurance programme and, embracing Keynesian economic management, set out a number of other radical policies, including the nationalization of key industries. Labour, the new government told the country, 'stands for order as against the chaos which would follow the end of all public control', and was committed to 'positive constructive progress as against the chaos of economic do-as-they-please anarchy'. The British people 'wanted a new start', Attlee later concluded. The Tories 'were looking towards the past', Labour 'towards the future'.

Labour was also much better prepared than the Conservatives for the return to something approaching normal party politics. While the Tories had suspended their national conference during the first half of the war, Labour maintained strong ties with local organizations and trade unions, whose co-operation had been an essential part of the war economy. Moreover, Labour had become adept at using the media to promote their credentials as reformers and a genuine party of government. Sympathetic newspapers such as the *Daily Mirror* banged the party drum. The party's intellectual supporters, including George Orwell and R. H. Tawney, had played a long game, contributing to projects like the Left Book Club, which issued a book a month throughout the 1930s and 1940s. Indeed, when Hayek reflected on why he lost his famous argument with Keynes during this period, he suggested that it was because socialists, dating back to Sidney and Beatrice Webb and their weekly dinner parties at their house in central London, had managed to capture the ear of the intellectual and governing classes.

Planning for important aspects of the transition to peace was well under way when Labour took over. Showing that a lesson had been learned from the aftermath of the First World War, rules for demobilizing the armed forces based on length of service and skills shortages back home had been drawn up. Moreover, new ministries, including one for national insurance, had been established in preparation for the kinds of changes indicated in the published White Papers. The economic situation, however, was precarious. Almost a third of Britain's wealth had been consumed by the war and the country had only made it through thanks to America's help. When the Lend-Lease agreement, which guaranteed US supplies of equipment and loans of around $30 billion, came to an abrupt end after Japan's surrender in August 1945, Britain was in trouble. The country had a massive trade deficit and a shortage of foreign currency, especially US dollars. Exports were the obvious answer to this problem but they needed to be increased by anything up to 75 per cent to solve it. The 62-year-old Keynes, whose health was failing under the pressure of negotiating arrangements for the new world economy, was sent to Washington to secure a loan. He returned with $3.75 billion, plus a further $1 billion from Canada. The money had major strings attached: it had been loaned at commercial rates of interest and on the conditions that Britain opened up its imperial markets to US companies and made sterling convertible to the dollar within two years. The country had until mid-1947 to fix its balance-of-payments problem. Keynes was under no illusions about the likelihood of that happening, but he thought the country had no choice. There would be no social reconstruction without the loan.

By the time it had to make good on these promises, Britain's economic situation had not improved. With more than one and a half million men still stationed overseas, 1947 had begun with the worst winter of the century, which brought the country to a virtual standstill. Snow fell in Britain for fifty-five consecutive days, with snowdrifts reaching seven metres high in Scotland. The army cleared roads and supplies had to be airdropped in to some areas. When the snow melted, flooding followed, compounding the effects of a predictable fuel shortage with coal supplies running down. Then, in July, came the moment of truth: sterling could now be converted into dollars. As almost everyone had expected when the American loan was made, Britain was nowhere near ready. There was a run on the pound and convertibility had to be suspended after less than two months.

Attlee faced calls to step down, with Ernest Bevin, the former head of the Transport and General Workers' Union touted as a likely replacement. Arguing that reality could not be bent to fit Labour's socialist idealism and that such chaos was inevitable, the Tories claimed that Labour had no choice but to step back from the ambitious social reconstruction they had promised the public in 1945. Attlee, however, stood firm. He conceded that reconstruction would need to feature austerity and that his Cabinet would have to be reshuffled to accommodate those who doubted him. However, Britain was going to get what it had voted for, not only because it was right, Attlee argued, but because, contrary to what the Conservatives believed, it was possible.

'STUFFED THEIR MOUTHS WITH GOLD'

Despite Attlee's resolve, Labour continued to struggle to forge a new set of economic policies that would support their plans for social reconstruction and social security. Their most immediate problem was to increase exports – but that goal was really a symbol of the need to create a growing economy in which businesses and industries, emerging from a wartime period in which there had been a 100 per cent excess profits tax, were prepared to invest in plant and infrastructure. Echoing the ideas about a new relationship between planning and finance that Beveridge had explored in *Full Employment in a Free Society*, Labour had retained the Economic Section, a legacy of the Economic Advisory Council of the early 1930s, and in 1947 had turned it into the Central Economic Planning Staff. This offered the government informed opinions on matters relating to its economic responsibilities and aims. They had also introduced an annual economic survey, separate from the annual budget, to help them monitor what was happening. Physical controls remained – most famously food rationing, which continued until July 1954 – and the government fulfilled its promise to nationalize key organizations and industries by the end of the 1940s, including the Bank of England, coal, gas, electricity, the railways, and iron and steel. Yet Britain did not become a command economy. Labour's 'thermostatters', who were of a Keynesian economic management persuasion, managed to hold off the party's 'Gosplanners', who derived their nickname from the title of the Soviet economic planning agency.

Meanwhile, Labour had set about trying to fulfil the central plank of its manifesto: to create a nationwide social security system by a self-imposed deadline of mid-1948. This system was to include not only the eye-catching promises about a national health service but a raft of legislation that plugged holes in the social security framework, such as the Industrial Injuries Act, passed in 1946. Yet economic uncertainty looked like it might scupper these plans. The school-leaving age was due to increase to fifteen by April 1947 but there was a shortage of building materials needed for new schools – a pressure made more acute by efforts to build new houses for demobilized soldiers and bombed-out civilians. The Labour Cabinet considered pushing back the date in January 1947 but, under pressure from the Minister of Education, Ellen Wilkinson, who pointed out that the economic circumstances were going to be far from ideal for some time to come, decided to plough ahead. (Less than a month after this decisive intervention, Wilkinson was dead due to an accidental overdose of medication for pneumonia.)

The Cabinet's decision to push ahead with their programme despite the difficulties they were faced with signalled the beginning of a new phase for the Labour government. Attlee had appointed Stafford Cripps (1889–1952), a lawyer and nephew of Beatrice Webb, Minister for Economic Affairs – a new and somewhat vague position – during the reshuffle that was intended to placate his party opponents. In

November 1947, six weeks later, Cripps was appointed Chancellor of the Exchequer after Hugh Dalton had been forced to resign, having let a journalist in the Commons lobby know details of his budget (which enabled London's *Star* to tell the public all about it before MPs had been briefed on its contents). Cripps combined his old and new roles, expanding the Chancellor's remit to include the new concern with economic planning. With the help of leading officials on the government's economic planning staff, Cripps fashioned a clearer Keynesian approach to the economy. Taxes were kept high, particularly on unearned incomes such as inheritances, with estates over £21,500 subject to a 75 per cent levy (increased to 80 per cent in 1950). A deal was also done with the Trades Union Congress to keep wages down so that a lid could be kept on inflation. Physical controls on food, clothing and furniture continued, largely in preference to further taxes on profits. There were further bumps in the road, including a devaluation crisis in 1949, but with the advent of the Marshall Plan, which saw the Americans commit more than $12 billion to rebuilding European economies, in part to combat the threat of communism, the British economy began to recover.

Cripps, a tall, bespectacled, teetotal vegetarian and renowned intellectual, whom many observers assumed had little interest in fun, also presided over spending cuts. He believed austerity was needed. The main casualty was Labour's plan to build up to 5 million homes within a decade – a decision with serious human consequences. Evacuees who had been moved out of Britain's cities during the early stages of the war wanted to return home; however, as late as March 1946, 38,000 of them still had nowhere to return to. This situation was made worse by a birthrate that had started to climb thanks to a baby boom that began during the second half of the war, meaning there were going to be more people to house than expected. Rather than build new homes, the government now channelled money into a programme to repair damaged properties and put up 125,000 prefabs – temporary buildings assembled on site from ready-made pieces – all over the country.

Despite these cuts, Labour was serious about tackling the working classes' housing problems, which had gone unsolved during the private house-building boom of the 1930s. To almost everyone's surprise,

Attlee had appointed Aneurin Bevan (1897–1960), the fiery left-wing former miner from south Wales, known as Nye to his friends, to health, the ministry that had been responsible for housing since its creation after the First World War. The egotistical Bevan was considered something of a loose cannon, more concerned with making his point than getting things done. However, he was committed to better working-class housing as a pillar of post-war reconstruction. Bevan had spent his childhood and youth in the coalfields of the Sirhowy Valley, where two-thirds of the men in his home town worked for the Tredegar Iron and Coal Company. Life had been tough. Four of his nine siblings had not made it to adulthood and his father, like many of the men he worked with, had died from pneumoconiosis, a lung disease contracted after years spent inhaling dust underground. Bevan believed that people like his father had not only built Britain, they had put their lives on the line to save the country twice during the previous three decades. The least they deserved, he felt, were houses with indoor toilets and rooms large enough for families to sit together.

Bevan prioritized local authority house-building projects, and insisted on mixed communities where different social classes were expected to rub shoulders. The Town and Country Planning Act of 1947 planned for substantial new towns in places such as Crawley, Hemel Hempstead, Stevenage, Harlow and Basildon. Progress was slow, mainly because there were so many different departments and organizations with the ability to block or defer decisions, but also because Cripps kept a tight grip on the finances, which came under pressure when Bevan increased the basic size requirements for new properties from 750 to 900 square feet, simply because he thought people were entitled to something better than the existing standards. More than 195,000 houses were completed each year from 1949 to 1951, in addition to the 227,000 that were completed in 1948. This was in many ways impressive but still fell short of the country's needs.

Although housing was a subject close to Bevan's heart, it paled in comparison to his passion for the proposed National Health Service. Bevan's lack of previous Cabinet-level experience made civil servants in the Ministry of Health apprehensive. The proposed National Health Service was going to be as big an institution as Britain had ever known, comparable in size to the National Coal Board, which took over more than 1,600 of the country's mines in 1948, and Labour had given themselves just three years to get it up and running. The challenge was massive, and civil servants, not to mention his colleagues in the Labour Party, wondered if Bevan was out of his depth.

To the surprise of most, Bevan turned out to be an astonishingly good organizer. After passing the National Health Service Act for England and Wales in 1946, with similar acts for Scotland and Northern Ireland following the year after, he had a number of highly technical and administrative problems to solve. The National Health Service was not being built from scratch; Britain already had numerous different types of healthcare provision, all of which had different models of ownership reflecting different user groups and expectations. The major challenge was integrating these institutions, not to mention the people who worked in them, into a single system. Bevan believed full nationalization was the only option but, like his colleagues in government, he was acutely aware of what had worked and what had not over the past century of poor relief and social insurance provision. He concluded that a system controlled from Whitehall was unlikely to work. Rather, such a diverse range of interests would have to be incorporated in a much more complex system, composed of a number of largely independent parts, in which local health authorities, regional institutions and contractors, such as pharmaceutical services, reported back to the Ministry of Health. In his system, local health authorities would maintain responsibility for social care – services such as maternity and child welfare and vaccination – while hospitals would come under the jurisdiction of regional hospital boards. In order to keep the best equipped and most prestigious institutions of their kind on board, Bevan was even prepared to let teaching hospitals have their own boards of governors who reported directly to the Ministry of Health.

Bevan wagered that everyone got at least something from this system and, for the most part, he was proven right. Even *The Economist*, a publication hardly renowned as a supporter of state-driven solutions, endorsed the overall package. The Tories were also satisfied with much of what Labour proposed. Yet they continued to argue that too much power and responsibility were being taken away from local authorities and decided that, as a point of principle, they would vote against the National Health Service Act on its second and third readings – a decision that had significant and long-lasting implications for public perceptions of their attitudes towards free and universal healthcare. The new system's most vehement opponent, however, and one with the power to obstruct it, was the British Medical Association, which threated not to co-operate with Bevan. The association's concerns were as old as health insurance in Britain: doctors' relationship with the government. Would a National Health Service mean doctors would be banned from selling their services and instead become fully-fledged government employees, like civil servants? If so, the British Medical Association argued, doctors were facing an assault on their freedoms and professional standing. As the association's former secretary, Alfred Cox, put it in a letter to the *British Medical Journal* in 1946, reviving the language that had caused Churchill so many problems a year earlier, critics thought the National Health Service looked like 'the first step ... towards National Socialism as practised in Germany'.

The British Medical Association took to balloting its members to gauge support. As late as January 1948, just six months before the National Health Service was due to start, almost 90 per cent voted against the government's proposals. Bevan was in no mood for threats, though. He told doctors he would retaliate by cutting their capitation fees – the money they received for each insured patient they treated – and went as far as organizing a motion in the Commons to demonstrate he had a democratic mandate. For all his posturing, though, Bevan wanted a negotiated solution. The British Medical Association had built its position around general practitioners, the organization's major faction, so he set about trying to bring them over to his side. He did so via a third party, consultants, whom he won over and then used as messengers. As he freely admitted, Bevan bought consultants off – 'stuffed their mouths with gold', as he later put it – by promising them both a National Health Service salary and that they could keep beds for their private patients within NHS hospitals. Turning to general practitioners, he offered what looked like an equally clever and elegant solution that would ensure they were neither salaried staff nor expected to become entrepreneurs within a nationalized system: they would be paid according to the number of NHS patients they had on their lists. It was a deal that hinted at a well-remunerated future for general practitioners – if they were prepared to co-operate.

The British Medical Association had no choice but to put the proposal to its members in April 1948, just three months before the NHS's start date. Bevan's gamble paid off. Although the majority of members were still against signing up, the number of GPs who were against him had almost halved, to below 10,000, forcing the association into a rapid U-turn. Bevan was triumphant. After three years of compromise – a quality he was not previously known to possess – he finally gave in to urges he had hitherto kept under control. Addressing a Labour Party rally in Manchester on 4 July, the night before the NHS's launch, he gave an emotional account of the poverty he had seen and experienced in south Wales. 'First-class people' had been condemned to 'semi-starvation', he explained, as he recalled how he had been forced to spend periods living off his sister's meagre wages. Emigration, and the prospect of leaving everyone he knew and loved behind for good, had sometimes seemed like the only way out. He knew exactly where blame for this distressing situation lay. 'No amount of cajolery, and no attempts at ethical or social seduction' came close to removing from his 'heart a deep burning hatred for the Tory Party that inflicted those bitter experiences on me', he told his audience. In a turn of phrase many of his colleagues thought quite regrettable, Bevan was blunt: the Tories were 'lower than vermin'. But his own experiences would be a thing of the past. On Monday, 5 July 1948, things would change.

Conclusion

This New Entity Composed of Old Elements

The south London comedian Tommy Trinder made it big after winning a music hall talent show when he was just thirteen. Tall and slim, sporting his trademark double-breasted suit and a trilby hat, he was hired by the Ministry of Information in early 1948 to star in a minute-long public information film. It was set in the hallway of a house that looked like one of the hundreds of thousands that had been built in Britain's suburbs during the 1930s. As the camera focused on the front door, a small booklet dropped through the letterbox onto a mat. A woman wearing a long skirt, blouse and apron knelt to retrieve it, stood up, glanced at the front cover, and made as if to throw the booklet away. Trinder, dapper as always, appeared from a side room and told her to stop. Turning to the camera, he spoke in rhyme.

> While I'm here in the hall, I'll talk to you all,
> So sit up and please pay attention.
> Are you haggard and old? Are you rolling in gold?
> Are you hard up and right on the rocks?
> Are you just newly wed or confined to your bed,
> Knitting wee little white woolly socks?
> Do you walk with a stick, are you limping or sick?
> You think that can't happen? Alright.
> Well, it can or it can't, or it shall or it shan't,
> Maybe it won't. But it might.
> Now the point of this tale is to drive home a nail
> You'll be getting a booklet like this.
> Although it's quite small, it affects one and all,

Every master, and misses, and miss.
So please everyone try, by the 5th of July,
To have read the booklet right through.
Put it safely away, you might need it one day.
And then you can read what to do.

The scene Trinder had been asked to act out was about to become familiar to people across the country. Millions of copies of the *Family Guide to the National Insurance Scheme* – a small, 32-page booklet printed in dark navy ink – were posted to homes up and down Britain in the months before the appointed day. It told people about the basic mechanics of the scheme they were all going to be enrolled in, from how they would be making contributions to how they would be able to claim benefits when they needed them. Meanwhile, the Ministry of National Insurance was scrambling to get the scheme's bureaucracy in place. Among other things, it had to issue documents to people who had not previously been covered by a government scheme, print millions of insurance stamps for employers to buy, and send out to post offices lists of medical practitioners whom people would now be able to see. 'The success of this great Insurance Scheme depends on the willing co-operation of every one of us,' wrote James Griffiths, the Minister of National Insurance, in his foreword to the *Family Guide*. The scheme was, he stated, more than an Act of Parliament; 'it is an act of faith in the British people'.

The new national insurance scheme was only one part of the story of 5 July 1948, known as the 'appointed day'. After three years of frantic activity, a whole raft of interrelated legislation was in effect. The school leaving age was now fifteen and local authorities had been handed a wide range of responsibilities, from planning for new housing developments to the care of vulnerable children. The creation of the National Health Service, though, was undeniably the biggest change.

Immediately, anyone in the country could make an appointment to see a doctor, an optician or a dentist and be prescribed medicine without having to pay. In the view of many, the NHS was – as one fifty-year-old woman, a metal polisher, put it to an interviewer from Mass-Observation – 'one of the finest things that ever happened in this country'. 'In the past there's many a man had to think twice before seeing a doctor even if he was very ill,' she explained. 'There are old people who went about for years half blind because they couldn't afford spectacles. I've seen them using bits of magnifying glass to read newspapers with and buying cheap 2 shilling glasses, which spoilt their eyes more than ever.' The NHS was 'a godsend' for people like them.

Not everyone was happy. Some people believed the government had ruined what was essentially a decent system. Individuals and businesses complained about red tape, especially when it came to filling out claims forms and waiting for benefits to arrive by post. Others resented contributions coming out of their wages, especially at the relatively high rates the government had set. There were also predictable and often apocryphal reports about waste and profiteering. One common story involved dentists who performed unnecessary procedures so they could rake in higher fees. Another featured overweight women feigning back pain and demanding their new GP prescribe a corset. Then there was discontent among sections of the middle classes. Despite Beveridge's claims, some thought the government had indeed created a 'Santa Claus' state – one that was handing out gifts to the poor, paid for by them. If that was not bad enough, they believed, the effect of the newly formed NHS was to downgrade the services they had been happy to pay for in the past. Doctors were now so busy they often dispensed with the rituals, like tea and biscuits, that had been part of visits before the war.

Many of these complaints were not new. They often had deep historical roots and reflected an anxiety about what looked like a final and dramatic stage in a century-long process of development. A little over a century earlier, reformers had tried to stigmatize the idea of unemployment benefit, making the act of receiving it from the public purse a matter of shame. The authorities were supposed to maintain a welfare system that was so basic and threadbare that nobody could possibly want to use it – and that, if they did, they would want to get out of as soon as possible. From the 'appointed day', though, welfare services were part of ordinary and everyday business. Everyone contributed and, one way or another, everyone used them. As the Labour government also embarked on an ambitious programme of nationalization, with coal, railways, iron and steel, electricity, gas and the Bank of England all being taken into state hands, it looked like a new balance had been struck between public and private. The country might have almost broken itself winning a war. But it looked like everyone really was in it together when it came to putting things back together.

Some observers believed they had lived through events that could be compared to the great political transformations of the eighteenth century. A compulsory contributory national insurance scheme was a natural and logical continuation of trends that had started almost half a century earlier, but the NHS and a commitment to full employment, which promised comprehensive and universal provision, gave the whole package of reforms a profoundly different meaning. According to T. H. Marshall, the sociologist whom Beveridge had hired to teach social work at the London School of Economics during the 1920s, his old boss's description of 'a British revolution' was apt.

Looking back on the 'appointed day' two decades later, by which point he had become one of the country's most important sociologists, Marshall was filled with a deep sense of awe. What Britain had seen, Marshall argued in *Social Policy*, one of his most famous books, was 'the logical development and natural evolution of ideas and institutions' that transformed everything. The revolution 'consisted in the welding together of the measures of social policy into a whole which, for the first time, acquired thereby a personality of its own and a meaning that had hitherto been only vaguely glimpsed'. The fundamental character of this new whole was, Marshall explained, that social services were not to be seen as 'regrettable necessities', to be kept only until the capitalist system had been reformed. On the contrary, 'they were a permanent and even a glorious part of the social system itself. They were something to be proud of, not apologise for.'

Others were not quite so sure that the coming of the 'welfare state' was a moment of great transformation. On the contrary, these critics argued, the advent of the welfare state was something of a missed opportunity because it stopped short of changing the social, political and economic order. The state may very well have been committed to keeping as many people in work as possible, key industries might have been nationalized, and benefits were certainly much more generous than they had been in the past. But national insurance was still built on contributions as the basis for entitlement, while capitalism was simply being managed. As far as critics were concerned, the state was now doing little more than providing people with a crutch to rest on so that they could be exploited once again.

Michael Young, director of Labour's research department and an author of *Let Us Face the Future*, the party's 1945 general election manifesto, thought the welfare state had serious failings. Politicians were, he felt, so enthusiastic about their new powers over society and the idea they could use them to engineer change that they paid little attention to the damage they could cause in the process. Governments were part of the solution to problems like economic depressions, Young argued, but they could not always bring about improvement from above. Ordinary people needed to be given a voice and an opportunity to participate in the process of change, rather than simply expected to accept what was given to them.

So disillusioned was Young that he resigned from his position in the Labour Party in 1951, returning to the world of social research and activism he had been part of before 1945. He went back to the London School of Economics, where he had been an undergraduate, to study for a Ph.D. under Richard Titmuss, the 'high priest of the welfare state'. Young was convinced that for all the material improvements wrought by the new system, the state was wilfully disregarding things ordinary people thought were valuable. In his 1957 book, *Family and Kinship in East London*, co-written with his colleague Peter Willmott, Young argued that the effort to move working-class people from city slums to new towns and estates showed little regard for the communities they were part of. There might have been nicer houses in places like Debden in Essex, one of the new estates built after the war, but the wider family networks and social interactions that had provided meaning in people's lives were gone. More famous, though frequently misunderstood, was Young's *The Rise of the Meritocracy* (1958), a dystopian social science fiction. Reflecting on the new educational ladder and a society that seemed intent on conferring economic rewards and social status on those who climbed it, Young suggested that a narrow understanding of intelligence, allied with a belief that it could be inherited, threatened to disenfranchise a whole class of people who might one day rebel against their social superiors.

In many respects, these differences of opinion were a testament to what Marshall called the welfare state's 'mixed parentage'. Labour had been responsible for the final and decisive push, bringing the whole framework into existence when the Tories might very well have conceded defeat in the face of a precarious economic situation, as well as seemingly intransigent opposition from groups like the British Medical Association. Yet Labour did not pluck ideas and legislation out of thin air. Much was already in place, with versions of the bureaucratic infrastructure, customs and practices initiated by the Liberal and Conservative governments during the first four decades of the twentieth century providing solid and useful foundations. The fact there were Labour, Tory and Liberal fingerprints on the welfare state was an important reason why it was not instantly dismantled by the Tories when they regained power in the 1951 general election. By the same token, the welfare state's heterogeneous beginnings also explain why there were people across the political spectrum who were never going to be happy with it. The welfare state was neither straightforwardly maximalist, in the sense of trying to achieve the best outcome for everyone in every set of circumstances, nor minimalist in providing a safety net and nothing else. Thanks mainly to Labour, however, the welfare state was universal and comprehensive, meaning a level of national unity on social policy that had never been tried before – or, indeed, since.

The welfare state was a maturing of a particular set of ideas about the relationship between individuals and the state, not to mention the state and the economy, which had been developing for more than a hundred years. Thinkers and commentators who had argued that Britain needed an approach to the economy that was better than simply leaving it alone had played their part. But those who thought the country needed an economic policy that was fully integrated with social policy had been most influential. In some ways, this was nothing new. The Poor Law reformers of the 1830s had seen the economic, social and government spheres as deeply connected; nevertheless, they believed the state could do little more than create dependency and stunt character. Their successors, however, including the majority of liberals, had been converted to the idea that state action was often better than inaction, meaning it was sometimes necessary to spend money now in order to save it further down the line.

As the likes of Edwin Chadwick had shown, these converts were far from sentimental when it came to the problems they wanted to fix. There was certainly no shortage of thinkers – especially among new liberals at the turn of the twentieth century – whose belief that the state could do more to help the poor had been fired by what they had witnessed in the East End of London and other areas of acute deprivation. But they were counterbalanced by the likes of Beveridge and Keynes, among liberals, and by socialists, including the Webbs, who were motivated by concerns about economic and social efficiency. All, however, accepted that a problem such as spiralling bills for poor relief could not be reduced to a single cause like individuals' character. People's lives, they believed, were complex constructions that could be badly affected by seemingly small changes or events in their social environment. If those people were going to stand a good chance of becoming the self-reliant, hard-working individuals that politicians and social commentators desired, then it looked like the state would have to do the best it could to put a barrier between its citizens and forces that had the power to alter their lives for the worse.

Nevertheless, the system that emerged after 1945 was only possible because a wide enough group of people had been convinced that it was possible, practically speaking, and compatible with their political convictions. Few embraced the most radical or extreme ideas, such as economic planning, but by the end of the Second World War, and under Keynes's influence in particular, economic management was popular with both politicians and the public. Government and citizens alike knew unemployment was a feature of modern life and that it could never be eliminated completely. But they thought it was within the state's power to stop the problem from getting out of hand through both pre-emptive action and help for those who found themselves casualties of it. This conviction was the most obvious and important example of a wider confidence in the ability of people, via the state, to influence – if not perfectly control – events in ways that pushed society in desirable directions.

These ideas were embraced as a necessary means of making the new vision of a good society a practical and workable reality. In this sense, the welfare state was the culmination of an intergenerational project focused on the question of how to adapt Britain to the realities of the modern world. By the end of the Second World War, the country had industrialized and urbanized and had a population four times the size it had been a century earlier. Some people had done well out of these processes; others had not. Most lived very different lives to those of their ancestors as a result. The welfare state was central to the twentieth century's answer to the question of how everyone was going to get along in such a way that social and economic order did not break down.

Of course, there are all manner of important questions about whether these convictions were borne out in practice, and whether the welfare state performed the function that it was intended to. The story of what happened to the welfare state after 1948 lies beyond the scope of this book. Yet it is worth pointing out that the welfare state has, in a sense, always been under construction. Affordability was a thorny issue from the outset – and an issue that critics have never been slow to raise since. Re-elected in 1950 with a tiny majority of five, and with Stafford Cripps demanding further budget savings, Labour introduced prescription charges, spelling the end for the pure vision of a health service that was free for all – and prompting Bevan's eventual resignation from the Ministry of Labour, where he had moved in 1951. By the 1960s the idea of comprehensive schools had become the new and sometimes controversial preference for political progressives. But all manner of other issues, from house-building rates to benefit scales to the pension qualification age, have been debated constantly since the 1940s.

One thing that can be said with certainty is that the welfare state's creation ushered in a unique era. The generation that came of age during the third quarter of the twentieth century had, to borrow Tory Prime Minister Harold Macmillan's phrase, 'never had it so good'. To be sure, they did not grow up in an age of uninterrupted expansion and progress. There were bumps in the road throughout the 1950s and 1960s, and the 1970s – when the Keynesian consensus established at the end of the war fell apart – are remembered as a period of acute economic difficulty. For many who grew up in the decades after 1948, however, it was a time when living standards rose immensely and opportunities were created that would, unbeknown to them, lay the foundations for comfort and prosperity for years to come. A new affluent society grew, a spirit of consumerism reached new parts of society and Britain became more equal than it ever had been before. Rates of social mobility increased as children born into the working class moved into the plethora of traditional middle-class jobs that became available as the economy expanded. Many members of the skilled working class who remained in their jobs saw their wages increase to the extent that they were able to enjoy some of the trappings of middle-class life, including home ownership, that had previously been out of reach. It was the era of social democracy, with parts of socialism blended into capitalism.

All this was underpinned by the welfare state, which was never simply a dull system of national insurance that paid out benefits to people who found themselves out of work but an interconnected system of institutions and policies, infused with ideas and values that had been debated and shaped for more than a century. Many of those who lived through the war and the difficult decades that preceded it greatly appreciated what had come into being by the end of the 1940s. Yet the generations that followed found it much easier to take for granted something that quickly became central to everyday life in Britain. It is too early to tell if those attitudes will lead to the welfare state unravelling. But as the 150 years before the end of the Second World War show, building something like the welfare state is immensely more difficult than allowing it to fall apart.

Essay on Sources

What follows are notes on reading related to each chapter. There are two aims. The first is to provide pointers for anyone interested in following up particular subjects. The second is to highlight books I have found particularly useful over the years and, in the absence of footnotes throughout the text, pay the necessary dues to historians whose work has influenced and informed my own. I have provided neither an account of everything I have read nor a comprehensive bibliography of the kind found at the end of academic treatises. I have also tried not to repeat myself. Some sources are mentioned more than once, but where a topic is discussed in more than one chapter I have provided suggestions for further reading just once. The essay has also been written in the knowledge that most readers will not have access to a university library or the expensive academic journals that they subscribe to. Most recommendations are books, though I have mentioned key articles where appropriate.

It is worth mentioning at the outset that the internet has transformed historical research. Although it is still necessary to travel to access most manuscript collections (though some notable exceptions are mentioned below), printed primary sources are accessible in a way that was difficult to imagine as recently as fifteen years ago. While most of the books that are mentioned in the text can be accessed via websites like www.archive.org, other institutions provide electronic versions of collections they store. This means things like the Fabian Society's pamphlets and photographic collections, including images of Sidney and Beatrice Webb and William Beveridge, are now freely available. Well-resourced public libraries will also have access to websites including www.parlipapers.chadwyck.

co.uk, through which you will be able to read things like reports of Royal Commissions (though older documents will be freely available online). Hansard is online (http://hansard.millbanksystems.com/), providing access to the parliamentary debates I have mentioned and which you may wish to investigate further.

There are also a wide range of general secondary works available online. Again, well-resourced public libraries will have access to resources including the *Oxford Dictionary of National Biography* (www.oxforddnb.com) – now no longer published on paper but updated at regular intervals in its new electronic form – which provides authoritative and concise essays on every individual mentioned in the preceding chapters. The Stanford Encyclopedia of Philosophy (www.plato.stanford.edu) is a hugely valuable but strangely under-publicized resource providing essays on most of the philosophers, political thinkers and their ideas mentioned in the text. All those essays are written by leading academics and therefore avoid many of the biggest problems associated with articles on more famous free websites.

None of this makes printed sources redundant. There are a number of excellent works on the history of the welfare state. Nicholas Timmins' *Five Giants: A Biography of the Welfare State*, 2nd edition (2001) is the best-known work and begins with events towards the end of my account. There are, however, many weighty academic tomes that cover the technical social policy details and often provide documentary resources as appendices. These include: Derek Fraser, *The Evolution of the Welfare State* (2009); Pat Thane, *The Foundations of the Welfare State* (1993); and David Vincent, *Poor Citizens: The State and the Poor in Twentieth-Century Britain* (1991). There are also a range of works dealing with the welfare state since 1948, including Margaret Jones and Rodney Lowe, *From Beveridge to Blair: The First 50 Years of Britain's Welfare State* (2002).

Economic and social statistics can be found in B. R. Mitchell, *British Historical Statistics* (1988) and A. H. Halsey, *Trends in British Society since 1900: A Guide to the Changing Social Structure of Britain* (1972). David Butler and Gareth Butler, *British Political Facts* (2010), a regularly updated work, provides the indispensable resource for the who, what and when of British politics. There are also collections, such as F. W. S. Craig, *British General Election Manifestos, 1900–1974* (1975), which provide key documents relating to that political history. There are numerous general works that provide illuminating and penetrating accounts of Britain over the period discussed in this book. It is impossible to mention them all. The ones I have found most valuable over the years are Martin Daunton's *Progress and Poverty: An Economic and Social History of Britain, 1700–1850* (1995) and *Wealth and Welfare: An Economic and Social History of Great Britain, 1851–1951* (2007) – brilliant excursions through the economic dynamics and social movements of the past 300 years; Peter Clarke, *Hope and Glory: Britain 1900–2000*, 2nd edition (2004) and Jose Harris, *Private Lives, Public Spirit: A Social History of Britain, 1870–1914* (1993), which both provide excellent and profoundly insightful surveys; and G. R. Searle, *A New England? Peace and War, 1886–1918* (2004).

1. ATMOSPHERIC IMPURITY

On the old Poor Law see Paul Slack, *The English Poor Law, 1531–1782* (1991), Keith Snell, *Annals of the Labouring Poor: Social Change and Agrarian England 1600–1900* (1988), J. R. Poynter, *Society and Pauperism: English Ideas on Poor Relief, 1795–1834* (1969), and Joanna Innes, 'The "Mixed Economy of Welfare" in Early Modern England: Assessment of the Options from Hale to Malthus (c. 1683–1803)', in Martin Daunton, ed., *Charity, Self-Interest and Welfare in the English Past* (1996). On the Scottish case see R. A. Cage, *The Scottish Poor Law 1745–1845* (1981). On the new Poor Law and its implementation see Anne Digby, *The Poor Law in Nineteenth-Century England and Wales* (1982), M. A. Crowther, *The Workhouse System: The History of an English Social Institution* (1981), and Peter Wood, *Poverty and the Workhouse in Victorian Britain* (1991). Sidney and Beatrice Webb's books on the Poor Law – *English Poor Law Policy* (1910) and *English Poor Law History* (1929) – are also immensely informative and a testament to their belief that knowledge is the first step towards reform.

There are numerous good works on the economic context. See G. R. Boyer, *An Economic History of the English Poor Law, 1750–1850*

(1990) and the essays in the first two volumes of Roderick Floud and Paul Johnson, eds., *The Cambridge Economic History of Modern Britain*, 3 vols. (2004) for analyses of different economic aspects of domestic and public life. Frank Trentmann, *Free Trade Nation* (2008) provides a clear and thought-provoking account of the centrality of free trade to political and cultural life in Britain during the nineteenth century. On arguments about different types of capitalism, particularly 'gentlemanly capitalism', see Peter J. Cain and Anthony G. Hopkins, *British Imperialism: Innovation and Expansion, 1688–2000*, 2nd edn (2001), and Boyd Hilton, *A Mad, Bad and Dangerous People? England, 1783–1846* (1989), as well as an early critique of their revisionism, which dated back to the mid-1980s: Martin Daunton, '"Gentlemanly Capitalism" and British Industry, 1820–1914', *Past and Present* 122 (1989). See William J. Ashworth, 'The British Industrial Revolution and the Ideological Revolution: Science, Neoliberalism and History', *History of Science* 52 (2014) for a recent succinct analysis of the flaws in the idea that free trade drove economic growth and technological innovation during the nineteenth century.

Classical political economy has been a popular research topic. There are a number of general works that cover the history of economic thought. Masterly and hugely accessible overviews include Roger Backhouse, *The Penguin History of Economics* (2002) and Robert L. Heilbroner, *The Worldly Philosophers: The Lives, Times, and Ideas of the Great Economic Thinkers*, 6th edition (1991). More technical but no less excellent and as broad in scope is Henry Spiegel, *The Growth of Economic Thought*, 3rd edition (1991). Most recent introductions to reprints of classic works contain excellent and lengthy introductions, such as Andrew Skinner's analytical essay in the Penguin edition of Adam Smith's *The Wealth of Nations* (1999). But there are also numerous biographies of key thinkers. For a study of David Ricardo's work see Samuel Hollander's *The Economics of David Ricardo* (1979) and Terry Peach, *Interpreting Ricardo* (2009). On Thomas Malthus see Donald Winch, *Malthus* (1987), the classic study of his ideas, and Robert J. Mayhew, *Malthus: The Life and Legacies of an Untimely Prophet* (2014), which traces Malthus's implications for subsequent generations of scholars and politicians. Much of this is put into context in Elie Halévy's classic *The Growth of Philosophic Radicalism* (1934/1972), Emma Rothschild, *Economic Sentiments: Adam Smith, Condorcet, and the Enlightenment* (2001), and Donald Winch, *Riches and Poverty: An Intellectual History of Political Economy in Britain, 1750–1834* (1996).

Utilitarianism is a hugely important and influential doctrine in British intellectual history. Halévy's *The Growth of Philosophic Radicalism* and William Thomas, *The Philosophic Radicals: Nine Studies in Theory and Practice, 1817–1841* (1979) are excellent starting points for the context out of which it developed, as is J. R. Dinwiddy, *Radicalism and Reform in Britain, 1780–1850* (1992). Jeremy Bentham is well covered in works like Philip Schofield, *Utility and Democracy: The Political Thought of Jeremy Bentham* (2006) and M. Mack, *Jeremy Bentham: An Odyssey of Ideas, 1748–1792* (1962). Every aspect of Bentham's thought has been covered by scholars from a myriad of different fields. As good a place to start as any is Gerald J. Postema, ed., *Bentham: Moral, Political and Legal Philosophy*, 2 vols. (2002). Particular projects receive attention in works like J. Semple, *Bentham's Prison: A Study of the Panopticon Penitentiary* (1993) and F. Rosen, *Jeremy Bentham and Representative Democracy: A Study of the Constitutional Code* (1983). University College London, home to both his auto-icon and his papers, has made a huge amount of his work available online for free, along with helpful essays and introductions at http://www.ucl.ac.uk/Bentham-Project.

There are two main biographies of Bentham's disciple Edwin Chadwick. While the classic work is S. E. Finer, *The Life and Times of Sir Edwin Chadwick* (1952/1970), Christopher Hamlin, *Public Health and Social Justice in the Age of Chadwick* (1998) provides a detailed analysis of Chadwick's technocratic leanings and historical context. The medical and scientific background to Chadwick's work can be picked up from a number of different sources. John Waller, *The Discovery of the Germ* (2002) is a breezy tour through the shift from miasmatic to germ theory in nineteenth- and twentieth-century science. Roy Porter – the most eminent and brilliant, not to mention prolific, historian of medicine of recent times – covers this territory in a number of places. The best are 'What is Disease?' in R. Porter, ed., *The Cambridge Illustrated History of Medicine* (1996) and *The Greatest Benefit to Mankind: A Medical History of Humanity from*

Antiquity to Present (1997). W. F. Bynum, *Science and the Practice of Medicine in the Nineteenth Century* (1995) is another brilliant general work that elucidates the relationship between medicine and scientific research during the period – a connection we now assume to be strong but was not so until the early twentieth century. On the public health history see Anthony Wohl, *Endangered Lives: Public Health in Victorian Britain* (1983) and, for a comparative international story, Dorothy Porter, *Health, Civilization, and the State: A History of Public Health from Ancient to Modern Times* (1999). Further information on hospitals and the Poor Law can be found in M. W. Flinn, 'Medical Services under the New Poor Law', in Derek Fraser, ed., *The New Poor Law in the Nineteenth Century* (1976).

2. BELOW THE POVERTY LINE

The public health context is closely related to the social science context, mainly via the growth of statistics. Lawrence Goldman, *Science, Reform, and Politics in Victorian Britain* (2002) provides an unmatched account of the Social Science Association, the people who attended its meetings, and its influence on government during the middle decades of the nineteenth century. Eileen Janes Yeo, *The Contest for Social Science: Relations and Representations of Class and Gender* (1996) covers similar territory but through to the early twentieth century. Martin Bulmer has edited several brilliant collections of relevant essays. These include *The Social Survey in Historical Perspective, 1880–1940* (1991), edited with Kevin Bales and Kathryn Kish Sklar, and *Essays on the History of British Sociological Research* (1985). David Englander and Rosemary O'Day, eds., *Retrieved Riches: Social Investigation in Britain 1840–1914* (1995) pays particular attention to Charles Booth and Seebohm Rowntree. These studies of social science should be read alongside investigations of social work during the period. While Robert Humphreys, *Sin, Organized Charity and the Poor Law in Victorian England* (1995) explores the voluntary organization context, Jane Lewis, *The Voluntary Sector, the State and Social Work in Britain: The Charity Organisation Society/Family Welfare Association since 1869* (1995) gives an excellent account of the COS.

Charles Booth's papers are housed at the London School of Economics. Many documents, including the famous colour-coded maps, have been made available online at http://booth.lse.ac.uk/, which also includes introductory essays. The standard biography is T. S. Simey and M. B. Simey, *Charles Booth: Social Scientist* (1961). See also B. Norman-Butler, *Victorian Aspirations: The Life and Labour of Charles and Mary Booth* (1972) and, on the survey itself, Rosemary O'Day and David Englander, *Mr Charles Booth's Inquiry: Life and Labour of the People of London Reconsidered* (1993). Asa Briggs, *Social Thought and Social Action: A Study of the Work of Seebohm Rowntree, 1871–1954* (1961) is the definitive and, somewhat strangely, only academic book on Rowntree's life. There are numerous other works, however, in which Rowntree, and the Rowntrees, feature. Gillian Wagner, *The Chocolate Conscience* (1987) tells the story of the Quaker families, including the Cadburys, whose social and political convictions permeated their business practices. Others, like Robert Fitzgerald, *Rowntree and the Marketing Revolution, 1862–1969* (1996) and L. F. Urwick, 'The Pioneers of Scientific Management: B. Seebohm Rowntree', in L. F. Urwick and E. F. L. Brech, eds., *The Making of Scientific Management* (1945), explore their contributions to business culture and innovation. Social policy researchers have been particularly interested in Seebohm Rowntree's work. J. H. Veit-Wilson has written extensively on the subject: see 'Paradigms of Poverty: A Rehabilitation of B. S. Rowntree', in O'Day and Englander's *Retrieved Riches* (1995). Jonathan Bradshaw and Roy Sainsbury, eds., *Getting the Measure of Poverty: The Early Legacy of Seebohm Rowntree* (2000) is also hugely valuable.

Given their importance to the history of the Labour Party, and British socialism in general, the Fabians are strangely under-represented in the historiography – a fact that probably tells us something about the sympathies of the historians who dominated the field during the late twentieth century. Norman MacKenzie and Jeanne MacKenzie, *The First Fabians* (1977) and A. M. McBriar, *Fabian Socialism and English Politics, 1884–1918* (1962) both provide excellent accounts of the society's early years and the broad political context. There are a number of good books on the Webbs, including: R. Harrison, *The Life and Times of Sidney and Beatrice Webb: The Formative Years,*

1858–1905 (2000) and Margaret Cole, ed., *The Webbs and their Work* (1949). There is, however, a large amount of primary material available in print. Beatrice Webb was a keen diarist and her often-revealing journals are available in published form – *The Diaries of Beatrice Webb*, 4 vols., ed. Norman MacKenzie and Jeanne MacKenzie (1982–5) – as are a collection of Sidney and Beatrice's letters, *The Letters of Sidney and Beatrice Webb*, 3 vols., ed. Norman MacKenzie. Beatrice produced two autobiographies based on those diaries: *My Apprenticeship* (1926) and *Our Partnership* (1948). Sidney and Beatrice Webb's clash with Bernard and Helen Bosanquet, and what it tells us about social-reforming tensions during the late nineteenth and early twentieth centuries, is explored brilliantly in A. M. McBriar, *An Edwardian Mixed Doubles: The Bosanquets versus the Webbs. A Study in British Social Policy, 1890–1929* (1987). McBriar also provides copious detail on, and insightful analysis of, the Royal Commission on the Poor Laws and Relief of Distress.

3. REINVENTING LIBERALISM

The political history of nineteenth- and early twentieth-century Britain is covered in countless books; certainly too many to list here. On the Tories see Robert Blake, *The Conservative Party from Peel to Thatcher*, 2nd edition (1985) and E. H. H. Green, *The Crisis of Conservatism: The Politics, Economics, and Ideology of the British Conservative Party, 1880–1914* (1995); on the Liberals G. R. Searle, *The Liberal Party: Triumph and Disintegration, 1886–1929* (1992). The standard work on Labour is Henry Pelling, *A Short History of the Labour Party*, 2nd edition (1991). Class is obviously an important dimension of that history. The classic work is, of course, E. P. Thompson, *The Making of the English Working Class* (1963), which sparked the enthusiasm for writing the social and cultural history of groups ignored by historians up until that point. Among many other subjects, Thompson provides insights into things like Owenism among the working classes. Mike Savage and Andrew Miles, *The Remaking of the British Working Class, 1840–1940* (1995) is a classic of more recent vintage, as are David Cannadine, *Class in Britain* (1984) and Patrick Joyce, *Visions of the People: Industrial England*

and the Question of Class c. 1848–1914 (1991). Ross McKibbin, *Classes and Cultures: England, 1918–1951* (1998) takes these stories into the twentieth century. David Howell, *British Workers and the Independent Labour Party, 1888–1906* (1983) is the authoritative study of the relationship between the working class and those who wanted a workers' party, though more books on the Labour Party are listed in essays on subsequent chapters. For studies of the evolution of British politics in response to all this see Martin Pugh, *The Making of Modern British Politics, 1867–1939* (1982) and Jon Lawrence, *Speaking for the People: Party, Language and Popular Politics in England, 1867–1914* (1998).

There are numerous excellent studies of the Liberals' social reforms during the first decade of the twentieth century, which are contextualized brilliantly in Richard Toye, *Lloyd George and Churchill: Rivals for Greatness* (2007). John Macnicol, *The Politics of Retirement in Britain, 1878–1948* (1998) weaves together the political story and an analysis of the statistics underpinning key decisions and is the standard work. Good accounts can also be found in Leslie Hannah, *Inventing Retirement: The Development of Occupational Pensions in Britain* (1986), Margot Jefferys, ed., *Growing Old in the Twentieth Century* (1989), and Jill S. Quadagno, *Ageing in Early Industrial Society: Work, Family, and Social Policy in Nineteenth-Century England* (1982). Christina Victor, *Old Age in Modern Society* (1987) and Paul Johnson and Jane Falkingham, *Ageing and Economic Welfare* (1992) provide more general studies of attitudes towards ageing. Martin Daunton, *Trusting Leviathan: The Politics of Taxation in Britain, 1799–1914* (2001) is a typically masterful study of the mechanics and meanings of taxation – a particularly important issue in connection with the 'People's Budget'. While Bruce K. Murray, *The People's Budget, 1909–10* (1980) surveys the economic and political context for Lloyd George's budget, Avner Offer, *Property and Politics 1870–1914: Landownership, Law, Ideology and Urban Development in England* (1981) and B. B. Gilbert, 'David Lloyd George: Land, the Budget, and Social Reform', *American Historical Review* 81 (1976) cover land reform. Gilbert's *The Evolution of National Insurance in Great Britain* (1966) is also an excellent study that puts the Liberals' reforms into the context of the story about national insurance. Essays in M. Gorsky and S. Sheard, *Financing Medicine: The British Experience since 1750* (2006) provide analysis of the situation health insurance was meant to address.

The intellectual history of politics and political ideas is also well covered. Mark Francis and John Morrow, *A History of English Political Thought in the Nineteenth Century* (1994) provides a useful overview of the forces that shaped key thinkers and political traditions, and H. S. Jones, *Victorian Political Thought* (2000) is a useful survey. Undoubtedly the best work on the subject, however, has been produced by three scholars. Stefan Collini, Donald Winch and J. W. Burrow, *That Noble Science of Politics: A Study in Nineteenth-Century Intellectual History* (1983) is a brilliant study that provides illuminating and insightful analysis of thinkers including Ricardo, Smith and the Mills and positions them clearly in the political and philosophical ferment of the early and mid-nineteenth century. No less excellent in this respect are Winch's two volumes of essays: *Riches and Poverty* (1996) and *Wealth and Life: Essays on the Intellectual History of Political Economy 1848–1914* (2009). Burrow's *Whigs and Liberals: Continuity and Change in English Political Thought* (1985) provides a lucid account of both traditions and explains their eighteenth-century roots. Boyd Hilton, *The Age of Atonement: The Influence of Evangelicalism on Social and Economic Thought, 1795–1865* (1988) explores the other side of the intellectual coin, helping us to make sense of thinkers like Malthus.

The development of utilitarianism after Bentham's death is probably best covered and most easily accessible via the work on John Stuart Mill. Mill receives extensive attention in Collini, Winch and Burrow, *That Noble Science of Politics*. His economics is covered by Winch, *Wealth and Life* and Samuel Hollander, *The Economics of John Stuart Mill*, 2 vols. (1985). There are several biographies, including M. St J. Packe, *The Life of John Stuart Mill* (1954), but by far and away the best is Richard Reeves, *John Stuart Mill: Victorian Firebrand* (2015), which is insightful, lucid and thought provoking.

New liberalism has been a popular topic of study among historians and political philosophers alike. The standard historical work is Michael Freeden, *The New Liberalism: An Ideology of Social Reform* (1978); his *Liberalism Divided: A Study in British Political Thought, 1914–1939* (1988) takes the story up to the Second World War. Stefan

Collini, *Liberalism and Sociology: L. T. Hobhouse and Political Argument in England, 1880–1914* (1979) is an unparalleled study of new liberalism's leading thinker and his historical context. The relationship between social reform and the Empire – particularly that of men like Joseph Chamberlain – is covered by H. C. G. Matthew, *The Liberal Imperialists: The Ideas and Politics of a Post-Gladstonian Elite* (1973) and Bernard Semmel, *Imperialism and Social Reform: English Social-Imperial Thought 1895–1914* (1960). There is also a great deal of excellent work on the relationship between new liberalism and socialism. Peter Clarke, *Liberals and Social Democrats* (1978) is a brilliant survey of the interactions of leading new liberal thinkers, including J. A. Hobson, and their socialist friends, including the Webbs. Ben Jackson, *Equality and the British Left: A Study in Progressive Political Thought, 1900–64* (2007) is an exceptional study of progressive British political thought during the early twentieth century. Andrew Vincent and Raymond Plant, *Philosophy, Politics, and Citizenship: The Life and Thought of the British Idealists* (1984) and Peter P. Nicholson, *The Political Philosophy of the British Idealists: Selected Studies* (1990) look at developments, including T. H. Green's work, from the perspective of political philosophy. All of this is connected to the history of the welfare state by Jose Harris, 'Political Thought and the Welfare State, 1870–1940', *Past and Present* 135 (1992).

4. THE HEALTH OF THE NATION

The best and most accessible starting point for the history of evolutionary thought is Peter J. Bowler, *Evolution: The History of an Idea*, 3rd edition (2003). A path-breaking study that connects politics, radicalism and evolutionary ideas in their mid- and late nineteenth-century British context is James A. Secord, *Victorian Sensation: The Extraordinary Publication, Reception, and Secret Authorship of* Vestiges of the Natural History of Creation (2000). Daniel Kevles, *In the Name of Eugenics: Genetics and the Uses of Human Heredity* (1995) is the standard work on the history of eugenics in an international context. Pauline Mazumdar, *Eugenics, Human Genetics and Human Failings: The Eugenics Society, its Sources and its Critics in Britain* (1992) tells the early twentieth-century story in a specifically British context, as do

Greta Jones, *Social Hygiene in Twentieth Century Britain* (1986) and Mathew Thomson, *The Problem of Mental Deficiency: Eugenics, Democracy, and Social Policy in Britain, c.1870–1959* (1998). There are a number of biographies of Francis Galton, the best of which is Nicholas W. Gillham, *A Life of Sir Francis Galton: From African Exploration to the Birth of Eugenics* (2001). Galton's entire oeuvre is also available at the impressively comprehensive www.galton.org, which includes his disciple Karl Pearson's biography, *Life, Letters, and Labours of Francis Galton*, 3 vols. (1914–30). The relationship between demography, eugenics and politics is explored in Richard A. Soloway's magisterial *Demography and Degeneration: Eugenics and the Declining Birthrate in Twentieth-Century Britain* (1995). Simon Szreter, *Fertility, Class, and Gender, 1860–1940* (1996) is an awe-inspiring study of the interaction of statistics, politics and social administration, which covers T. H. C. Stevenson and events around the fertility census. All of this is connected to the era's debates about women and their social roles in Angelique Richardson, *Love and Eugenics in the Late Nineteenth Century: Rational Reproduction and the New Woman* (2003). Ian Hacking, *The Taming of Chance* (1990) is an accessible and insightful account of the development of statistical thinking.

Daniel Pick, *Faces of Degeneration: A European Disorder, c.1848–c.1918* (1989) is a comparative international account of the medical background to theories of degeneration. This should be read alongside the literature on British society during the late nineteenth and early twentieth centuries. Gareth Stedman Jones, *Outcast London: A Study in the Relationship Between Classes in Victorian Society* (1971) is the classic account of a society riven with conflict and mistrust. John Welshman, *Underclass: A History of the Excluded since 1880*, 2nd edition (2013) is a brilliant survey of attitudes towards the working classes and the belief that there is a significant subgroup that threatens the rest of society. For more on Arnold White see G. R. Searle's introduction to the reprint of *Efficiency and Empire* (1901/1973) and Searle's 'Critics of Edwardian Society: The Case of the Radical Right', in Alan O'Day, ed., *The Edwardian Age: Conflict and Stability, 1900–1914* (1979). While Soloway, *Demography and Degeneration*, is a good starting point for more about the outcry over army recruits during the Boer War, Bentley B. Gilbert, 'Health and

Politics: The British Physical Deterioration Report of 1904', *Bulletin of the History of Medicine* 39 (1965) provides a useful analysis of the Interdepartmental Committee on Physical Deterioration.

The school meals debate is covered from a variety of different angles. John Welshman, 'School Meals and Milk in England and Wales, 1906–45', *Medical History* 41 (1997) is a useful survey of developments. While Roderick Floud, Kenneth Wachter and Annabel Gregory, *Height, Health, and History: Nutritional Status in the United Kingdom, 1750–1980* (1990) provides an exploration of living standards in connection with these issues, James Vernon, *Hunger: A Modern History* (2007) is an exceptional account of how our understanding of what hunger is and what causes it has changed over the past two centuries.

5. THE WELL-BEING OF THE WHOLE

G. R. Searle, *The Quest for National Efficiency: A Study in British Politics and Political Thought, 1899–1914* (1971) is an excellent account and analysis of – and is the standard work on – the cross-party national efficiency movement. H. C. G. Matthew, *The Liberal Imperialists* (1973) and Bernard Semmel, *Imperialism and Social Reform* (1960) are also useful on this topic. See A. M. McBriar, *Fabian Socialism and English Politics, 1884–1918* (1962) for more on the national minimum idea and the Fabian context for the national efficiency movement.

Michael Sanderson, *Educational Opportunity and Social Change in England* (1987) is an excellent account. Andy Green, *Education and State Formation: The Rise of Education Systems in England, France and the USA* (1990) puts the issue in international perspective (as the national efficiency movement itself did); Adrian Wooldridge, 'The English State and Educational Theory', in S. J. D. Green and R. C. Whiting, eds., *The Boundaries of the State in Modern Britain* (1996) provides an excellent analysis of the state's approach to educational systems and curriculums.

The debate about family allowances has been the subject of a number of excellent and informative studies. The best is Susan Pedersen, *Family, Dependence, and the Origins of the Welfare State: Britain and France, 1914–1945* (1993). Like his work on pensions, John Macnicol's *The Movement for Family Allowances, 1918–45: A Study in Social Policy Development* (1980) provides a robust and inform-ative analysis of the social policy debate and developments. Stephen Brooke, *Sexual Politics: Sexuality, Family Planning and the British Left from the 1880s to the Present Day* (2011) links many of these discussions up with left-wing politics, which has frequently had a pre-carious relationship with the topic for cultural as much as economic reasons. Work on Eleanor Rathbone, the leading figure in the British family allowances movement, also provides numerous insights into the issue. See M. D. Stocks, *Eleanor Rathbone: A Biography* (1949), Johanna Alberti, *Eleanor Rathbone* (1996), and Brian Harrison, 'Constructive Crusader: Eleanor Rathbone', in his *Prudent Revol-utionaries: Portraits of British Feminists between the Wars* (1987).

Barry Doyle, *The Politics of Hospital Provision in Early Twentieth-Century Britain* (2014) argues that many people were quite happy with the services they had access to and that they responded well to local need. Jane Lewis, *Women in England, 1870–1950: Sexual Divi-sions and Social Change* (1984) is an authoritative study on the gender context for these services and should be read alongside Martin Pugh, *Women and the Women's Movement in Britain, 1914–1959* (1992). Anne Digby, 'Poverty, Health and the Politics of Gender in Britain, 1870–1948', in Anne Digby and John Stewart, eds., *Gender, Health and Welfare* (1996) is an excellent starting point for questions about gender and health, as are Ellen Lewin and Virginia Olesen, eds., *Women, Health and Healing: Toward a New Perspective* (1985), essays in G. Bock and Pat Thane, eds., *Maternity and Gender Poli-tics: Women and the Rise of European Welfare States 1880s–1950s* (1991), and Dorothy Porter, *Health, Civilization and the State* (1999). The relationship between domestic and public spheres is tackled by Jane Lewis in 'Women, Social Work, and Social Welfare in Twentieth-Century Britain: From (Unpaid) Influence to (Paid) Obliv-ion', in Martin Daunton, ed., *Charity, Self-Interest and Welfare in the English Past* (1996) and Joanna Bourke, 'Housewifery in Working-Class England, 1860–1914', *Past and Present* 143 (1994). The connections between these issues and the welfare state are explored in Miriam Cohen and Michael Hanagan, 'The Politics of Gender and the

Making of the Welfare State, 1900–1940: A Comparative Perspective', *Journal of Social History* 24 (1991).

6. THE GREATEST ARGUMENT FOR SOCIALISM EVER PRODUCED

The First World War is a subject on which there are plenty of books and articles to choose from. I will not list any here – see any of the general works listed in the introduction to this essay as starting points. There are a number of works tackling the conflict's impact that have some bearing on the issues discussed in this chapter, however. Richard Overy, *The Morbid Age: Britain and the Crisis of Civilization* (2010) is a quite brilliant study that tackles the conflict's impact on the nation's intellectual and cultural life. Jay Winter, *The Great War and the British People* (1985), explores the demographic impact and connects it with the improvements in public health during the 1920s and 1930s. David Edgerton, *Warfare State: Britain, 1920–1970* (2006) is a superb and myth-busting account of the British state's relationship with the military and its exceptional levels of spending in that area compared to welfare.

There is a huge array of books on the political context discussed in the chapter. To name a few useful starting points: Richard Toye, *Lloyd George and Churchill: Rivals for Greatness* (2007) is a lively and accessible insight into the converging lives and careers of two of the era's dominant figures. Both Lloyd George and Churchill are well covered, of course. On the former see Thomas Jones, *Lloyd George* (1951) and, on the period under discussion, John Grigg, *Lloyd George: From Peace to War, 1912–1916* (1985) and *Lloyd George: War Leader, 1916–1918* (2002). On Churchill see Paul Addison, *Churchill on the Home Front, 1900–1955* (1992) and Norman Rose, *Churchill: An Unruly Life* (1994). Kenneth O. Morgan, *Consensus and Disunity: The Lloyd George Coalition Government, 1918–22* (1979) is essential reading on the post-war administration.

On the economic issues confronting governments during and after the war, Martin Daunton, *Wealth and Welfare* (2007), and Jim Tomlinson's books, including *Problems of British Economic Policy, 1870–1945* (1981) and *Public Policy and the Economy since 1900*

(1990), provide the best overviews. Frank Trentmann, *Free Trade Nation* (2008) considers the creeping doubts about free trade, previously a unifying economic policy. For more focused studies see Alan Sykes, *Tariff Reform in British Politics, 1903–13* (1979), D. E. Moggridge, *British Monetary Policy, 1924–1931* (1972), and Donald Winch, *Economics and Policy: A Historical Study* (1969), which provide excellent analyses of the debate about the gold standard, among other issues. See Andrew McDonald, 'The Geddes Committee and the Formulation of Public Expenditure Policy, 1921–1922', *Historical Journal* 32 (1989) on the Geddes axe. It is worth consulting Alan Lee, *The Origins of the Popular Press in England, 1855–1914* (1976) and Stephen Koss, *The Rise and Fall of the Political Press in Britain*, 2 vols. (1981, 1984) on the rise of newspapers like the *Daily Mail*, which played such an important part in shaping public perceptions of events.

On the welfare policies of the post-war years see Anne Digby, 'Medicine and the English State, 1901–1948', in S. J. D. Green and R. C. Whiting, eds., *The Boundaries of the State in Modern Britain* (1996) for a general discussion of the Ministry of Health, on which see also Arthur Newsholme, *The Ministry of Health* (1925). On education see Michael Sanderson, *Educational Opportunity and Social Change in England* (1987) and Gillian Sutherland, *Ability, Merit and Measurement: Mental Testing and English Education 1880–1940* (1984). For studies of working-class housing during the nineteenth century see Martin Daunton, *House and Home in the Victorian City: Working-Class Housing, 1850–1914* (1983) and Anthony Wohl, *The Eternal Slum: Housing and Social Policy in Victorian London* (1977). Mark Swenarton, *Homes Fit for Heroes: The Politics and Architecture of Early State Housing in Britain* (1981) provides an excellent close analysis of the post-First World War house-building programme.

7. THE MAN YOU CAN TRUST

The politics of the interwar years is well covered in the historical literature. See Ben Jackson's *Equality and the British Left* (2007) for a brilliant study of the politics of the left and centre-left of the period from an intellectual perspective, with further detail on things like the Liberal Summer School. Trevor Wilson, *The Downfall of the Liberal*

Party, 1914–35 (1966) takes the story of the Liberals' decline through to their final pre-war collapse. Duncan Tanner, *Political Change and the Labour Party, 1900–1918* (1990) and Ross McKibbin, *The Evolution of the Labour Party, 1910–1924* (1975) are standard works on the build-up to Labour's emergence as a parliamentary force. These should be read alongside Jon Lawrence, 'Labour and the Politics of Class, 1900–1940', in David Feldman and Jon Lawrence, eds., *Structures and Transformations in Modern British History* (2011). David Marquand, *Ramsay MacDonald* (1977) provides a sympathetic account of a much-maligned figure. Laura Beers, *Your Britain: Media and the Making of the Labour Party* (2010) explores the Labour Party's under-appreciated relationship with and use of the media on its journey into political modernity. Ross McKibbin, *Parties and People: England, 1914–1951* (2010) puts much of this in context by considering how party politics played out in an era of mass democracy.

On the Tories, see Robert Blake, *The Conservative Party from Peel to Thatcher*, 2nd edition (1985) for a general account. See Philip Williamson, *Stanley Baldwin: Conservative Leadership and National Values* (1999) for a study of the era's shrewdest and most influential Conservative. On the figure who would later become for the Tories what MacDonald is for Labour, see David Dilks, *Neville Chamberlain*, vol. 1 (1984) and Robert Self, *Neville Chamberlain: A Biography* (2006). John Macnicol, *The Politics of Retirement in Britain* (1998) and Bentley B. Gilbert, *British Social Policy 1914–39* (1970) provide close analysis of Chamberlain's pensions reforms.

Housing has been the subject of historical investigation from a number of different angles. While Martin Daunton, *A Property-owning Democracy? Housing in Britain* (1987) is a hugely valuable survey of the housing market across the twentieth century, Helen Meller, *Towns, Plans and Society in Modern Britain* (1997) provides an overview of urbanization across the twentieth century. Peter Hall, *Cities of Tomorrow: An Intellectual History of Urban Planning and Design in the Twentieth Century*, 3rd edition (2002) is the standard and quite brilliant work that puts architects like Raymond Unwin into historical perspective. Ross McKibbin, *Classes and Cultures, England 1918–1951* (1998) offers valuable insights into both working- and middle-class housing and habits. Ben Jackson, 'Property-Owning

Democracy: A Short History', in Martin O'Neill and Thad Williamson, eds., *Property-Owning Democracy: Rawls and Beyond* (2012) is an incisive account of the origins and history of an idea that played such an important role in late twentieth-century politics.

8. WILL THE MACHINE WORK?

Unemployment – both the phenomenon and ideas about it – has been studied extensively. The central challenges are to understand the forces that produced the kinds of unemployment witnessed by the early twentieth century, the debates about what constituted an appropriate response, and what this meant for the status of unemployment as a problem for the state. José Harris, *Unemployment and Politics: A Study in English Social Policy, 1886–1914* (1972) is a superb account of how unemployment became a central social administration problem. While W. R. Garside, *British Unemployment, 1919–1939* (1990) takes the story up to the Second World War, Jim Tomlinson, *Public Policy and the Economy since 1900* (1990) and *Problems of British Economic Policy, 1870–1945* (1981) are authoritative surveys of the policy responses throughout the twentieth century. Jose Harris's *William Beveridge: A Biography*, 2nd edition (1997) is much more than a biography of the era's leading authority on unemployment: it is an analysis of an emerging new world. This can be read alongside Beveridge's own reflections, *Power and Influence* (1953). Richard Overy, *The Morbid Age: Britain and the Crisis of Civilization* (2010) is a superb history of interwar Britain that puts the idea of unemployment in the context of broader social, cultural and political concerns about decline.

Economic thought during the first half of the twentieth century – a particularly fascinating and fertile time, largely because of the problems economists were trying to explain – has been studied extensively. While Roger Backhouse, *The Penguin History of Economics* (2002) provides a good accessible general survey, Mary S. Morgan, 'Economics', in Theodore M. Porter and Dorothy Ross, eds., *The Cambridge History of Science*, Volume 7: *The Modern Social Sciences* (2003) provides a typically powerful and insightful analysis of the reshaping of economic thought and the discipline itself. For more on those latter issues, see Mary Morgan, *The History of Econometric Ideas* (1990) and *The World in the Model: How Economists Work and Think* (2012), both of which I have found indispensable in my time studying these topics. Welfare economics is well covered by the essays in Roger E. Backhouse and Tamotsu Nishizawa, eds., *No Wealth but Life: Welfare Economics and the Welfare State in Britain, 1880–1945* (2010) and the later essays in Donald Winch, *Wealth and Life* (2009).

Mike Savage, *Identities and Social Change in Britain since 1940: The Politics of Method* (2010) is a compelling and now hugely influential account of the intellectual milieu from which the dominant post-war strands of social science emerged. James Hinton, *The Mass Observers: A History, 1937–1949* (2013) tells the story of Mass-Observation. While E. P. Hennock's essay in Martin Bulmer, Kevin Bales and Kathryn Kish Sklar, eds., *The Social Survey in Historical Perspective, 1880–1940* (1991) explores Booth and Bowley's London surveys, numerous contributions to Martin Bulmer, ed., *Essays on the History of British Sociological Research* (1985) examine different surveying traditions. Mark Roodhouse, ' "Fish-and-Chip Intelligence": Henry Durant and the British Institute of Public Opinion, 1936–63', *Twentieth-Century British History* 24 (2013) considers the emergence of polling in Britain. There are a number of excellent works on social science at the London School of Economics and the hugely influential thinkers who worked there. The best general work is Ralf Dahrendorf, *LSE: A History of the London School of Economics and Political Science, 1895–1995* (1995). Lawrence Goldman, *The Life of R. H. Tawney: Socialism and History* (2013) is both a biography and the story of the emergence of a particularly influential strand of British socialism. Susan Howson, *Lionel Robbins* (2013) is an epic account of an economist who played an important role in economics and politics in Britain during the middle decades of the twentieth century. Ann Oakley, *Man and Wife: Richard and Kay Titmuss* (1996) and David Reisman, *Richard Titmuss: Welfare and Society* (1977) provide insights into the man most closely associated with the emergence of the field of social policy in Britain.

9. IN THE LONG RUN WE'RE ALL DEAD

On the second Labour government, national government and the economy see Ross McKibbin, *The Ideologies of Class: Social*

Relations in Britain, 1880–1950 (1990), Philip Williamson, *National Crisis and National Government: British Politics, the Economy and Empire, 1926–1932* (1992), Andrew Thorpe, *The British General Election of 1931* (1991), and, on the much-maligned Labour leader's decision-making, David Marquand, *Ramsay MacDonald* (1977) and Reginald Basset, *1931: Political Crisis* (1958/1986). Donald Winch, *Economics and Policy: A Historical Study* (1969) is the standard work on the development of economic policy during the period and is particularly illuminating on the 'Treasury view'. There are a number of excellent studies of the influential debates about planning. The two best works on the British context are Richard Toye, *The Labour Party and the Planned Economy, 1931–1951* (2003) and Daniel Ritschel, *The Politics of Planning: The Debate on Economic Planning in Britain in the 1930s* (1997). See also the Keynesian Robert Skidelsky's *Oswald Mosley* (1975) for more on Mosley's efforts to develop an economic policy in this context, and Richard Cockett, *Thinking the Unthinkable: Think-Tanks and the Economic Counter-Revolution, 1931–1983* (1994) for the non-governmental organizations where planning ideas were first developed.

There a number of excellent studies of economic knowledge and expertise in government during the early twentieth century. Essays in Mary Furner and Barry Supple, eds., *The State and Economic Knowledge* (1990), particularly those by Peter Clarke and Donald Winch, are a good starting point, as is G. C. Peden, 'Economic Knowledge and the State in Modern Britain', in S. J. D. Green and R. C. Whiting, eds., *The Boundaries of the State in Modern Britain* (1996). While Roy MacLeod, ed., *Government and Expertise: Specialists, Administrators and Professionals, 1860–1919* (1988) and Martin Bulmer, *The Uses of Social Research: Social Investigation in Public Policy-Making* (1982) are excellent accounts of the emerging role of social science in government, Andrew Hull's unpublished Ph.D. thesis, 'Passwords to Power: A Public Rationale for Expert Influence on Central Government Policy Making. British Scientists and Economists, *c.* 1920–*c.* 1925' (University of Glasgow, 1994) explains why economic knowledge was valued rather more than other sciences during the period in question. Susan Howson and Donald Winch, *The Economic Advisory Council, 1930–1939: A*

Study of Economic Advice during Depression and Recovery (1977) is the authoritative and brilliant study of the first effort to insert economists into day-to-day government decision-making.

The figure towering over all these developments is John Maynard Keynes. While Peter Clarke, *Keynes: The Twentieth Century's Most Influential Economist* (2009) is an excellent and accessible introduction to the man and his ideas, Roger Backhouse and Bradley W. Bateman, eds., *The Cambridge Companion to Keynes* (2006) contains essays on different aspects of his life and work. There are a number of biographies of varying lengths, not all of which I will list here. His former student Robert Skidelsky's *John Maynard Keynes*, 3 vols. (1992–2001) is unparalleled in depth and, of course, its insider knowledge, but there are other studies, such as D. E. Moggridge, *John Maynard Keynes: An Economist's Biography* (1992), that focus on his ideas and career. There is a vast literature on the development of Keynesian thinking, some of which is mentioned in the essay on chapter eleven. However, Peter Clarke, *The Keynesian Revolution in the Making, 1924–1936* (1988) provides an account of the debates and developments leading up to the publication of *The General Theory*.

Keynes does need to be understood in relation to his most vocal opponent, Friedrich Hayek, who lost out during the 1930s and 1940s but captured the imagination of policy-makers during the 1970s. Bruce Caldwell, *Hayek's Challenge: An Intellectual Biography of F. A. Hayek* (2004) is the best and most authoritative study. Nicholas Wapshott, *Keynes Hayek: The Clash that Defined Modern Economics* (2012) is an accessible and informative account of the Keynes/Hayek debate and its consequences. The early twenty-first century has also seen a boom in writing about the history of neoliberalism, a slippery but no less real idea, which Hayek helped shape. Keith Tribe, 'Liberalism and Neoliberalism in Britain, 1930–1980', in Philip Mirowski and Dieter Plehwe, eds., *The Road from Mont Pèlerin: The Making of the Neoliberal Thought Collective* (2009) is excellent on the British context. More general works, which take in the international context, include Angus Burgin, *The Great Persuasion: Reinventing Free Markets since the Depression* (2012) and Daniel Stedman Jones, *Masters of the Universe: Hayek, Friedman, and the Birth of Neoliberal Politics* (2012).

10. HALF-WAY TO MOSCOW

There are countless books on the Second World War. The most relevant ones for the story told in this chapter are Angus Calder, *The People's War* (1969) and Paul Addison, *The Road to 1945: British Politics and the Second World War*, revised edition (1994). James Cronin, *The Politics of State Expansion* (1991), Jim Tomlinson, *Employment Policy: The Crucial Years, 1939–1955* (1987), and Alan T. Peacock and Jack Wiseman, *The Growth of Public Expenditure in the United Kingdom* (1961) analyse a key period in the growth of the British state and attitudes towards what it was capable of doing – a crucial aspect of changing attitudes in both Whitehall and the country towards more extensive welfare policies.

Nicholas Timmins, *The Five Giants: A Biography of the Welfare State*, 2nd edition (2001) is the best general account of policy development during the war years. C. L. Dunn, *The Emergency Medical Services*, vol. 1 (1952) is an official account of the government's extension of hospital care. This is also tackled in Richard Titmuss, *Problems of Social Policy* (1950), which is very long and a somewhat dry read, but also contains an informative account of numerous other aspects of wartime policy, including evacuation. Jose Harris, *William Beveridge: A Biography*, 2nd edition (1997) tackles the debate about social reconstruction and provides a detailed account of the behind-the-scenes manoeuvrings that eventually led to the Social Insurance and Allied Services Report, which illuminates Beveridge's own version of events, *Power and Influence* (1953). This should be supplemented with Jose Harris, 'Political Ideas and the Debate on State Welfare, 1940–45', in Harold L. Smith, ed., *War and Social Change: British Society in the Second World War* (1986).

While Frank Whitehead, 'The Government Social Survey', in Martin Bulmer, ed., *Essays on the History of British Sociological Research* (1985) and James Hinton, *The Mass Observers: A History, 1937–1949* (2013) provide important insights into the deployment of social science on the Home Front, Mark Abrams, *The Population of Great Britain* (1945) provides a fascinating look at Britain, as seen by one of the post-war era's most important market researchers. The question of whether people were that enthusiastic about what Beveridge proposed is tackled in José Harris, 'Did British Workers Want the Welfare State? G. D. H. Cole's Survey of 1942', in Jay Winter, ed., *The Working Class in Modern British History: Essays in Honour of Henry Pelling* (1983). This should be read alongside Rodney Lowe, 'The Second World War, Consensus, and the Foundation of the Welfare State', *Twentieth-Century British History* 1 (1990).

II. CONSTRUCTIVE PROGRESS

The debate about the National Health Service is well covered. The standard works on the early years of the NHS are Charles Webster, *The National Health Service: A Political History*, new edition (2002) and Frank Honigsbaum, *Health, Happiness, and Security: The Creation of the National Health Service* (1989), which take the story through to the late twentieth century. There are a number of biographies of Aneurin Bevan, the man who turned the NHS from a principle into an institutional reality. While the future Labour leader Michael Foot, Bevan's friend and colleague, wrote the extensive *Aneurin Bevan: A Biography*, 2 vols. (1962–73), Dai Smith's *Aneurin Bevan and the World of South Wales* (1993) recovers the local context that shaped his views, and Nicklaus Thomas-Symonds, *Nye: The Political Life of Aneurin Bevan* (2015) is a superb, insightful and accessible recent account of a difficult but profoundly important politician.

On education and the Education Act of 1944 see Gillian Sutherland, 'Education', in F. M. L. Thompson, ed., *The Cambridge Social History of Britain, 1750–1950*, vol. 3 (1990), Michael Sanderson, *Educational Opportunity and Social Change in England* (1987), and Deborah Thom, 'The 1944 Education Act', in Harold L. Smith, ed., *War and Social Change: British Society in the Second World War* (1986). For more on R. A. Butler see Anthony Howard, *RAB: A Life of R. A. Butler* (1987), as well as Butler's own account, *The Art of the Possible: The Memoirs of Lord Butler* (1971). House building is well covered in Peter Hall, *Cities of Tomorrow* (2002), Helen Meller, *Towns, Plans and Society in Modern Britain* (1997), and Patrick Dunleavy, *The Politics of Mass Housing in Britain, 1945–1975: A Study of Corporate Power and Professional Influence in the Welfare State* (1981).

The shift towards economic management is covered in many of the works mentioned in the essay on chapter five. These can be supplemented with Alec Cairncross, *Years of Recovery: British Economic Policy, 1945–51* (1985), Susan Howson, *British Monetary Policy, 1945–51* (1993), and Peter Clarke, 'The Keynesian Consensus', in David Marquand and Anthony Seldon, eds., *The Ideas that Shaped Post-War Britain* (1996). Richard Toye, 'Winston Churchill's "Crazy Broadcast": Party, Nation, and the 1945 Gestapo Speech', *Journal of British History* 49 (2010) and Richard Cockett, *Thinking the Unthinkable* (1994) provide important insights into the intellectual and political context of those shifts.

There are a number of biographies of Attlee, including Kenneth Harris, *Attlee* (1982), Trevor Burridge, *Clement Attlee* (1985), and, most recently, John Bew, *Citizen Clem: A Biography of Attlee* (2016). On the post-1945 government see Peter Hennessy, *Never Again: Britain 1945–51* (1992), Kenneth O. Morgan, *Labour in Power, 1945–1951* (1984), Henry Pelling, *The Labour Governments, 1945–51* (1984), and Steven Fielding, Peter Thompson and Nick Tiratsoo, *'England Arise!' The Labour Party and Popular Politics in 1940s Britain* (1995). While Ross McKibbin, *Parties and People: England, 1914–1951* (2010) puts the government into a slightly longer-run history, Correlli Barnett, *The Lost Victory: British Dreams, British Realities, 1945–1950* (1995) provides a somewhat different and much less positive account of Labour's efforts. Jim Tomlinson, *Democratic Socialism and Economic Policy: The Attlee Years, 1945–1951* (1996) and Richard Toye, 'Gosplanners versus Thermostatters: Whitehall Planning Debates and their Political Consequences, 1945–1949', *Contemporary British History* 14 (2000) provide conflicting takes on economic policy. Martin Daunton, *Just Taxes: The Politics of Taxation in Britain, 1914–1979* (2002) explores the seemingly dry and niche interest of fiscal policy but offers a lucid and important account of how ideas like justice and fairness are embedded into it. David Kynaston, *Austerity Britain, 1945–1951* (2007) is an important and influential social history of the period that uncovers how people lived through these developments.

Acknowledgements

I owe thank-yous to numerous people for their help, encouragement and constructive criticisms during the writing of this book. My agent, Andrew Gordon, listened patiently and with a straight face as I described a very different book to the one I ended up writing. He explained exactly where I was going wrong through various iterations of the book proposal and provided incredibly helpful comments on an earlier draft. A whole host of people at Penguin have used all their expertise and wisdom to get the book from that point to the printed page. My editor, Thomas Penn, was of great assistance when it came to understanding how to write for a new audience. He supplied immensely helpful thoughts on the earliest drafts of the first two chapters, much more detailed advice on subsequent drafts, and gently persuaded me that few other people would be interested in reading either long passages drawn from the works of nineteenth-century technocrats or largely irrelevant musings on Jeremy Bentham. Charlotte Ridings grappled with my often clunky prose, turning it into a much more precise and, frankly, grammatically correct text. Chloe Currens and Pen Vogler have also been fantastic in guiding me through everything else that comes with publishing a book of this kind.

Many current and former colleagues have helped me, either directly or indirectly. I owe Nicholas Guyatt the biggest thanks. He spent hours talking about my ideas over many pints and even more packets of crisps and offered sage advice at various stages. Stuart Carroll was a hugely understanding head of department who steered my department through an immensely challenging period and helped provide a supportive environment when I was considering taking on this project. Mark Roodhouse discussed a number of important issues that crop up in the book, whether he actually knew it at the time or not. Alex Goodall has been, and continues to be, a constant source of thought-provoking debate on contemporary politics, particularly the question of how we should make sense of the twentieth century as a historical period, whose ideas I do take seriously, regardless of what I tell him. While Lawrence Black read and provided very helpful comments on an early draft of the book, he was also able to explain quite concisely why I was wrong about Ramsay MacDonald every time I had latched on to a new idea. Mike Finn provided a number of important points of detail about the history of medicine. Alex Buckley took on the onerous task of being the non-historian reader of an early draft. His thoughts were an invaluable part of trying to understand what someone who does not spend most of their waking moments thinking about history might want to know about particular topics.

As always, however, it is my immediate family who deserve the biggest thanks. My wife, Clare, has been a source of immense support throughout my career and has displayed patience and understanding during the three years it took to turn *Bread for All* from an idea to a physical object. This book is, however, for my daughter, Ivy, who arrived on the scene shortly before I started writing it. Ivy has made me think long and hard about the things I have benefitted from in my own lifetime. Friends and family, in particular my parents, Shelagh and Stephen, helped me along the way and made sure I ended up, both literally and metaphorically, in the right places at the right time. Yet I, like so many others, have much to thank strangers for. The events I discuss in *Bread for All* provided the platform for my parents to make a good life for not only themselves but my sister and me too. Everyone worked hard, but nobody could have achieved any of it without the state institutions we collectively support. The state gave me an education, it has patched me up when I needed help, and it has made sure both Clare and Ivy are around to see the words on these pages. And for those things I will always be grateful.

Index

Addison, Christopher, 138, 141,
    142, 146, 152, 157, 162
air force, 130–31
Albert, Prince, 37
alcohol, 54, 123, 134, 173, 184
Alden, Percy, 176–7
Anderson, Sir John, 165
Andover, Hampshire, 35
Anglo-Japanese Alliance (1902), 108
Anson, William, 101
Anti-Waste League, 145–6
army
    Boer War recruitment scandal,
        95–7, 98–9, 102, 104, 105,
        109, 113
    Boer War tactics, 95, 128
    cheap edition of Beveridge
        Report, 233
    Liberal Party reforms, 60
    officer class, 95, 106, 114
    WWI conscription, 130, 134
    WWI volunteers, 129
Army Medical Corps, 95–6, 98–9
Arnott, Neil, 29–30
Arts and Crafts Movement, 67
Asquith, Herbert, 65, 73–4, 91,
    107, 127–8
    and 'coupon election' (1918), 137
    forms coalition (1915), 129–30,
        132–3
    and Independent Liberals, 147,
        148, 151
    ousted as Prime Minister
        (1916), 130
Association of Approved Societies,
    220
Astor, David, 240
Astor, Waldorf, 141
Attlee, Clement, 5, 235, 237, 238,
    239, 252, 254
    becomes Prime
        Minister (1945), 249
    and sterling convertibility
        suspension (1947), 251
Australia, 126

Baden-Powell, Robert, 108
Baldwin, Stanley, 149, 150, 203
    'national' conservatism,
        158–69, 192
    'Safety First' slogan, 195–6
    and tariff reform, 150, 159, 161
Balfour, Arthur, 48, 72–3, 97–8,
    100, 101, 113, 195
Balfour, Sir Arthur (steel
    manufacturer), 199

Bank of England, 194, 252, 261–2
Bayer (German company), 108
Becontree, 143, 163
benefits system, 3, 4–5
  Beveridge links to subsistence,
    225, 234
  Beveridge's rationalized scheme,
    223–5, 267
  contributory principle, 8, 78, 79,
    80, 82, 166–7, 223–4, 261, 262
  and housing costs, 227–8
  and means testing, 76, 102, 165,
    166, 173, 205, 219, 225
  'milking the system' worries, 227
  rules and regulations, 8
  and stigmatization, 205, 261
  as target for critics, 7, 227
Bentham, Jeremy, 6, 14–15, 20, 183
  An Introduction to the Principles
    of Morals and Legislation
    (1789), 15
Besant, Annie, 90
Bevan, Aneurin 'Nye', 162, 235,
    254–7, 266
Beveridge Report (Social Insurance
    and Allied Services)
  Churchill's response to, 3, 234–5,
    237, 246
  compulsory nature of scheme,
    224, 234, 262
  'five giants' of, 4, 215
  general public responses to,
    230–32
  implementation of proposals, 9,
    248, 252–3
  and 'national minimum', 225, 226
  need for near full employment,
    228, 229
  Parliament debates, 1–2, 4–5,
    233–4

problems, 225–8
publication of (1 December
    1942), 222
rationalized scheme proposed,
    223–5, 267
recommendations, 4–5, 214–15,
    222–5
rents and housing costs, 227–8
sales of, 1–2, 3–4, 214, 230
subsistence concept, 225, 226,
    227, 234
supports contributory scheme,
    223–4, 232, 234
'three assumptions', 228–9, 239,
    241–2
universality of proposed scheme,
    224–7, 228, 256, 262
wartime context of, 232–3
Beveridge, William
  background and early life, 172
  at Board of Trade, 79, 171,
    177–8, 191
  The Brains Trust appearances,
    214, 220
  'bread for all . . .' quote, 7
  consultants, 241–2
  early career, 5, 170, 172–4
  and efficiency, 265
  and eugenics, 2, 109
  excluded from implementation of
    proposals, 248
  and family allowances, 121
  during First World War,
    131, 217
  as Liberal MP, 5, 248
  as LSE director, 121, 158, 187–8,
    190, 215
  as Master of University College,
    Oxford, 216, 239
  on need for economists, 195

and 'organised fluidity of labour',
175–80, 193
and Second World War, 1,
216–19, 220–22, 229–30,
235–6, 239–42
tour of USA (1943), 235–6
and Toynbee Hall, 49, 170,
172–4, 177
and unemployment, 170–71, 172,
173–80, 216, 239–42
and welfare economics, 182
*Full Employment in a Free
Society* (1944 report), 242
*Unemployment: A Problem of
Industry* (1909), 173–6, 188
Bevin, Ernest, 218, 251
Birmingham, 33–4, 49, 86, 114,
163, 164, 167, 191
Bismarck, Otto von, 70–71, 108
Blackett, Sir Basil, 208
Board of Trade, 54, 79, 170–71,
177–8, 179, 180, 191
Boer War, Second (1899–1902), 69,
72, 95, 108, 118
financial impact, 74, 83,
107, 113
recruitment scandal, 95–7, 98–9,
102, 104, 105, 106, 109, 113
social policy impact, 83, 97–103,
104, 113
Bolton, 2, 24, 187, 189
Bonar Law, Andrew, 129, 133,
136–7, 149–50
Bondfield, Margaret, 197
Booth, Charles, 42–5, 47, 50, 67,
75, 88, 98, 119, 174
colour-coded maps, 44, 187
and falling birthrate, 90
Llewellyn Smith updates work of
(1928–32), 186–7

and Beatrice Potter (Webb),
43, 50
researchers of, 43–4, 46, 49, 50,
178, 187
*The Life and Labour of the
People in London* (1889–1903),
44, 94, 178, 182–3
Bosanquet, Bernard, 51
Bosanquet, Helen, 51–2, 53, 56,
76, 109
Bowley, Arthur, 187, 190
Bracken, Brendan, 238, 239
Bradford, 23–4, 25, 27, 117
Bradlaugh, Charles, 90
The Brains Trust (BBC radio
programme), 214, 220
British Association for the
Advancement of Science, 99
British Empire
administration of, 117
Empire free trade, 73,
205–6, 208
Imperial Economic Conference
(Ottawa, 1932), 206
'imperial preference', 168, 196,
198, 204–5
Liberal Imperialists, 107
and new liberalism, 69, 70, 157
and Arnold White, 94, 95, 96
British Institute of Public Opinion,
190, 231
British Medical Association, 79,
124, 138, 220, 256–7, 264
British Union of Fascists, 207
Brookings Institution, 180
Bryce, Lord, 112
bushido (Japanese moral
code), 108
Butler, R. A., 245–8
Buxton, Noel, 67

Caird, Mona, 120
Cambridge University, 60, 156, 183, 189, 199, 241
Cameron, David, 161
Campbell-Bannerman, Henry, 73, 74, 97, 101
Campbell, J. R., 153
Canada, 206
capitalism, 7, 8, 116, 133, 140, 158, 181, 262–3
  era of social democracy, 267
  'gentlemanly', 38
  industrial, 38, 39–41, 48, 59, 61
  and Labour Party, 197–8, 249
  and new liberalism, 69, 70
  and planning, 206
  and welfare economics, 182
Carr-Saunders, Alexander, 208
Cazalet-Keir, Thelma, 247–8
census (1911), 91, 92
Chadwick, Edwin
  belief in centralization, 22, 31–2, 33, 138
  character of, 20, 32
  as commissioner of General Board of Health, 32
  'conversion'/'U-turn' of, 28–9, 31–2, 55, 59, 139, 229, 265
  elite connections, 20, 30, 41, 105
  focus on illness and disease, 29, 30–32, 34, 36, 38, 40, 139, 229, 265
  and miasmatic theories, 29, 30, 33
  and 'national minimum' concept, 115
  Royal Commission on the Poor Law (1832–4), 20–23, 24, 34, 35, 49, 57, 58, 83

  and scientific approach, 20, 31, 33, 52–3, 100, 122
  as secretary to Poor Law Commission, 28–9
  Report on the Sanitary Condition of the Labouring Population of Great Population, 30–32
Chamberlain, Austen, 145, 163
Chamberlain, Joseph, 33–4, 72, 110, 163
  and education reform, 113, 114
  'tariff reform' campaign, 49, 73, 76, 202
Chamberlain, Neville, 5, 163–8, 169, 216–17, 224
  as Chancellor of the Exchequer, 205–6
Chamberlain, Richard, 163
Chambers, Robert, Vestiges of the Natural History of Creation (1844), 84–5
Chandler, Francis, 55
channel tunnel idea, 199
Charity Organisation Society, 43, 49, 50, 51, 55, 76, 83, 98, 102–3, 109, 173
Chartist movement, 60–61
chemical engineering, 73, 107–8, 131, 243
Chester, Daniel, 220
cholera, 29, 32, 33
Churchill, Winston, 1, 107, 139, 217
  and 1945 election, 5, 237–8
  as Chancellor of the Exchequer, 159–60, 165–6, 169
  crosses floor over free trade, 73
  and First World War, 126, 127, 128, 129, 130, 132, 249

meets Beveridge at the Webbs
(1908), 170–71, 177, 217
as President of Board of Trade,
79, 170–71, 177–8
response to Beveridge Report, 3,
234–5, 237, 246
return to gold standard (1925),
160, 161, 169, 199, 200
returns to Conservatives,
157, 159
civil service, 50, 60, 79, 131, 220,
221, 222, 231, 254–5
competitive examinations, 87,
117, 178
pensions, 75
Civil War, American (1861–65), 26
Civil War, English, 61
Clarke, William, 67
Clay, Henry, 194
Co-Efficients Club, 106
co-operative movement, 40, 61,
92, 150
coal industry, 194, 195–6, 252, 254,
255, 261–2
and general strike (1926), 160–61
Cobbe, Frances Power, 124
Cole, G. D. H., 199, 235
Combination Laws (1799,
1800), 40
competition
between countries, 64, 70, 97,
107, 108–9, 110, 160, 161,
194, 196
between individuals, 97, 110, 178
and welfare economics, 183
Conan Doyle, Arthur, 93
Conservative Party
and 1918 'coupon election', 137
and 1922 election, 148
and 1924 election, 153

and 1929 election, 169
and 1931 election, 204
Baldwin's governments, 149, 150,
158–69
Baldwin's 'national'
conservativism, 158–69, 192
Balfour's government (1902–5),
72–3, 97–101, 113–14, 244
Bevan's 'lower than vermin'
comment, 257
House of Lords as bastion, 78
Liberal Unionist alliance, 48
local organization, 155
and National Health Service Act,
255–6
'property-owning democracy'
concept, 8, 161–2
during Second World War, 249
splits over free trade, 48–9, 73
'The 1922 Committee', 146
constitutional crisis (1909–11), 78,
82
contraception, 90, 93
Corn Laws, abolition of (1846), 25,
37–8, 88, 212
Coventry, 139
Cox, Alfred, 256
Cripps, Stafford, 252–3, 254
Crystal Palace, Hyde Park, 37

Daily Express, 150, 202, 237, 240
Daily Mail, 145–6, 150, 202
'Zinoviev letter', 153
Daily Mirror, 249
Daily News, 74
Daily Telegraph, 91, 173, 222
Dalton, Hugh, 253
Darwin, Charles, On the Origin of
Species (1859), 64, 83–4, 85, 86
Darwin, Erasmus, 84, 85

Debden, Essex, 263
degeneration, 93–7, 109, 188
   and Boer War recruits, 95–9,
      102, 104
   Interdepartmental Committee on
      Physical Deterioration,
      97–101, 102, 119
   and role of women, 120
demography
   and Beveridge Report, 226
   birth rate, 3, 89–93, 228–9, 253
   fertility question on 1911 census,
      91, 92
   increased life expectancy, 74–5,
      89, 105, 165
   infant mortality rates, 99, 122
   population forecasts, 2, 88–9
   population growth, 89, 266
   social class and average height,
      99, 100, 102
   trend towards smaller families,
      2–3, 90–93
   WW2 baby boom, 253
dentists, 260, 261
department stores, 181
Dickens, Charles, 40, 41, 74
the Diggers, 61
disability insurance, 71
Disraeli, Benjamin, 59
distribution
   Interdepartmental Committee on
      Physical Deterioration,
      99–100
   and J. S. Mill, 63, 71, 181
   and theory of
      'underconsumption', 70, 157
   and welfare economics, 183, 184
doctors, 33, 41, 78–9, 80, 224,
      230–31, 261
   barring of women from
      profession, 124

capitation fees, 138, 256
dispensaries, 27
female, 123, 125
opposition to NHS, 256–7, 264
Dower, John, 208
Durant, Henry, 190, 231

East End of London, 29, 42, 67,
      94–5, 139, 173, 265
   battle of Cable Street, 207
East India Company College,
      Hertfordshire, 17
Economic Journal, 177
economics
   classical, 13, 15, 17, 40, 171–2, 181
      see also Ricardo, David; Smith,
      Adam
   economic liberalism, 7, 39, 67,
      101, 132, 133, 212–13
   Fabian 'national minimum',
      115–17, 184, 225
   free trade, 25–6, 36–7, 38, 48–9,
      59, 60, 73
   funding of First World War,
      131–4, 140–41
   gold standard, 133, 140–41, 144,
      159–60, 161, 169, 198, 199,
      200, 201, 204
   IS-LM model, 211–12
   Keynes' General Theory (1936),
      210–11, 241
   macroeconomics, 6, 211, 241,
      242, 253
   'marginal utility', 182
   market failure, 183–4
   and J. S. Mill, 63, 71, 181
   'multiplier effect', 200, 210, 241
   'national dividend' concept, 184
   'neoclassical', 182
   new consensus in 1940s, 240–41
   positive and normative, 63

'Tariff reformers', 48–9, 73, 76, 202, 205–6
theory of consumption, 181–2
theory of 'underconsumption', 70, 157
trade cycle, 180–81
The Economist, 60, 255
economy
  Capital Issues Committee (WWI), 133
  Central Economic Planning Staff, 251–2
  Cripps' austerity, 253, 254
  deflation after return to gold standard, 160, 161, 169
  depression from early 1870s, 42, 64, 66–7, 88, 172, 182
  devaluation crisis (1949), 253
  and division of labour, 36–7
  at end of Second World War, 7, 250–51
  in first decades of welfare state, 266–7
  First World War, 133–4
  Geddes committee, 146, 147, 162, 202
  'Great Victorian Boom', 38, 42, 88, 172
  post-WWI boom, 137–8, 144
  post-WWI industrial decline, 194, 195–6
  post-WW2 rationing, 252, 253
  sharp downturn (1920), 144, 160
  sterling convertibility suspended (1947), 251
  and winter of 1947, 251
Ede, James Chuter, 245
Edgar, Florence, 70
Edinburgh Review, 60
education
  1940s reform, 243–8
  adult education classes, 113
  Bryce Commission (1895), 112
  church schools, 111–13, 244, 245, 247
  Cockerton case, 113
  comprehensive, 266
  curriculum, 114
  early state funding, 110
  Education After the War ('Green Book', 1941), 243
  Educational Reconstruction (*White Paper*, 1943), 246
  elected school boards, 111–13
  grammar schools, 111, 112, 113, 244, 247
  Hogben's statistical research, 188
  international comparisons, 110
  Local Education Authorities, 113–14, 117, 168
  Lord Taunton's Schools Inquiry Commission (1860s), 66, 110–11
  and J. S. Mill, 63–4
  and 'national efficiency', 110–15, 172
  nineteenth-century legislation, 43, 111, 113
  and non-conformism, 111–12, 244
  payment-by-results scheme, 112
  principle of basic schooling for all, 43
  private, 188
  public schools, 111, 114, 189, 244–6, 247
  school board visitors, 43–4
  school-leaving age, 112, 136, 243, 247, 252, 260
  school meals question, 57, 83, 100–103, 104, 117, 118, 119, 173

education – *cont.*
  secondary level, 111, 112–14, 244
  see also teachers
Education Act (1902), 113–14,
  136, 244
Education Act (1918), 136
Education Act (1944), 247
Education (Provision of Meals) Act
  (1906), 101–2
El Alamein, Allied victory at
  (1942), 233
electoral politics
  calls for universal male suffrage,
    60–61
  constitutional crisis (1909–11),
    78, 82
  electoral reform in nineteenth-
    century, 19, 60, 61, 105, 109,
    154–5
  Great Reform Act (1832), 19,
    60, 154
  property qualification for
    franchise, 19, 60, 61, 154
  Representation of the People Act
    (1918), 135, 155
  return of party politics (1922),
    146–7
  'rotten boroughs', 19, 37, 60
  Second Reform Act (1867),
    61, 88
  Third Reform Act (1884), 64, 68
  tiny electorate in early nineteenth-
    century, 19, 37, 60
  Tory domination (early 1780s to
    1820s), 18–19
  two-party political system, 59
  universal suffrage, 155, 169
  Whig ascendency from 1830s,
    19–20, 37, 64
electrical industry, 73

Elementary Education Act (1870),
  43, 111, 113
Elementary Education
  Act (1880), 43
elites, 6
  belief in power to shape society,
    8, 263, 265
  and education, 110, 114, 115,
    116, 189, 244
  Galton's concerns, 104
  and land ownership, 60
  and traditional literary culture, 189
  and the Webbs, 106, 115, 116,
    170–71
empirical social research, 2, 41,
  43–8, 174, 178, 185–91
empiricism, 65
Endowed Schools Act (1869), 111
Engels, Friedrich, 41
  *The Condition of the Working
    Class in England* (1845), 40
Enlightenment, European, 13,
  14, 15
  and free trade, 25–6, 36–7
Epps, Sir George, 220
eugenics, 85–8, 99, 104, 141
  and degeneration theory, 96–7,
    109
  'eugenic feminists', 120, 121–2
  forced sterilization concept,
    96–7, 109
  physical discrepancies as
    environmental, 99–101, 102
Eugenics Society, 2, 3, 109
evolutionary theory, 83–6, 93,
  97, 110
expert knowledge, 31, 50, 56, 105,
  109–10, 115, 118
  economists, 194–5, 199–200
  imposition from above, 118

and Local Education
Authorities, 113–14
MacDonald's Economic Advisory
Council, 198–201, 251–2
and the Webbs, 110, 113–14,
115, 195

Fabian Society, 5, 43, 50–51, 52,
67, 70, 151, 154, 173, 220
and 'national minimum', 115–17,
184, 225
and professional economists, 195
Factory Acts (1830s/40s), 39,
71, 116
family allowances, 121–2, 228, 229
Family Endowment Society, 121–2
Fawcett, Millicent, 135
First World War
armed forces during, 129,
130–31, 134
Asquith forms coalition (1915),
129–30, 132–3
Beveridge during, 131, 217
expansion of state during, 126–7,
131, 132–4
funding of, 131–4, 140–41
Gallipoli campaign (1915), 126,
129, 249
and gold standard, 133, 140–41,
144, 159
and Kitchener, 128–9
Lloyd George becomes Prime
Minister, 130
Ministry of Reconstruction, 135
munitions scandal, 129
outbreak of (1914), 127–8
Fisher, H. A. L., 136, 146
food and diet
during First World War, 131
food prices, 16, 37–8, 73, 89, 131

and health visitors, 123
laws and regulations, 117
milk depots, 124
poor diets, 93, 99, 104, 109, 118,
119
repeal of Corn Laws, 25, 37–8
Rowntree's calorie calculation,
47, 225
school meals question, 57, 83,
100–103, 104, 117, 118, 119,
173
foreign policy
MacDonald and USSR, 152–3
naval 'two power standard', 74,
76–7, 108, 128, 130
and theory of
'underconsumption', 70, 157
Forster's Education Act (1870), 43
Fox, Colonel G. M., 97–8
free trade, 25–6, 36–7, 38, 48–9,
59, 60, 62, 69, 105, 193
and 1923 election, 151
and Bismarck's Germany, 70–71
and Conservatives in 1920s, 149,
150, 159–60, 161
Empire free trade, 73, 205–6,
208
gold standard as totemic,
159–60, 161
and Labour in 1920s, 150, 152,
198, 201–2
and 'national efficiency', 109
national government abandons,
205–6
and Political Economy Club, 106
and public health, 89
and 'Yellow Book' Liberals,
156–7
French Revolution (1789), 40
friendly societies, 54, 79, 223

Gallup, 190

Galton, Francis, 85–6, 87–8, 91, 99, 104, 109
  social class and average height, 99, 100
  Hereditary Genius (1869), 86–7

'garden cities', 142

Gatacre, General, 95

Geddes, Sir Eric, 146, 147, 162, 202

General Board of Health, 32–3

general election (1906), 73, 101, 113

general election (1918, 'coupon election'), 136–7

general election (1922), 146–7, 148

general election (1923), 151, 165

general election (1924), 153

general election (1929), 169, 195–7

general election (1931), 204

general election (1945), 5, 237–8, 248, 249

general election (1951), 264

general strike (1926), 160–61

Germany
  Bismarck's economic policy, 70–71, 108
  as competitor to Britain, 64, 70, 73, 107
  and labour exchanges, 79, 176–7
  science-based industries, 107–8, 243
  technical schools, 110
  and Versailles Treaty, 144, 156, 192

Gladstone, William, 59, 64, 68, 69, 71, 105

Glasgow, 141

Gloucester, 3

Gorst, Sir John, 112–13, 117

governmental and political system, 6

'Glorious Revolution' (1688), 13–14

'ministries' formed during WWI, 131

Parliament, 1–2, 4, 78, 82, 233–4
  payment for MPs, 80, 155
  size of Cabinet, 117
  Whig and Tory factions, 13–14
  see also civil service; electoral politics; local authorities

Grand, Sarah, 120

Great Depression, 8, 102, 197–9
  Keynes-Hayek disputes over, 238, 240–41, 250
  MacDonald's Economic Advisory Council, 199–201, 210, 217, 251–2

Great Exhibition (1851), 37

Great Famine, Irish, 38, 89

Great Reform Act (1832), 19, 60, 154

Green, Thomas Hill, 65–6, 67, 111, 176
  Principles of Political Obligation (1885), 66

Greenwood, Arthur, 220, 221–2, 234, 240

Griffiths, James, 260

Haldane, R. B., 69, 106, 107

Hale, Edward, 221

Hall, Noel, 208

Hamilton, Mary Agnes, 220

Hamilton, Walton, 182

Hardie, Keir, 67, 105

Harrisson, Tom, 2, 189

Hayek, Friedrich, 188, 212–13, 239, 241, 242, 250

The Road to Serfdom (1944),
    213, 238
health insurance, Beveridge
    proposals, 224, 256
health insurance, Liberal
    Government scheme,
    58, 78–9
  access to doctors, 78–9, 80, 224
  contributory nature of, 78,
    166, 224
  hospital treatment excluded, 80
  negotiations with doctors,
    79, 138
  sick pay, 78–9
  for wage earners only, 80, 125
  women's access to, 125, 166
Health, Ministry of, 138–9, 140–41
health services
  Neville Chamberlain's reforms,
    168–9
  dispensaries, 27
  free prescriptions, 8
  maternity and infant services,
    123–4, 125
  medical officers of health, 33
  Ministry of Health's remit, 138–9
  national blood transfusion
    service, 219
  Royal Commission on Poor Law
    (1905–9), 56
  shared resources during WW2,
    219–20
  spending on as in state's interest,
    8, 229
  unreported illness/disease, 80
Hegel, G. W. F., 65
Henderson, Arthur, 130, 203, 204
Hewins, W. A. S., 106
Hicks, John, 211–12
Hill, Octavia, 43, 49, 53, 141

history, Whig theory of, 14
Hobhouse, Emily, 69
Hobhouse, Leonard, 64–5, 67, 127,
    151, 156, 172, 178, 183
  and Boer War, 69
  The Labour Movement
    (1893), 69
  Liberalism (1911), 71
Hobson, John Atkinson, 67, 69–70,
    93, 157, 173, 176, 183,
    195, 207
  theory of 'underconsumption',
    70, 157
Hogben, Lancelot, 188
Home Rule question, 69, 71, 80,
    94, 128
Hopkins, Ellice, *The Power of
    Womanhood* (1899), 120
hospitals
  beds for private patients, 256
  care services for women, 125
  health outreach
    programmes, 122
  nineteenth-century, 27, 28
  WW2 Emergency Medical
    Service, 219–20, 232
House of Lords, 58, 78,
    80, 82
housing
  and Beveridge Report, 227–8
  built on outskirts of cities,
    142–3
  Conservative policy in 1920s/30s,
    162–3
  high rents in post-WW1
    developments, 143
  'homes fit for heroes',
    137–44, 162
  and Labour government
    (1945–51), 252, 253–4, 263

housing – *Cont.*
  Labour's subsidy (1924–33),
    152, 162
  Lloyd George halves
    targets, 146
  and local authorities, 141,
    143, 152
  Octavia Hill's projects, 49
  overcrowding and squalor, 29,
    30–31, 32, 36, 38
  post-WW1 building programme,
    127, 137–44, 162
  post-WW1 new towns,
    142–3
  post-WW1 rent strikes, 139–40
  post-WW2 new towns,
    254, 263
  post-WW2 prefabs, 253
  private house-building boom
    (1930s), 162–3, 209, 253
  'property-owning democracy'
    concept, 8, 161–2
  slum clearance, 34, 139
  Wheatley's Housing Act
    (1924), 152
Housing Act (1924), 152
Housing and Town Planning Act
    (1919), 141, 142–3
Hulton, Edward, 240
human nature, 6
Huxley, Julian, 208
Hyndman, Henry, 44

idealism, 65–6
ill health, 8, 80
  'germ theory of disease', 33
  miasmatic concept of disease,
    30, 33
  and Poor Law, 27, 29, 34, 36
immigration, 94

independence and self-reliance, 18,
    36, 49, 51, 59, 60, 68, 76, 92,
    102–3, 116, 173
Independent Labour Party, 55,
    67, 117
India, 206
Industrial Injuries Act (1946), 252
industrialization, 7, 29, 38, 39–41,
    59, 64, 181, 266
  campaigns to improve working
    conditions, 39
  and falling birthrate, 90
inflation, 134, 141, 144, 156,
    213, 253
insurance companies, private, 79, 83
Inter-Departmental Committee on
    Social Insurance and Allied
    Services, 218–19, 220–21, 234,
    239–40
Interdepartmental Committee on
    Physical Deterioration, 97–101,
    102, 119
interest rates, 144, 160, 162, 200,
    210, 211
International Health Exhibition,
    South Kensington, 87
Invergordon mutiny (1931), 203–4
Ireland
  Easter Rising (1916), 128
  Home Rule question, 69, 71, 80,
    94, 128
Irish Nationalist Party, 78, 80
Irish Repeal Party, 19, 59, 71

James II, King, 13–14
Japan, 108
Jennings, Humphrey, 2, 189
Jevons, W. S., 181–2
Jewish community, 72, 94
Joseph, Keith, 2, 7

Kahn, Richard, 200, 210
Kaldor, Nicholas, 240, 241
Kant, Immanuel, 65
Kay, James Phillips, 29–30
Keynes, John Maynard, 6, 105,
    109, 195, 197, 265
  background and early life, 192
  and Economic Advisory Council,
    199–201, 210, 217
  and Hayek, 212, 213, 238,
    241, 250
  influence in USA, 212
  and Liberal Party, 9, 156, 192–3,
    196, 199
  'liquidity preference' theory,
    210, 211
  and May Committee, 203
  obtains loan from US/Canada
    (1945), 250, 251
  and Second World War, 217
  and unemployment, 169, 193,
    196, 199
  *The Economic Consequences of
    Mr Churchill* (1925),
    160, 199
  *The Economic Consequences of
    the Peace* (1919), 156, 192
  The General Theory (1936),
    210–11, 241
  How to Pay for the War (1940),
    213
  A Tract on Monetary Reform
    (1923), 199
  A Treatise on Money (1930),
    209–10
Keynesian economics, 6, 209–12,
    241–2, 266
  and decline of Liberal Party, 9
  demand management, 210, 241,
    242, 249

  and Labour government
    (1945–51), 249, 252, 253, 265
  and theory of
    'underconsumption', 70, 157
Kitchener, Lord, 128–9
Koestler, Arthur, 240

Labour Exchange Bill (1909), 178
labour exchanges, 54, 79,
    176–80, 193
labour force
  casual labourers, 175
  and degeneration theory, 99
  discontent in 1880s, 42, 88,
    90, 151
  early trade-based bodies, 40
  'Great Victorian Boom', 38, 42,
    88, 172
  and increased life expectancy,
    74–5, 89
  and industrial capitalism, 38,
    39–41, 48, 59, 61
  marriage bars, 124
  matchgirl strikes (1880s), 90
  mobility due to Poor Law, 18
  Owen's New Lanark, 38–9
  post-WWI period, 135–6
  and return to gold
    standard, 160
  Rowntree paternalism, 45
  and Second World War,
    217–18
  Victorian campaigns over
    working conditions, 39
  women during First World War,
    129, 135
  working class women, 26, 39,
    119, 124–5
  workplace automation, 75
  see also wages

Labour government (1945–51), 5, 9, 249
  Central Economic Planning Staff, 251–2, 253
  Cripps' austerity, 253, 254
  devaluation crisis (1949), 253
  economic policy, 238–9, 249, 250–53
  economic problems, 250–51
  housing policy, 252, 253–4, 263
  implementation of Beveridge proposals, 252–3, 254–7
  nationalization programme, 249, 252, 261–2
Labour Party
  and 1892 election, 105
  and 1906 election, 73, 101
  and 1922 election, 147
  and 1924 election, 153
  and 1929 election, 197
  and 1931 election, 204
  and 1945 election, 5, 237, 238, 249
  and Beveridge Report, 234, 235
  emergence of, 59
  and enfranchisement of working classes, 154–5
  and First World War, 129–30, 145
  forms government (1923), 151–2, 165
  forms government (1929), 169, 197–8
  individual members, 151
  intellectual supporters, 249–50
  Keynes' rejection of, 192–3
  Lansbury as leader, 55
  Let Us Face the Future (1945 manifesto), 249, 263
  local organization, 155
  and national government, 203
  as official opposition after 1922, 146, 149
  and payment for MPs, 80, 155
  press hostility to, 150
  programme in 1920s, 150–51, 152, 198
  and Second World War, 219, 249–50
  supports free trade in 1920s, 150, 152
  trade union donations to, 80
  and the Webbs, 43, 151, 154–5
  WWI Cabinet appointments, 130
Labour Representation Committee, 72, 73, 97, 148, 155
Lamarck, Jean-Baptiste, 84
Lancashire cotton famine (1860s), 26–7, 38, 172
The Lancet, 89, 93
land nationalization, 138
land reform, 60
Lankester, E. Ray, 93
Lansbury, George, 55, 178
Laski, Harold, 234
Layton, Walter, 217
Lee, Kenneth, 240
Leeds, 14, 19, 29, 32, 96, 124
Left Book Club, 250
Letchworth, 142
the Levellers, 61
Liberal Government (1906–14)
  income tax reforms (1907), 73–4
  and Irish Nationalist Party, 78, 80
  Old Age Pensions Act (1908), 74, 76, 80, 89, 125
  'People's Budget' (1909), 77–8, 82, 128, 179
  school meals' question, 101–3
  social policy, 5, 57, 58–9, 74–81, 82, 89, 101–3, 125, 179

Liberal Party
  and 1906 election, 73, 113
  and 1918 'coupon election', 137
  and 1922 election, 147, 148
  and 1924 election, 153
  and 1945 election, 238
  Asquith's Independents, 147, 151
  Britain's Industrial Future
      ('Yellow Book', 1928), 156–7
  decline from 1920s, 9, 148–9,
      153–4, 155
  defections from in 1920s, 157–8
  intellectual establishment, 156
  'Lib-Lab' system in late
      nineteenth century, 68, 72, 82
  Lloyd George's Independents,
      204
  nineteenth-century programme,
      59–60
  and non-conformism, 60,
      111–12, 244
  post-WWI threat from Labour,
      147, 148–9
  split over Home Rule, 69, 71–2
  We Can Conquer
      Unemployment (1929), 196
  weak local organization, 155–6
  Whig origins of, 57, 59
Liberal Summer School, 156, 192–3
Liberal Unionists, 69, 72, 94, 113,
    163
liberalism, 9, 62–3, 117, 157, 158
  'advanced liberalism' of Mill,
      63–4, 69, 83, 182
  classical, 36–7, 60, 64, 181
  and democracy, 61
  economic, 7, 39, 67, 101, 132,
      133, 212–13
  and entrenched privileges, 60
  and evolutionary theory, 85, 88
  and idealism, 65–6
  neoclassical, 182
  and religious education, 113
  and role of state, 58–9, 63–4, 66,
      69, 115–16, 126–7, 132, 264–5
  and socialism, 62, 63, 67–8
  tariff reform and social welfare,
      49, 76
  thrift and hard work, 36, 51, 60
  transformation of, 58–9, 193
  woven into welfare state's
      identity, 9
  see also new liberalism
Lincoln, Abraham, 26
Lindsell, H. M., 98
Liverpool, 26, 29, 121, 191, 232
Llewellyn Smith, Hubert, 178,
    179–80, 186–7, 194
Lloyd George, David, 5, 59, 156,
    192, 233, 234
  and 1918 'coupon election',
      136–7
  and 1924 election, 153–4
  and 1929 election, 169
  and 1931 election, 204
  backs Labour after 1923 election,
      151
  becomes Prime Minister (1916),
      130
  on Neville Chamberlain, 164
  as Chancellor of the Exchequer,
      77–8, 79, 82, 83
  coalition/National Liberals, 147,
      148, 151
  Geddes axe, 146, 147, 162, 202
  'homes fit for heroes', 137–44,
      162
  ousts Labour government (1924),
      153, 165
  rhetorical brilliance, 83

local authorities
administration, 117
Neville Chamberlain's reforms,
167–9, 196
committees for maternal/child
welfare, 124
elected school boards, 111–13
and Geddes axe, 146
health outreach programmes,
122, 123–4
and housing, 141, 143, 152, 254
and industrial pollution, 33
maternity clinics, 123–4
'municipal socialism', 33–4, 72,
163
new responsibilities (5 July 1948),
260
'Poplarism', 167–8
and poverty relief, 56
public health powers expanded,
139
and public works, 27
and school meals' question,
101–2
and waste removal, 29–30, 32,
116, 139
Local Education Authorities,
113–14, 117, 168, 179
Local Government Act (1929),
168–9
Local Government Board, 24, 122,
142
Loch, Charles S., 49, 53, 98, 102–3,
109
Locke, John, 65
Two Treatises of Government
(1689), 14
Lodge, Oliver, 114
London
Booth's investigation, 42–5, 46, 50

immigrant Jewish community, 12
and Mass-Observation, 2, 3, 189
overcrowding, 141
underground train network, 142
London County Council, 167
London School of Economics, 106,
185, 200, 208, 234, 240, 263
Beveridge as Director, 121, 158,
187–8, 190, 215, 262
founding of, 43, 51
Hayek at, 212, 238, 241
Lopokova, Lydia, 191

Macaulay, Thomas Babington, 42
MacDonald, Ramsay, 67, 72, 93,
173, 176
becomes Prime Minister (1923),
151–2, 165
becomes Prime Minister (1929),
169, 197
and economic crisis (1929–31),
197–203
evolutionary view of socialism,
151
forms national government
(1931), 203
as leader of the opposition, 148,
151
and May Committee, 202, 203
and Oswald Mosley, 207
Mackinder, Halford, 106
Maclay, Joseph, 131
Macmillan, Harold, 238, 266
Madge, Charles, 2, 189
Malthus, Thomas, 17, 88–9, 105
An Essay on the Principle of
Population (1798), 17–18
Manchester, 19, 26, 29, 32, 40, 96,
99, 109, 123
Manchester Guardian, 67, 127, 156

Mansfield House, Canning Town, 176
Marshall, Alfred, 183, 184, 195
Marshall Plan, 253
Marshall, T. H., 190, 262, 264
Marx, Eleanor, 67
Marx, Karl, 38, 41, 61
Mary II, Queen, 14
Mass-Observation, 2–3, 189–90, 231
Masterman, Charles 'Charlie', 74
materialism, 14
Maternity and Child Welfare Act (1918), 124
Maurice, General Frederick, 119
May, George, 202, 203
McKenna, Reginald, 133, 152, 159
means tests
  Beveridge opposes, 173, 225
  for Old Age Pensions, 76, 165, 166, 219
  and school meals' question, 102
  and Unemployment Act (1934), 205
Mearns, Andrew, *Bitter Cry of Outcast London*, 41
Metropolitan Police, 167
military expenditure
  and Boer War, 74, 83, 107, 113
  and First World War, 131–4, 140–41
  rearmament in 1930s, 209
  during Second World War, 250
  'two power standard', 74, 76–7, 108, 128, 130
Mill, James, 62, 105
  An Essay on Government (1820), 15
Mill, John Stuart, 6, 41, 62, 88, 90

'advanced' liberalism of, 63–4, 69, 83, 182
economic science-government distinction, 195
and education, 63–4
production and distribution, 63, 71, 181
and socialism, 63
On Liberty (1859), 63, 83
Principles of Political Economy (1848), 63, 182
Utilitarianism (1863), 62
Mises, Ludwig von, 180, 212
Mond, Sir Alfred, 146
Money, Leo Chiozza, 77
Montgomery, Lieutenant-General, 233
Morning Post, 173, 177
Morris, William, 142
Mosley, Oswald, 206–7, 209
Mussolini, Benito, 207

Napoleonic wars, 18
The Nation and Athenaeum, 156, 195
national assistance, 205, 227
National Birth-Rate Commission, 92–3
National Coal Board, 255
National Council of Public Morals, 92–3
'national efficiency', 106–9, 117–18, 125, 141, 189, 243
  and democratic state, 109–10
  and education reform, 110–15, 172
  and 'national minimum', 115–16, 225
  and role of women, 119–21

national government (1931–40)
  comes off gold standard
    (1931), 204
  and 'Empire Free Trade',
    205–6
  formed by MacDonald (1931),
    203–4
  unemployment benefit reforms,
    204–5, 214, 227
National Health Service
  administrative structure, 255
  'appointed day' (5 July 1948),
    260–61, 262
  Beveridge Report proposes, 4,
    228, 229, 231
  implementation of proposals, 9,
    248, 252, 254–7
  opposition to, 256–7, 261, 264
National Health Service Acts
  (1946/47), 255, 256
National Institute of Economic and
  Social Research, 215–16
National Insurance Act (1911),
  78–9, 179
national insurance, Beveridge's
  scheme
  bureaucracy of, 250, 259, 260
  compulsory nature of, 224,
    234, 262
  contributory nature of, 261, 262
  The Family Guide to the
    National Insurance Scheme,
    259–60
  see also Beveridge Report (Social
    Insurance and Allied
    Services)
national insurance, Liberal
  Government scheme
  and Beveridge, 5, 79, 170–71,
    177–80, 217

contributions systems, 78, 80, 82,
  166, 224
delayed in House of Lords, 179
and expanding base of provision,
  124–5
as 'fact of life' by 1920s, 149
and Great Depression, 199
intellectual rationale, 156
Lloyd George introduces, 77,
  78–80
and 'national efficiency', 118
new bureaucracies created
  by, 118
opposition to, 79, 80–81, 82,
  125, 138
and pensions scheme, 82
and private providers, 79–80, 83
as regressive tax, 82–3
and Royal Commission report
  (1909), 57, 58
stamps inside insurance books,
  80
two parts of 1911 Act, 78–80,
  179
National Insurance Statutory
  Committee, 205
nationalism and patriotism
  and Boer War, 69, 95
  and First World War, 128
Naval Defence Act (1889), 74
navy
  Dreadnought-class ships,
    76–7, 128
  Invergordon mutiny (1931),
    203–4
  'two power standard', 74, 76–7,
    108, 128, 130
New Earswick, York, 45, 142
New Harmony, Indiana, 38–9
New Lanark, 38–9, 141

new liberalism, 58, 64–71, 74, 101,
    148, 156, 173, 195
  and British Empire, 69, 70, 157
  and Lloyd George, 83, 138
  Manchester Guardian as voice
    of, 67, 127, 156
  and socialism, 67–9, 127,
    148, 151
  and the state, 66, 71, 111, 127,
    138, 265
  T. H. Green as inspiration for,
    111
  see also Hobhouse, Leonard
New Statesman, 151, 156, 189
New York Times, 212
New Zealand, 126
News Chronicle, 222
Newsholme, Arthur, 122
Nicholson, Edward Max, 208, 209
Nightingale, Florence, 28
non-conformists, 42, 60, 111–12,
    113, 244
Nordau, Max, 93
Northcliffe, Baron (Alfred
    Harmsworth), 145–6
Northcote–Trevelyan Report
    (1854), 75
Norwood, Sir Cyril, 243
Notification of Births Act (1907), 123
Nuffield, Viscount, 216
Nunn, Thomas Hancock, 49

Observer newspaper, 240
O'Connell, Daniel, 19, 71
old age pensions
  Beveridge as campaigner for, 173
  Beveridge scheme, 214–15, 224,
    226, 230, 231
  civil service and government
    employees, 75

pre-1909 opposition to, 49, 54
  and tariff reform, 49, 76
  trade union schemes, 75
old age pensions, Liberal
    Government scheme, 57, 58,
    74, 76, 80, 89, 125
  additional spending (1940), 219
  Anderson Committee, 165
  Neville Chamberlain's reforms,
    164–7, 224
  coalition's increases (1919), 165
  cost of, 76–7, 226
  as 'fact of life' by 1920s, 149
  funding of, 75–6
  intellectual rationale, 156
  made contributory (1925),
    166, 167
  and means testing, 76, 165,
    166, 219
  and national insurance scheme, 82
  non-contributory nature of, 76,
    125, 165
  Old Age Pensions Act (1908), 74,
    76, 80, 89
  qualifying age, 76, 165,
    166, 219
  and Royal Commission report
    (1909), 54
Old Oak estate,
    Hammersmith, 143
opinion polling, 190, 231
Orwell, George, 250
Owen, Robert, 38–9, 141
Oxford University, 60, 172, 189,
    216, 239, 243
  extension scheme, 70

Palmerston, Viscount, 59
parenthood and families
  crèches, 125

parenthood – *cont.*
  family allowances, 121–2, 228, 229
  family size, 2–3, 90–93, 109
  ideal of nuclear family, 119–20
  income tax abatements, 121
  maternity allowance, 79, 225
  maternity clinics, 123–4
Pareto, Vilfredo, 185
Parker, Barry, 142
Parliament, 1–2, 4, 78, 82, 233–4
Parliament Act (1911), 78, 128
Pasteur, Louis, 30
Peabody Trust, 141
Pearson, Karl, 89–90, 97, 110
Peel, Robert, 37, 38, 59
Penguin, 222
pharmaceuticals, 108
philosophy, political
  Baldwin's 'national' conservativism, 158–69, 192
  contract principle, 14
  empiricism, 65
  Enlightenment, 36–7
  idealism, 65–6, 111, 176
  individual rights, 13, 14, 158, 213, 239
  as not static entity, 9
  radical thought, 14–15
  see also liberalism; Mill, John Stuart; new liberalism; socialism; Spencer, Herbert; utilitarianism
Picture Post, 240
Pigou, Arthur Cecil, 183–5, 200–201
Pitt, William, the Younger, 18–19
planning, 109, 206–9, 212
  Hayek's rejection of, 212–13
police, 167

pensions, 75
Political and Economic Planning (PEP), 207–9, 220
Political Economy Club, 105–6
politics, electoral *see* electoral politics
pollution, industrial, 33, 100
Poor Law
  1834 reforms, 11–12, 20–23, 35, 54, 57, 58, 59, 71, 167, 264
  the '43rd of Elizabeth', 11, 15, 22
  as about destitution, 55–6
  Boards, 24, 54, 117
  centralized control, 22, 24, 27–8, 33
  and corn tariffs, 25, 38
  Guardians, 29, 30, 56, 124, 139, 167–8
  indoor relief, 16, 22
  Lancashire cotton famine (1860s), 26–7, 38, 172
  local administration of, 15–16, 18, 20–21, 22
  and mobile workforce, 18
  in northern industrial areas, 23–4, 26–7
  outdoor relief, 16, 17, 21, 24, 25
  Poor Law Unions, 22, 24, 25, 26, 27–8, 54
  'Poplarism', 167–8
  and 'poverty cycle', 48
  principle of less eligibility, 21–2, 24–5, 27, 28, 35, 167, 261
  principle of 'setting the poor to work', 16, 22
  Royal Commission on (1905–9), 11, 48, 49–57, 58, 116, 119, 125, 168, 170, 177
  Settlement Act (1662), 15–16, 17

'Speenhamland system' (1795),
  16–17
and warding off of rebellion,
  11, 18
and waste removal, 29–30, 139
popular movements, 6, 60–61
poverty
  Beveridge at Toynbee Hall, 173–4
  Booth's investigation, 42–5, 46,
    50, 88, 90, 174, 182–3
  children as wage earners, 90
  factors beyond individuals'
    control, 16, 26–31, 34, 36
  and family size, 90, 228
  later nineteenth-century debates
    on, 41–6
  and Lloyd George's 'People's
    Budget' (1909), 77–8
  Masterman's work on, 74
  moral judgements about, 16, 18,
    36, 44–5, 47, 51–2, 54–5, 56,
    94–5, 115–16, 118–19, 227
  moralizing of Chadwick and
    Senior, 21, 22, 32, 35, 36, 172
  moralizing rejected by Beveridge,
    173, 174, 227
  and 'national efficiency', 110
  poor relief abroad, 52
  'poverty cycle', 6, 47–8, 55, 90,
    186, 228
  'poverty line' concept, 47,
    187, 202
  quantitative research, 185–7, 225
  Rowntree's 'primary poverty', 47,
    52, 90, 186, 187
  Rowntree's survey, 46–8, 90,
    174, 182–3, 228
  Royal Commission on Poor Law
    (1905–9), 11, 48, 49–57, 58,
    116, 119, 125, 168, 170, 177
  and Social Science
    Association, 41
  and Victorian working classes,
    38–42
  and Webb's 'national minimum',
    115
prescription charges, 266
Pretyman, Ernest, 142
Priestley, J. B., *English Journey*
  (1934), 143
progress, notions of, 1–2, 99–100,
  110
  and 1945 Labour manifesto,
    249–50
  and classical economists, 37
  and 'eugenic feminists', 120
  and Poor Law Amendment Act
    (1834), 23
  and social science, 189
  in Victorian era, 7, 38, 41, 85, 88,
    110, 142
  Whig theory of history, 14
progressive politics, 6–7, 107, 142,
  148–9, 195, 266
  and Beveridge, 2, 234, 248
  and dinner parties, 105–6,
    170–71, 176, 177, 250
  and falling birthrate, 90
  and First World War, 128,
    129–30, 145
  and Hayek, 212–13
  and Keynes, 192–3, 212, 213
  Progressive Alliance, 72, 82
  see also Fabian Society; Labour
    Party; Liberal Party; liberalism;
    new liberalism; radicalism,
    Nineteenth-century;
    socialism
'property-owning democracy', 8,
  161–2

Proudhon, Pierre-Joseph, 61–2
psychology, 85, 87, 181–2
Public Assistance Committees, 54,
    168, 205
public health
  and Boer War recruits, 95–9,
    102, 104
  and green public spaces, 100
  health visitors, 122–4
  local authority powers increased,
    139
  and 'national minimum', 115–16
  nineteenth-century
    improvements, 89, 115–16
  physical discrepancies as
    environmental, 99–101, 102
  preventative health programmes,
    122–4
  Sanitary Act (1866), 33
  sanitation in Victorian cities,
    29–32, 89, 115–16, 139
  vaccination programmes, 28, 89,
    116
  workhouse infirmaries, 27–8, 168
  see also health services
Public Health Act (1875), 33
Public Works (Manufacturing
    Districts) Act (1864), 27

Quakers, 45, 46, 47
quantitative research, 185–7, 225

radicalism, nineteenth-century,
    14–15, 59
  and land reform, 60
  self-interest principle, 15
  and Whigs, 19–20, 58, 59–60,
    67–8, 69
railways, 105, 196, 252, 261–2
Rainbow Circle, 67, 173

Rathbone, Eleanor, 121–2, 220
Reeves, William Pember, 67
Registrar General, Office of, 88,
    91–2
religious dissenters, 72
Representation of the People Act
    (1918), 135, 155
revolutions of 1848 in Europe, 61
Ricardo, David, 12–13, 25, 51, 62,
    105, 181
  and class conflict, 37–8
  as MP for Portarlington, 19
  and Poor Law, 15, 17
  and rent seeking, 74
  and unemployment, 171–2
  *Principles of Political Economy
    and Taxation* (1817), 13
roads, 183, 196
Robbins, Lionel, 185, 188, 200,
    201, 206
Robertson, J. M., 69
Robinson, Joan, 240, 241
Rochdale Society of Equitable
    Pioneers, 40
Rockefeller Foundation,
    187–8, 235
Roosevelt, F. D., 212, 235
Rosebery, Lord, 96, 108, 110, 114
Rothermere, Lord, 146
Rousseau, Jean-Jacques, 17
Rowntree, Joseph, 45, 142
Rowntree, Seebohm, 6, 45–6, 98,
    119, 156, 173, 174, 202,
    220, 228
  and Boer War recruits, 96
  calorie calculation, 225
  and falling birthrate, 90
  and Liberal Party, 196
  repeats survey of York (1936–41),
    185–6, 226

The Human Needs of Labour (1918, 1937), 185–6
Poverty: A Study of Town Life (1901), 46–8, 52, 182–3
Royal Commission on the Poor Law (1832–4), 11, 20–22, 24–5, 35
Royal Commission on the Poor Laws and the Relief of Distress (1905–9), 11, 48–57, 58, 116, 119, 170
Royal Statistical Society, 43
Ruskin, John, 141
Russell, Bertrand, 106
Russell, Lord John, 29
Russian Revolution (1917), 135, 152–3, 206
Russo-Japanese War (1905), 108

Salisbury, Lord, 72
Salter, Arthur, 217
Salvation Army, 51
Samuel, Herbert, 67, 203
Saturday Review, 208
schools *see* education; teachers
Schumacher, E. F., 240
science, technology and engineering, 92, 93, 99, 109, 115, 142, 172, 181, 188, 231
Chadwickian approach, 20, 31, 33, 35, 52–3, 100, 122
Darwinian theory, 64, 83–5, 86, 110
during First World War, 131, 134
science and technical education, 108, 110, 114–15, 243, 244, 247
science-based industries, 73, 107–8, 131, 243
technological innovations, 87, 105, 183, 194
Scientific and Industrial Research, Department of, 131
Scott, C. P., 67
Second World War, 4, 213, 215, 217–18
Beveridge during, 1, 216–19, 220–22, 229–30, 235–6, 239–42
demobilizing the armed forces, 250
electoral truce during, 235
Emergency Medical Service, 219–20, 232
evacuation during, 232, 253
Lend-Lease agreement, 250
Normandy Landings (1944), 248
outbreak of, 216–17
post-war reconstruction thinking during, 219–22, 235, 243–8
self-employed, 225
Senior, Nassau, 20–22, 23, 35, 57
Shaftesbury, Earl of, 14
Shaftesbury, Lord, 39
Shaw, George Bernard, 50, 107
Sheffield, 96
Sieff, Israel, 208
Simon, John, 33
Sims, George, *How the Poor Live*, 41
Skelton, Noel, 161
slavery, 26
smallpox, 33
Smiles, Samuel, 60
Smith, Adam, 15, 17, 25, 51, 181
and division of labour, 36–7
and education, 63
and unemployment, 171–2
The Wealth of Nations (1776), 13

Snow, John, 33
Snowden, Philip, 201–2, 203
social class
  and average height, 99, 100, 102
  Booth's categories, 44
  conditions for Victorian working
    classes, 38–42
  and Conservative housing policy,
    162–3
  defining, 91–2
  and degeneration theory, 95–7,
    98, 99–101
  and falling birthrate, 90, 91–2
  and franchise extensions, 154–5
  and health visitors, 122–3
  increased social mobility, 266–7
  physical discrepancies as
    environmental, 99–101, 102
  and post-WW1 new towns, 143
  post-WW2 housing policy, 254,
    263
  'professional model of', 92
  and responses to Beveridge
    Report, 230–32
  and responses to welfare
    state, 261
  Ricardo's ideas on, 37–8
  and social science, 189
'social Darwinism', 85
social democracy, era of, 266–7
Social Democratic Federation, 44,
  66–7, 151
'social housing', 141
social policy (academic discipline),
  190–91
social science, 188–9, 216
  and London School of
    Economics, 187–8, 190
  Mass-Observation, 2–3, 189–90
Social Science Association, 41

Social Security League, 235, 241
socialism, 59, 61, 82, 242
  democratic, 62, 63
  and new liberalism, 67–9, 127,
    148, 151
  Owen's New Lanark, 38–9, 141
  and Ramsay MacDonald, 151
  revolutionary, 61–2
  Social Democratic Federation,
    66–7
  and the Webbs, 50–51, 52–3,
    116, 151, 154, 265
Socialist League, 142
South Africa, 69, 206
the Spectator, 41, 161
'Speenhamland system' (1795),
  16–17
Spencer, Herbert, 50, 60, 88, 93, 97
  Synthetic Philosophy, 85
the state
  administration, 117
  'advanced Liberal' view of,
    63–4, 69
  and Helen Bosanquet, 51
  changing liberal view of, 58–9,
    66, 71, 115–16, 264–5
  and economic intervention, 193
  and education reform, 110–11
  during First World War, 126–7,
    131, 132–4
  Hayek's view of, 213
  and the individual, 49, 54, 102–3,
    264
  and J. S. Mill, 63–4, 69
  and 'national efficiency', 109–10,
    117
  and new liberalism, 66, 71, 111,
    127, 138, 265
  nineteenth-century growth
    of, 117

Royal Commission's view of
(1909), 49, 51, 53, 54–5, 57
'top down' nature of Beveridge
proposals, 263
and unemployment, 171, 176,
265
statistical analysis, 178, 188
Statistical Society, 41
Stead, Alfred, 108
steel industry, 194, 195–6, 252
Stevenson, T. H. C., 89, 91–2
Stopes, Marie, 93
suffragette movement, 121
Swing Riots (1830s), 19

Taff Vale Railway Company,
72, 97
Tatham, J. F. W., 98
Tawney, R. H., 158, 172, 188, 199,
234, 250
taxation
abatements related to children,
121
business relief from local rates,
169, 196
differentiated income tax, 73–4,
82, 132
during First World War, 132
graduated income tax, 77, 82,
132
land and death duties, 77
national business rate, 169
as still high in post-WW1 period,
144–5
and welfare economics, 184–5
Taylor, Harriet, 63
Taylor, Sir William, 98–9
teachers
in church schools, 112, 244
female, 247–8

pensions, 75
salaries, 136, 202, 247–8
The Times, 35, 129, 145, 150, 215,
217, 222, 232–3
Titmuss, Richard, 190,
232, 263
Tory faction
dominance from early 1780s to
1820s, 18–19
and Liberal Unionists, 72
principles of, 13, 14, 39
split over Corn Laws, 38
and Whig ascendency from
1830s, 19–20
Tower Hamlets, 43
Town and Country Planning Act
(1947), 254
Toynbee, Arnold, 65
Toynbee Hall, 49, 67, 170, 172–4,
177, 178
trade and commerce
competition from Germany and
USA, 64, 70, 73, 107
Empire free trade, 73,
205–6, 208
'imperial preference', 168, 196,
198, 204–5
international networks, 25–7,
36–7
lost overseas market post-WW1,
144, 156
trade cycle, 180–81
trade unions, 54, 55, 67, 92, 121,
173, 175
and Beveridge, 217–18
closed shops, 180
donations to Labour Party, 80
expansion of, 68
and First World War, 129
general strike (1926), 160–61

and labour exchanges, 177, 180
and Labour Party policy, 150
'Lib-Lab' system in late
    nineteenth century, 68,
    72, 82
nineteenth-century forerunners, 40
pension schemes, 75
Taff Vale decision (1901), 72, 97
trade disputes in 1880s, 42, 88
Trades Union Congress, 220, 253
Trafalgar Square riots (1886), 42,
    88, 151
transport infrastructure, 183,
    196, 197
Trevelyan, Charles, 157
Trinder, Tommy, 259–60
typhoid, 33

unemployment
    in 1924/25 period, 152, 160
    and 1929 election, 196
    and Beveridge, 170–71, 172,
        173–80, 216, 239–42
    and Beveridge Report, 228,
        229, 241–2
    and classical economists, 171–2
    cyclical, 173–4
    falling levels in 1930s, 209
    Full Employment in a Free
        Society (1944 report), 242
    Great Depression, 8, 102,
        197–203
    high levels in 1920s, 144, 156–7,
        160, 169, 194, 195
    and Hobson, 70
    labour colonies in mainland
        Europe, 176
    long-term, 7–8, 205
    and 'organised fluidity of labour',
        175–80, 193

passes 2 million (1930), 169
profoundly debilitating effects of,
    56–7
Unemployment Act (1934),
    204–5
Unemployment Assistance
    Boards, 205
unemployment benefits
    Assistance Boards, 205
    Beveridge's rationalized scheme,
        223, 224, 225, 267
    Beveridge's 'tolerated' rate of
        unemployment, 229
    exhaustion of entitlement, 196,
        199
    during Great Depression, 201,
        202–3, 204
    introduced by Liberal
        government, 79, 80
    and labour exchanges, 179
    Labour manifesto (1929), 196
    national government reforms
        (1934), 204–5, 214, 227
    as target for critics, 7
unemployment insurance
    Beveridge scheme, 224, 225, 229,
        234–5, 239–42, 265
    pre-1909 provision, 75, 112
    and Royal Commission report
        (1909), 54
unemployment insurance, Liberal
    Government scheme, 5, 58,
    217
    as Board of Trade responsibility,
        179, 180
    compulsory nature of, 79, 80
    contributory nature of, 79, 224
    national government reforms
        (1934), 204–5, 214
    and voluntary organizations, 54

United States of America (USA),
64, 70, 73, 107, 144, 197
Beveridge's tour of (1943), 235
Lend-Lease agreement, 250
Marshall Plan, 253
Roosevelt's New Deal, 212, 235
and sterling convertibility,
250, 251
universities
in Germany, 108
'redbrick', 114, 191
Unwin, Raymond, 142
urbanization, 29, 105, 181, 266
and building regulations, 100
USSR, 152-3, 206-7
utilitarianism, 6, 14-15, 62-3,
64-5
and welfare economics, 183
utilities
'municipal socialism', 33-4,
72, 163
nationalization of, 252, 261-2

venereal disease, 93
Versailles peace conference (1919),
137, 144, 156, 192
voluntary organisations
and Helen Bosanquet, 51, 52
and hospital care, 27
and post-WW1 social housing,
141
and poverty relief, 49-50, 54-5
preventative health programmes,
122-3
and Royal Commission report
(1909), 54-5

wages, 76, 92, 144, 175, 213, 239,
253, 267
and Beveridge, 216, 217-18, 228

children as wage earners, 90
and classical economists,
17, 116
and family allowances, 121, 228
and Great Depression, 200-201,
202, 203-4
and high rents in post-WW1
developments, 143
levels in nineteenth-century, 38,
44, 71
national minimum wage
proposals, 116, 173, 184
and return to gold standard, 159,
160-61
and Rowntree's 'poverty cycle',
47-8
and tax burden, 73-4, 77
women as wage earners, 26, 39,
119, 124-5, 247-8
Wakefield, H. Russell, 55
Wall Street Crash (1929), 197
Wallace, Alfred Russel, 84
Webb, Beatrice (née Potter), 5,
43, 67
adversarial style, 52-3
as Booth's assistant, 43, 50
relationship with Sidney, 50
Royal Commission on Poor Law
(1905-9), 50, 51, 52-3, 55-7,
58, 116, 168, 177
Webb, Sidney, 5, 43, 50-51, 67, 187
Co-Efficients Club, 106
and experts, 110, 113-14,
115, 195
as Labour MP for Seaham, 154
and science education, 114
The Decline in the Birth-Rate
(1907), 91
'The Necessary Basis of Society'
(1908), 110

the Webbs (Beatrice, Sidney) (where
mentioned jointly)
and 1902 Education Act, 113–14
and Beveridge, 170, 173, 177
dinner parties, 170–71, 177, 250
and elites, 50, 106, 115, 116,
170–71, 250
and experts, 110, 113–14,
115, 195
and Fabian Society strategy,
50–51, 52–3, 116, 151, 154
founding of *New
Statesman*, 151
and Labour Party, 43, 151, 154–5
and Liberal Party, 68
National Birth-Rate
Commission, 93
and 'national minimum', 115–17,
173, 225
and socialism, 50–51, 52–3, 116,
151, 154, 265
*Soviet Communism: A New
Civilisation?* (1935), 206–7
Week-End Review, 208
welfare economics, 182–5, 213
welfare state
affordability issue, 266
'appointed day' (5 July 1948),
260–61, 262
and capitalism, 7, 262–3, 267
contributory nature of, 8, 78, 79,
80, 82, 166–7, 223–4, 261,
262
as intergenerational project, 6–7,
265–6
liberalism woven into identity
of, 9
as 'missed opportunity', 262–3
'mixed parentage' of, 264,
265–6

as underpinning social
democracy, 267
universality of, 28, 224–7, 228,
248, 256, 262, 264
Michael Young's criticism, 263–4
see also Beveridge Report (*Social
Insurance and Allied
Services*)
Wellington, Duke of, 19
Wells, H. G., 50, 97, 106, 107
A Modern Utopia (1905), 108
Westminster Review, 60
Wheatley, John, 152
Whig faction
ascendency from 1830s, 19–20,
37, 64
Grey administration (1830–34),
19
and Liberal Party, 57, 59
Lichfield House Compact (1835),
19, 59, 71, 78, 128
principles of, 13–14
and radicalism, 19–20, 58,
59–60, 67–8, 69
theory of history, 14
White, Arnold, 94, 100
and Boer War, 95–6, 109
Efficiency and Empire (1901),
118–19
The Problems of a Great City
(1886), 94–5
Wicksell, Knut, 180
Widows, Orphans, and Old Age
Pensions Act (1925), 164–7
Wilkinson, Ellen, 252
William III, King, 14
Willmott, Peter, 263
Willoughby de Broke,
Lord, 82
Wilson, Harold, 216

women
  and bathhouses, 122
  'civic/eugenic motherhood'
    movement, 120
  contraceptive habits, 90, 93
  enfranchisement of some (1918),
    135, 155
  equal pay issues, 247–8
  'eugenic feminists', 120, 121–2
  and falling birthrate, 89–93,
    228–9
  family allowances, 121–2, 228,
    229
  in First World War labour force,
    129, 135
  franchise equality, 169, 197
  in higher education, 51
  and ideal of nuclear family,
    119–20
  and low paid work, 26, 39, 119,
    124–5
  marriage bars, 124
  and medical profession, 124
  moral judgements on mothers,
    118–19
  and 'national efficiency', 119–21
  Octavia Hill's view of role, 49
  opportunities in public
    administration, 124
  poor deal from pension reforms
    (1925), 166
  and Poor Law, 119
  suffrage campaign, 49, 61, 121,
    135
Wood, Kingsley, 246
Woolf, Virginia, 192
Woolwich, 139
Wootton, Barbara, 240
Workers' Weekly, 153
workhouse, 11–12, 22, 24–5,
  27, 56
  appalling conditions in, 25,
    28, 35
  infirmaries, 27–8, 168
  segregation rules, 22, 25, 28,
    48, 75
Wythenshawe, 143

York, 45–6, 96, 142, 185–6
Young, Michael, 263–4

ALLEN LANE
an imprint of
PENGUIN BOOKS

Also Published

Michael Pollan, *How to Change Your Mind: The New Science of Psychedelics*

David Christian, *Origin Story: A Big History of Everything*

Judea Pearl and Dana Mackenzie, *The Book of Why: The New Science of Cause and Effect*

David Graeber, *Bullshit Jobs: A Theory*

Serhii Plokhy, *Chernobyl: History of a Tragedy*

Michael McFaul, *From Cold War to Hot Peace: The Inside Story of Russia and America*

Paul Broks, *The Darker the Night, the Brighter the Stars: A Neuropsychologist's Odyssey*

Lawrence Wright, *God Save Texas: A Journey into the Future of America*

John Gray, *Seven Types of Atheism*

Carlo Rovelli, *The Order of Time*

Mariana Mazzucato, *The Value of Everything: Making and Taking in the Global Economy*

Richard Vinen, *The Long '68: Radical Protest and Its Enemies*

Kishore Mahbubani, *Has the West Lost It?: A Provocation*

John Lewis Gaddis, *On Grand Strategy*

Richard Overy, *The Birth of the RAF, 1918: The World's First Air Force*

Francis Pryor, *Paths to the Past: Encounters with Britain's Hidden Landscapes*

Helen Castor, *Elizabeth I: A Study in Insecurity*

Ken Robinson and Lou Aronica, *You, Your Child and School*

Leonard Mlodinow, *Elastic: Flexible Thinking in a Constantly Changing World*

Nick Chater, *The Mind is Flat: The Illusion of Mental Depth and The Improvised Mind*

Michio Kaku, *The Future of Humanity: Terraforming Mars, Interstellar Travel, Immortality, and Our Destiny Beyond*

Thomas Asbridge, *Richard I: The Crusader King*

Richard Sennett, *Building and Dwelling: Ethics for the City*

Nassim Nicholas Taleb, *Skin in the Game: Hidden Asymmetries in Daily Life*

Steven Pinker, *Enlightenment Now: The Case for Reason, Science, Humanism and Progress*

Steve Coll, *Directorate S: The C.I.A. and America's Secret Wars in Afghanistan, 2001 - 2006*

Jordan B. Peterson, *12 Rules for Life: An Antidote to Chaos*

Bruno Maçães, *The Dawn of Eurasia: On the Trail of the New World Order*

Brock Bastian, *The Other Side of Happiness: Embracing a More Fearless Approach to Living*

Ryan Lavelle, *Cnut: The North Sea King*

Tim Blanning, *George I: The Lucky King*

Thomas Cogswell, *James I: The Phoenix King*

Pete Souza, *Obama, An Intimate Portrait: The Historic Presidency in Photographs*

Robert Dallek, *Franklin D. Roosevelt: A Political Life*

Norman Davies, *Beneath Another Sky: A Global Journey into History*

Ian Black, *Enemies and Neighbours: Arabs and Jews in Palestine and Israel, 1917-2017*

Martin Goodman, *A History of Judaism*

Shami Chakrabarti, *Of Women: In the 21st Century*

Stephen Kotkin, *Stalin, Vol. II: Waiting for Hitler, 1928-1941*

Lindsey Fitzharris, *The Butchering Art: Joseph Lister's Quest to Transform the Grisly World of Victorian Medicine*

Serhii Plokhy, *Lost Kingdom: A History of Russian Nationalism from Ivan the Great to Vladimir Putin*

Mark Mazower, *What You Did Not Tell: A Russian Past and the Journey Home*

Lawrence Freedman, *The Future of War: A History*

Niall Ferguson, *The Square and the Tower: Networks, Hierarchies and the Struggle for Global Power*

Matthew Walker, *Why We Sleep: The New Science of Sleep and Dreams*

Edward O. Wilson, *The Origins of Creativity*

John Bradshaw, *The Animals Among Us: The New Science of Anthropology*

David Cannadine, *Victorious Century: The United Kingdom, 1800-1906*

Leonard Susskind and Art Friedman, *Special Relativity and Classical Field Theory*

Maria Alyokhina, *Riot Days*

Oona A. Hathaway and Scott J. Shapiro, *The Internationalists: And Their Plan to Outlaw War*

Chris Renwick, *Bread for All: The Origins of the Welfare State*

Anne Applebaum, *Red Famine: Stalin's War on Ukraine*

Richard McGregor, *Asia's Reckoning: The Struggle for Global Dominance*

Chris Kraus, *After Kathy Acker: A Biography*

Clair Wills, *Lovers and Strangers: An Immigrant History of Post-War Britain*

Odd Arne Westad, *The Cold War: A World History*

Max Tegmark, *Life 3.0: Being Human in the Age of Artificial Intelligence*

Jonathan Losos, *Improbable Destinies: How Predictable is Evolution?*

Chris D. Thomas, *Inheritors of the Earth: How Nature Is Thriving in an Age of Extinction*

Chris Patten, *First Confession: A Sort of Memoir*

James Delbourgo, *Collecting the World: The Life and Curiosity of Hans Sloane*

Naomi Klein, *No Is Not Enough: Defeating the New Shock Politics*

Ulrich Raulff, *Farewell to the Horse: The Final Century of Our Relationship*

Slavoj Žižek, *The Courage of Hopelessness: Chronicles of a Year of Acting Dangerously*

Patricia Lockwood, *Priestdaddy: A Memoir*

Ian Johnson, *The Souls of China: The Return of Religion After Mao*

Stephen Alford, *London's Triumph: Merchant Adventurers and the Tudor City*

Hugo Mercier and Dan Sperber, *The Enigma of Reason: A New Theory of Human Understanding*

Stuart Hall, *Familiar Stranger: A Life Between Two Islands*

Allen Ginsberg, *The Best Minds of My Generation: A Literary History of the Beats*

Sayeeda Warsi, *The Enemy Within: A Tale of Muslim Britain*

Alexander Betts and Paul Collier, *Refuge: Transforming a Broken Refugee System*

Robert Bickers, *Out of China: How the Chinese Ended the Era of Western Domination*

Erica Benner, *Be Like the Fox: Machiavelli's Lifelong Quest for Freedom*

William D. Cohan, *Why Wall Street Matters*

David Horspool, *Oliver Cromwell: The Protector*

Daniel C. Dennett, *From Bacteria to Bach and Back: The Evolution of Minds*

Derek Thompson, *Hit Makers: How Things Become Popular*

Harriet Harman, *A Woman's Work*

Wendell Berry, *The World-Ending Fire: The Essential Wendell Berry*

Daniel Levin, *Nothing but a Circus: Misadventures among the Powerful*